THEATRE OF SHADOWS: SAMUEL BECKETT'S DRAMA 1956–76

THEATRE OF SHADOWS:
Samuel Beckett's Drama 1956–76

From *All That Fall* to *Footfalls* with commentaries on the latest plays

ROSEMARY POUNTNEY

COLIN SMYTHE
Gerrards Cross

First published in 1988 by Colin Smythe Limited
Gerrards Cross, Buckinghamshire SL9 8XA
First published in paperback, 1998

British Library Cataloguing in Publication Data

Pountney, Rosemary
Theatre of shadows : Samuel Beckett's
drama 1956-76 From All that fall to Footfalls
(With commentaries on the latest plays)
1. Beckett, Samuel—Criticism and interpretation
I. Title
822'.912 PR6003.E282Z/

ISBN 0-86140-407-6

Produced in Great Britain
Printed and bound by Guernsey Press Co. Ltd, Guernsey, C.I.

To my mother and father

CONTENTS

ACKNOWLEDGEMENTS

I gratefully acknowledge a scholarship from St. Cross College, Oxford, in the early stages of preparing this book, also funding from the Irish Department of Foreign Affairs (Cultural Relations Committee) and University College Dublin which enabled me to visit Beckett manuscript collections in America in 1981. More recently I have been most grateful for a grant towards research expenses from King Alfred's College, Winchester, and to Jesus College, Oxford, for generous hospitality and help with typing costs. Part of the discussion of *Play* appears in *Modern Drama*, Vol. 19, No. 3 (University of Toronto, 1976) and of *Lessness* in the *Review of Contemporary Fiction*, Illinois, 1987, and I am indebted to the editors of both journals.

The curators of manuscript collections at the following universities have been most helpful in providing material: Harvard Theatre Collection, Harvard College Library; the Ohio State University Libraries; the Humanities Research Center, the University of Texas at Austin; the Samuel Beckett Papers, Washington University Libraries, St. Louis, Missouri; the Beinecke Rare Book and Manuscript Library, University of Yale. Professor Breon Mitchell, Indiana University and McMaster University Library, Hamilton, Ontario, have also kindly sent material. The painstaking help of the staff of the Beckett archives at Reading University and Trinity College, Dublin has been greatly appreciated.

I wish to thank Mr. Francis Warner for his encouragement and generosity during the preparation of the thesis on which this book is based and Dr. John Pilling for additional supervisory help. I am also most grateful for the encouragement of many friends and colleagues, without which the end would not have been reached, in particular the late Professor Richard Admussen, John Beckett, Professor James Knowlson, Professor Jay Macpherson, Dr. James Mays, Colin Smythe, Professor Katharine Worth and Dr. Nicholas Zurbrugg; also to Elsie Callander for help in translation and Margot Levy for editorial assistance. I am especially indebted to Professor Jay Macpherson for preparing the index. Finally, I should like to thank my students for much stimulating discussion and Samuel Beckett himself, not only for unfailing help in answering questions and for permission to quote from the manuscripts, but for giving me the invaluable opportunity of attending several weeks of rehearsal when he was directing *Endgame* in London and for his help and encouragement with the role of May, prior to Gordon Macdougall's production of *Footfalls* at Oxford Playhouse in 1980.

FOREWORD

This book is based on a doctoral thesis for the University of Oxford. With the exception of the draft studies of *Theatre I, Theatre II, That Time* and *Footfalls* and the commentaries on the latest plays, the work was completed in 1978. That it has not emerged before is due to my being entirely without research time in which to work on additional drafts until the summer of 1984. Since the bulk of the study was completed earlier, however, I have thought it best to allow the discussion to develop in its original form, which has its own internal logic rather than to change the focus by attempting to include reference to subsequent critical material.

The initial purpose of the thesis was to establish whether extreme precision is Beckett's customary practice in planning a work, having seen in manuscript his extraordinary scheme for the structuring of *Sans/Lessness* (reproduced on p.237) which reads like a mathematical formula. Through the cooperation of university libraries in England, Ireland, Canada and America I was able to gain access to the mss. of almost all Beckett's published plays and this led to the possibility of making a more comprehensive study than at first envisaged. Working on a substantial body of mss. (all the plays of the years 1956-76), afforded most interesting insight into Beckett's creative process. It became apparent that not only is strict, often rigorous patterning a common feature of the structural organisation of his finished work, but that he customarily moves from a concrete approach to a subject in the early drafts of a play, towards more abstract and ambiguous expression. It thus emerged that what Beckett himself has described in the drafts of *Happy Days* as a ''vaguening'' of the text is an integral part of his dramatic vision.

Since ambiguity as well as structure proved such promising lines of approach to his dramatic writing, it seemed appropriate to gain as complete a view of Beckett's creative process as possible by exploring both areas. In publishing the work the study of structure is placed first, in order to familiarise a student readership with the texts as printed, before going on to discuss the "vaguening" process of the genesis of the plays in some depth. The analysis of stagecraft which follows is a logical development from text to stage, arising from the importance of looking at a play not only on the page, but in the context of performance also. The intention here, having gained insight into the text in preceding chapters, is to draw the plays together in a discussion of the various aspects of Beckett's theatrical technique. As a trained actress, the radical innovations of Beckettian theatre have always been a particular interest of mine and while working on this book my appreciation of the difficulties and rewards for the actor in playing pieces of such unique precision and depth was considerably increased when opportunities arose of performing in *Not I* and *Footfalls*. Where an actor would normally build up a character through a process of close observation and intuition, it became clear that the Beckett actor's task is to strip away all preconception, all idea of "character", almost every movement and inflection, in a probing towards "the thing itself". In emptying himself of all but his identification with the language, he becomes at best an open channel of communication — and it is the resulting active fusion of actor and text with the audience that seems to produce the extraordinary intensity of Beckett's theatre.

After teaching Beckett to students at the universities of Oxford, University College, Dublin and U C Berkeley since 1972, I had a student readership largely in mind in writing this book, although the detailed work in Appendix VII is likely to be of more interest to scholars. It has been my experience that students at both undergraduate and postgraduate level are stimulated by discussion of Beckett's dramatic innovation and patterning. Many of these (especially at postgraduate level) also develop an interest in the genesis of the plays. It is the intention of this book to provide, for such students, as comprehensive an approach as possible to Beckett's drama of 1956–76. Excellent specialist studies of individual plays have begun to appear (such as that of *Krapp's Last Tape* in the Theatre Workbook series, edited by James Knowlson). This book has a wider focus, however, and attempts a perspective view of the work of a twenty year period, from three separate, yet complementary angles: structure, ambiguity and stagecraft.

There is so much draft material for most of Beckett's plays that it soon became evident it would be impossible to consider it all in a single volume. It seemed appropriate instead to begin this study with Beckett's return to writing in English as a first language, since the early plays in French have received considerably more critical attention than the later work. This book therefore both defines and takes as its subject the middle period of Beckett's dramatic writing and explores all the plays written between *All That Fall* in 1956 and the publication of *Footfalls* twenty years later, with the exception of Robert Pinget's play *La Manivelle* (translated by Beckett as *The Old Tune*). Evidence of developing ambiguity in the mss. of the early plays in French is briefly discussed prior to the exploration of the English drafts, in order both to set the middle period in context, and to establish the fact that Beckett's dramatic method has remained consistent. Certain unpublished fragments are also considered, where they have a bearing on the published texts. A chart showing the extent and whereabouts of the mss. of the middle period is given at Appendix 1.

There are still some years of work to be done before a second volume, containing a ms. study of the plays that follow *Footfalls* can be produced. Since, however, Beckett has been particularly prolific in recent years (as revealed by the publication of the *Collected Shorter Plays* in 1984) and there is as yet no critical discussion of plays such as *Nacht und Träume* and *What Where,* this book ends with a series of commentaries on the latest work and these plays are also included in the analysis of stagecraft. Discussion of Beckett's latest plays in the epilogue helps to define the middle period of his dramatic writing and to set it in context, since the recent work shows a growing awareness of the theatrical possibilities of televison. The transmission of *Ghost Trio* and . . . *but the clouds* . . . by the BBC in 1977 first showed Beckett's developing interest in the visual potential of images on a screen and these two plays thus make a natural starting point for consideration of his latest work. The latest plays present certain problems for students, since some of them rely largely on directions for camera action rather than speech, and are thus difficult works to read. It is hoped however, that insights gained into Beckett's patterning and stagecraft in earlier chapters will assist in such reading.

There are certain inevitable difficulties in presenting ms. material to the reader. In the first place what is shown is governed by the writer's choices and there is a fine line to be drawn between too little detail and too much. I have tried to counter this problem by largely pointing to the "vaguening" of the text in Chapters 6–10, but including a detailed analysis of four plays in Appendix VII, so that the reader can have a fuller idea of the material if he so wishes and appreciate the kinds of choices that have to be made. Some of the ms. drafts are naturally livelier than others; but although a statement of the extent and content of the material as a whole is required of a manuscript study, I have concentrated on the drafts that contain the most radical alterations, or reveal the strongest evidence of the dramatist's shaping hand. The editorial note explains how Beckett's handwritten alterations have been translated into typescript, while the chronology sets the plays in the context of his other writing.

Rosemary Pountney

Jesus College
Oxford
April 1985

Foreword to 1998 reprint

It is now twenty years since this book was completed as a doctoral thesis – apart from the epilogue on the late plays, added in 1984 (shortly after these appeared) when preparing the book for publication. This is a reprint not a new edition, since the many subsequent studies of Beckett's drama and manuscript (in particular the excellent 'Theatrical Notebooks of Samuel Beckett' series) provide comprehensive accounts of individual plays which would prove impossible to incorporate into a single volume. Moreover, Beckett studies having moved on since this book was commissioned in 1977, means that an attempt to include subsequent work would dislocate the rationale of the original, in which form it is still being requested. As it stands therefore *Theatre of Shadows* is a study of Beckett's dramatic writing from *All That Fall* (1956) to *Footfalls* (1976), a period that can now be seen following his death as comprising the bulk of Beckett's work for the theatre, his experiments with radio and his first works for the camera. Paperback publication thus makes available to students in one volume detailed studies of the genesis of all but Beckett's earliest and very late plays.

On initial publication the book was stated by one critic to be short on critical theory – to which there can only be a Beckettian response: 'No theory where none intended' (see *Addenda* to *Watt*). It so happens that genetic criticism is now considered a branch of critical theory, but the book was not conceived in order to propound a particular formula. Studying the Beckett manuscripts proved my early hypothesis that he customarily 'vaguened' his material in the course of developing it in order to introduce deliberate ambiguity of expression, often radically cutting drafts on the principle less = more. My major concern, however, while working on the manuscripts became the attempt to reflect Beckett's own creative process, how he customarily developed his material – from the first glimmering of ideas for a play through the shaping process of drafting it until arriving at the published text – and its subsequent realisation in performance.

As Beckett when writing worked steadily towards giving his plays maximum openness and ambiguity, it becomes a hazardous process to introduce the generally more explicit nature of their origins since, though a fascinating and rewarding study in itself, this can result in a kind of 'closure' of the richness of possibility inherent in the published text. It is especially evident since Beckett left vestiges of his initial ideas in the final versions as, for example, in *Come and Go*. Thus investigating the early drafts of a play can appear a violation, like trying to place the worn out husk of its seed on top of a flower which, in the process of gestation, has clearly transcended its origins. Beckett, however, in preserving his manuscripts and draft notebooks certainly anticipated that they would be studied, and even drew my attention to where he thought they could mostly be traced, when giving permission to work on them in 1973.

The analysis of Beckett's stagecraft in Chapter 11 is particularly addressed towards actors, directors and students looking for ways of approaching Beckett's theatre.

Rosemary Pountney
Jesus College, Oxford
December 1997

EDITORIAL NOTE

Beckett's handwriting varies between a neat and careful script when making a fair copy and (in the early stages of a work in particular, when composition is in full flow) a fast hand verging on illegibility. Virtually all the plays begin with a manuscript draft (holograph) followed by several typescript drafts with handwritten emendations. It has been my practice throughout to indicate Beckett's revisions by crossing out with a single line and to use **bold type** for alterations. For convenience of presentation instead of writing the altered word above the line, it has been placed, wherever possible, immediately beside the word or words crossed out. An example from the holograph of *Eh Joe* illustrates this practice:

~~Leave the rest to your imagination~~ **Now imagine ...**

Where nothing has been crossed out but a phrase of bold type appears in the text, it means that the phrase was an addition to the manuscript, following an omission mark. Where certain words have been crossed out but no amended words appear in bold italics, it shows that Beckett was simply pruning the manuscript. Where a word in the MS. is illegible, it is indicated thus: xxx. If a reading has been attempted but is uncertain, it is underlined (as here) by a broken line. Omission from a continuing quotation is marked by square brackets, thus: [ ]. It is not possible to indicate separate stages of revision (as, for example, the use of different inks) without printing in colour. Should particular emphasis be required anywhere in the text, ordinary italics are used, as also for stage directions. Page references are normally to the standard Calder editions of the novels and Faber editions of individual plays. Where any other text (such as the Faber collected edition *Ends and Odds*) has been used, reference is made in the notes.For all the latest plays (in the epilogue) the *Collected Shorter Plays* (Faber,1984) is used.

CHRONOLOGY OF BECKETT'S WRITING:
Drama, Prose Fiction and Verse.*

1929
''Dante...Bruno. Vico..Joyce'', Paris, 1929.
Assumption, Paris, 1929.
Che Sciagura, T.C. Dublin, 1929.

1930
Whoroscope, Paris, 1930.
Proust, London, 1931.

1931
The Possessed, T.C. Dublin, 1931.

1932
Dante and the Lobster, Paris, 1932.
Sedendo et Quiescendo, The Hague, 1932.
Text, Paris, 1932.

1933
More Pricks than Kicks, London, 1934.

1934
A Case in a Thousand, London, 1934.

1935
Echo's Bones and Other Precipitates, Paris, 1935.

1935–36
Murphy, London, 1938.

1936–37
Human Wishes, (fragment) Princeton, 1980.

*Works are listed under date of writing and of first publication.
The chronology is restricted to volumes of verse and (*Whoroscope* apart) contains collected editions in French and English rather than single poems. The short stories are included, as are the critiques of Joyce and Proust and the *Three Dialogues with Georges Duthuit*; for the remainder of Beckett's criticism the reader is referred to the valuable collection in *Disjecta*, edited by Ruby Cohn (John Calder, 1983). Where English is not the first language of publication, the date of the English translation is added in brackets. Beckett's translations from other authors and his unpublished work are not included.

1937–39
Poèmes 38–39, Paris, 1946, (*Poems in English*, London, 1961).

1943–44
Watt, Paris, 1953.

1946
L'Expulsé, Le Calmant, La Fin, Paris, 1955 (London 1967).
Premier Amour, Paris, 1970 (London 1973).
Mercier et Camier, Paris, 1970 (London 1974).

1947
Molloy, Paris, 1951 (English translation Paris, 1955).

1947–48
Trois Poèmes, Paris, 1948 (Dublin, 1949).

1948
Malone meurt, Paris, 1951 (New York, 1956).

1948–49
En attendant Godot, Paris, 1952 (New York, 1954).

1949
Trois Poèmes, Paris, 1955 (London, 1977).
Three Dialogues with Georges Duthuit, Paris, 1949 (London, 1965).

1949–50
L'Innommable, Paris, 1953 (New York, 1958).

1950–51
Textes pour rien, Paris, 1955 (London, 1967).

1953–56
Fin de partie, Paris, 1957 (London, 1958).

1955
From an Abandoned Work, T.C. Dublin, 1956.
Acte sans paroles I, Paris, 1957 (London, 1958).

1956
Acte sans paroles II, Frankfurt, 1963 (New York, 1959).
All That Fall, London, 1957.
Fragment de théâtre, Paris, 1974 (*Theatre I*, London, 1977).

1958
Fragment de théâtre, Paris, 1976 (*Theatre II*, London, 1977).
Krapp's Last Tape, London, 1959.

1959
Embers, London, 1959.

1959–60
Comment c'est, Paris, 1961 (London, 1964).
"années 50":
Foirade, Paris, 1972.
Foirades II and III, Paris, 1973.
Foirade IV, Paris, 1973.
"années 60":
Foirade V (with *Foirade* IV), Paris, 1973.
(*For to End Yet Again and Other Fizzles*, London, 1976).
Pochade radiophonique, Paris, 1975 (*Radio II*, London, 1977).

1960–61
Happy Days, New York, 1961.

1961
Words and Music, London, 1964.
Esquisse radiophonique, Paris, 1973 (*Radio I*, London, 1977).
Cascando, Frankfurt, 1963, (New York, 1963).

1962–63
Play, (German translation, *Spiel*, Frankfurt, 1963 (London, 1964).

1963
Film, London, 1967.

1963–64
All Strange Away, Gotham Book Mart, 1976.

1965
Come and Go, Frankfurt, 1966 (with German translation).
Eh Joe (London, 1967) *Dis Joe*, Paris, 1966.
Imagination morte imaginez, Paris, 1965, (London, 1967).
Assez, Paris, 1966 (London, 1967).
Le Dépeupleur, Paris, 1970 (London, 1972).

1966
Bing, Paris, 1966 (*Ping*, London, 1967).
circa 1966:
Breath, London, 1970.
Dans le cylindre, Paris, 1967.
circa 1967:
L'Issue, Paris, 1968.

1968
Poèmes, Paris, 1968 (*Collected Poems in English and French*, London, 1977).

1969
Sans, Paris, 1969 (*Lessness*, London, 1970).
circa 1970:
The North, London, 1972.
Séjour, Paris, 1970.

1971
Abandonné, Paris, 1972.

1971–75
Pour finir encore, Paris, 1976 (London, 1976).

1972
Not I, London, 1973.

1972–73
Still, Milan, 1974 (Italian/English parallel texts).
Sounds, London, 1978.

1973
Still 3, London, 1978.
As The Story Was Told, Frankfurt, 1975.

1974–75
That Time, London, 1976.

1975
La Falaise Montpellier, 1975.
Footfalls, London, 1976.
Ghost Trio, London, 1976.

1976
. . . but the clouds. . ., London, 1977.
Neither, London, 1977.
Poèmes, Paris, 1976 (London, 1977).

1976–78
Mirlitonnades, Paris, 1978.

1930–1976
Collected Poems in English and French, London, 1977.

1977
A Piece of Monologue, Ohio, 1979.

1977–79
Company, London, 1980.

1979–80
Mal vu mal dit, Paris, 1981 (London, 1982).
Rockaby, New York, 1981.

1980
Ohio Impromptu, New York, 1981.
circa 1980:
Quad, London, 1984.

1981
Worstward Ho, London, 1983.

1982
Catastrophe, Paris, 1982 (New York, 1983).
Nacht und Träume, London, 1984.

1983
What Where, London, 1984.

CHAPTER 1
INTRODUCTION

In an article by Israel Shenker in the *New York Times* of 6 May 1956 (two days before the première of Osborne's *Look Back In Anger* heralded the new wave of British theatre) Beckett is described as finding himself in an impasse, a situation not merely of writer's block, but of total negation:

> In the last book — *L'Innommable* — there's complete disintegration. No 'I', no 'have', no 'being'. No nominative, no accusative, no verb. There's no way to go on. The very last thing I wrote — *Textes pour rien* — was an attempt to get out of the attitude of disintegration, but it failed.[1]

These comments are revealing. With hindsight it can be seen that Beckett's dramatic career, a career that would change the face of modern theatre far more radically than the apostles of the kitchen sink, had already begun by this time — unrecognised by himself.

This chapter begins by considering Beckett's early dealings with the theatre — prior to 1956, when drama in various forms began to absorb his main attention. It is clear that in the mid-fifties Beckett did not regard the stage — least of all involvement in dramatic productions — as anything more than a relaxation from the demands of his work as a novelist. He told Colin Duckworth that he wrote his first plays, *Éleuthéria* and *En attendant Godot* as a deliberate attempt to relieve his mind from the weight of the novel.[2] *Éleuthéria* was written in 1947, the same year as *Molloy* and *En attendant Godot* was begun in 1948, the year of *Malone meurt*. The idea of drama as 'relaxation' may have stemmed from Beckett's love of the silent cinema and the antics of Chaplin, Keaton and Laurel and Hardy, as well as his light-hearted experience of theatre while a lecturer at Trinity College, Dublin. Two of his earliest publications, which were written for the college newspaper, are in dramatic form — the dialogues *Che Sciagura* and *The Possessed*. The former, which transforms the

Irish contraception problem into a matter of linguistics, is signed D.E.S.C., thus describing the author as 'd'essere senza coglioni' (without balls); the latter is a reply in Joycean style to the reviewer of his play *Le Kid*. Beckett wrote *Le Kid*, a parody of Corneille's *Le Cid*, with a colleague — Georges Pelorson — for a Trinity College Modern Language Society production in 1931; he also acted in the production.

Beckett naturally visited the Abbey Theatre as a young man in Dublin. In 1904, as is well known, this theatre had become the headquarters of the Irish National Theatre Society, founded by W. B. Yeats and Lady Gregory to encourage the work of Irish dramatists. The theatre repertoire included their own plays, as well as those of Synge and, sometime later, of O'Casey. Beckett's appreciation of the new drama is evident from his response in 1956 to a request for a tribute to G. B. Shaw, on the centenary of his birth. Beckett replied:

> I wouldn't suggest that G.B.S. is not a great play-wright,
> whatever that is when it's at home.
> What I would do is give the whole unupsettable apple-
> cart for a sup of the Hawk's Well, or the Saints', or
> a whiff of Juno, to go no further.
> Sorry.[3]

The later plays of Yeats, from *At The Hawk's Well* (1916) onwards, particularly appealed to Beckett; indeed the spare, stylised form of Yeats's plays for dancers, based on the Japanese Noh Theatre, has a good deal in common with the stark world of Beckettian drama, as will be seen in ensuing chapters.

In the summer of 1936 Beckett became marginally involved in both the professional and amateur theatre in Dublin. He helped his cousin Mary Manning Howe reshape her play *Youth's The Season*, prior to its production at the Gate Theatre by Hilton Edwards and Micheál MacLiammóir. He also discussed ideas about theatre with the playwright Denis Johnston and attended several rehearsals of the Dun Laoghaire Theatre Group, as well as productions of the Drama League run by Mrs. W. B. Yeats and Lennox Robinson. Beckett even wondered at this time whether he might find a career in the silent cinema and wrote to Eisenstein offering himself as an unpaid apprentice, but received no reply.[4]

With his mind on the theatre, Beckett began to think of writing a play himself. His subject was a growing fascination with Dr. Johnson, what he described to George Reavey in 1937 as 'my efforts to document my Johnson fantasy'.[5] These 'efforts' included amassing two hundred pages of material on Johnson,[6] largely on his relations with Mrs. Thrale, and a good deal of brooding on his life. 'In a sense' Beckett wrote to Thomas McGreevy, Johnson 'was spiritually self-conscious, was a tragic figure, i.e. worth putting down as part of the whole of which oneself is part . . .'.[7] When he came to try to write the play, however, Beckett found himself unable to develop the material to his satisfaction and managed only part of the first scene, in which the various members of Johnson's household await his return from the funeral of Mr. Thrale in 1781. Her husband's death left Mrs. Thrale, with whom Johnson was in love, ostensibly free to remarry. Beckett's projected play was to have charted the Johnson/Thrale relationship from Mr. Thrale's death until Johnson's own death in 1784, the year of Mrs. Thrale's marriage to Gabriel Piozzi. It was to be called *Human Wishes,* echoing Johnson's satirical poem in imitation of Juvenal 'The Vanity of Human Wishes'.

The fragment of *Human Wishes,*[8] foreshadows Beckett's later drama in the use of silence liberally punctuating the text. The play opens with a conversation between three women; the exaggerated formality and high comedy of the language is echoed, nearly thirty years later, in the first draft (scene one) of *Come and Go.* In the drafts of both plays one of the women reads aloud to the others, who dissect the text with acuity. Both scenes break off abruptly and are abandoned. When Beckett resumed *Come and Go* he developed the play quite differently; *Human Wishes,* however, was abandoned altogether in 1937, just before Beckett's decision to make his home in Paris.

In France as in Ireland Beckett experienced attempts to find new directions in the theatre. The revolutionary Théâtre Alfred Jarry had been founded in Paris by Antonin Artaud and Roger Vitrac in 1926, two years before Beckett arrived there to take up a temporary post as lecteur at the École Normale Supérieure. When, moreover, ten years after abandoning *Human Wishes,* Beckett wrote *Éleuthéria,* his first completed though still unpublished play, Roger Blin, who had worked closely with Artaud in his Théâtre de la Cruauté in the mid-thirties was the director he eventually decided upon. After greatly admiring Blin's production of Strindberg's *Ghost Sonata* in 1949, Beckett sent him *Éleuthéria* and *En attendant Godot* and Blin accepted both plays. *Godot* was finally selected for production since its five characters and minimal set were a much cheaper proposition to stage than the seventeen characters and more complicated design of *Éleuthéria*. Financial problems even so prevented *Godot* from reaching the Paris stage until January 1953.

It was, however, as a novelist that Beckett decided to try to begin his writing career after relinquishing his academic post at Trinity College in 1932. Although his first novel *Dream of Fair to Middling Women* was never published as such, it shows Beckett's early awareness of the power and function of silence in a work, an awareness that was later to become so important a part of his theatrical technique. It was his aim to infiltrate his prose with silence:

> The experience of my reader shall be between the phrases, in the silence, communicated by the intervals, not the terms, of the statement.[9]

Beckett continued to meditate on the desirability of trying to go beyond language in his work, of breaking through a wall of words. In a letter to Axel Kaun in July 1937, when he was considering how to write *Human Wishes*, he commented:

> It is indeed becoming more and more difficult, even senseless, for me to write an official English. And more and more my own language appears to me like a veil that must be torn apart in order to get at the things (or the nothingness) behind it. Grammar and style. To me they seem to have become as irrelevant as a Victorian bathing suit or the imperturbability of a true gentleman. A mask. Let us hope the time will come, thank God that in certain circles it has already come, when language is most efficiently used where it is being most efficiently misused. As we cannot eliminate language all at once, we should at least leave nothing undone that might contribute to its falling into disrepute. To bore one hole after another in it, until what lurks behind it — be it something or nothing — begins to seep through; I cannot imagine a higher goal for a writer today.Or is literature alone to remain behind in the old lazy ways that have been so long ago abandoned by music and painting? Is there something paralysingly holy in the vicious nature of the word that is not found in the elements of the other arts? Is there any reason why that terrible materiality of the word surface should not be capable of being dissolved, like for example the sound surface, torn by enormous pauses, of Beethoven's Seventh Symphony, so that through whole pages we can perceive nothing but a path of sounds suspended in giddy heights, linking unfathomable abysses of silence?[10]

Beckett went on to consider how 'this literature of the unword, which is so desirable to me', 'An assault against words in the name of beauty'[11] might be expressed:

Of course, for the time being we must be satisfied with little. At first it can only be a matter of somehow finding a method by which we can represent this mocking attitude towards the word, through words. In this dissonance between the means and their use it will perhaps become possible to feel a whisper of that final music or that silence that underlies All.[12]

It was not until he embarked on the *trilogy* in 1947 that Beckett began a sustained attempt to get at 'the Nothingness'. Increasingly irked by the way in which his native language seemed to hinder expression, he released in himself a burst of creative energy by deciding to write the *trilogy* in French. He was already at work on the *trilogy* and beginning to bring about the desired breakdown of the word by the time he started writing his first plays. Although it took him some time to appreciate its full potentialities, he had found in the theatre an ideal means of breaking the language barrier — where words could be contradicted by action (as at the end of both acts of *Godot*) and where it was possible to reach beyond language by extending the action into silence. The theatre proved a tool such as he had wished for in the letter to Axel Kaun, once he discovered how to use it for his purposes, a means of expression that equalled the porosity of music and painting. Indeed in the strict sense of admitting silence as part of the work of art, Beckett found the theatre to be at least as effective as music. Silence is part of the theatre's natural language and as such can be used to counterpoint the spoken word — thus forming a subtext, or to communicate without words and through action alone.

Beckett's main preoccupation after completing the *trilogy* in 1950, was not excitement at the recognition of the possibilities of a new medium of expression, but despair at the apparent exhaustion of his fictional voice. This was a by-product of writing the three remarkable novels, indeed it could be said to be the logical outcome. Having deliberately used the *trilogy* in order to destroy conventional form, Beckett had brought his writing to an apparent dead end. Even before finishing *L'Innommable* Beckett had forecast in *Tal Coat*, the first of his three 'Dialogues' on art and the artist with Georges Duthuit, the dilemma of the artist encumbered with an 'obligation to express' yet with no power to say anything and indeed nothing to say. If the statement attributed to Beckett in Israel Shenker's article of 6 May 1956 is accurate, Beckett himself had reached such an impasse and he spent six years wrestling with the problem. After completing *L'Innommable*, the period 1950-55 yielded for publication only the

Nouvelles et Textes pour rien and a piece of prose with the unpromising title: *From an Abandoned Work*. Although by the summer of 1956 he had written three plays (*Fin de partie* was completed in that year, after a long and painful gestation) Beckett still had no idea of becoming a dramatist. He regarded himself as a novelist in a cul de sac, having blocked his own path. Instead of opening up a new direction for him, the *Textes pour rien* had led nowhere.

1956 was, however, to prove a crucial year in Beckett's creative development. It came about almost fortuitously. In June 1956, only a month after admitting that he felt he had come to the end of the road as a novelist, he was approached by the BBC with a request to write a play for the Third Programme. Beckett, who accepts no commissions, was nonetheless attracted by the possibilities of radio and *All That Fall* was completed three months later. The consequences were far reaching. Writing for English radio meant a return to English as a first language, while the challenge of the radio medium opened up a new channel for his creative energies and merged fruitfully with his developing experience of writing for the theatre. Beckett's next stage play after *All That Fall* is *Krapp's Last Tape*, in which he succeeds in bringing radio technique (recorded voices and a tape recorder) into the theatre.

Interestingly enough as Beckett's prose fiction dwindled following the *trilogy*, his plays increasingly adopted the stream of consciousness form of the novels. The possibilities for eavesdropping on the human consciousness that his introduction to radio opened up led inevitably to the use of the monologue form. The plays that follow *All That Fall* are, for the most part, monologues of various kinds, voices in the head. The writing of *All That Fall* in 1956 may thus be seen in retrospect to mark the beginning of an important new stage in Beckett's career and to be an appropriate starting point for a study of his later drama. Since 1956 plays have been Beckett's major output, written, like *All That Fall*, almost consistently in English as a first language.

In order to make a detailed study of Beckett's plays in English, it is clearly necessary to establish whether his dramatic practice has remained consistent, by some preliminary consideration of his first three plays in French. The two published plays *En attendant Godot* and *Fin de partie* are therefore included in the ensuing chapters whenever such a comparison becomes relevant. As there is already an enormous amount of criticism on both plays — (*Godot* in particular having received what might be called blanket coverage) such discussion has been kept to a minimum.[13] Since, however, the unpublished text of *Éleuthéria* is not readily accessible to the reader,[14] it is examined here briefly, in order to see whether it has anything in common with Beckett's later drama.

Éleuthéria (or *Freedom*) chronicles the attempts of Victor Krap's relations to lure him back to the family home, whereas his goal is to be free, more precisely to be 'tout simplement rien'. The family rift is expressed by a division of the stage, which consists of two separate sets: one is the Krap family home and the other Victor's hotel bedsitter. There is no dividing wall. The two sets exist separately onstage and yet are connected, emphasising the family web from which Victor has been unable wholly to extricate himself. Beckett describes in the opening stage directions how 'l'action principale et l'action marginale' exist simultaneously in the first two acts. In Act 1 the principal action takes place in the family home, but Victor, present at his own absence, can be seen in his room throughout. In Act 2 the situation is reversed, Victor's room becoming the main focus of attention. In the last act the latter takes over the whole stage, Victor having at last ousted the family: 'le côté Krap étant tombé dans la fosse à la suite du virement de la scene.'[15]. Beckett is thus already using the visual language of the theatre to express meaning, but the device is cumbersome compared with the subtlety of visual effect he was soon to achieve. In *Godot*, which followed only a year later, he is already expressing dual vision through pairs of characters, who reveal different points of view. The complexity of viewpoint is also enhanced in *Godot* because the separation of the characters is incomplete and is combined with their mutal interdependence.

Éleuthéria has three acts. Perhaps the main problem with the play is that Beckett relies too heavily on words (the tools of the novelist) and gives too little scope to the dramatic action. The play's reliance on language is prophetic, at the same time, of Beckett's subsequent stage monologues although the latter are combined with dramatic effects of such extraordinary originality that *Éleuthéria* seems elephantine by contrast. Nonetheless Victor's quest for freedom in *Éleuthéria* provides Beckett with the opportunity of raising several of the topics that remain his concern in the later plays. On the day of his death, for example, M. Krap senior ruminates:

Je suis la vache qui, devant la grille de l'abbatoir, comprend toute l'absurdité des pâturages. Elle aurait mieux fait d'y penser plus tôt, la-bas, dans l'herbe haute et tendre. Tant pis. Il lui reste toujours la cour à traverser. Ca personne ne pourra le lui ravir.[16]

Beckett rings many changes on this theme in subsequent plays. Hamm, for example, confronts his situation as squarely as M. Krap, Vladimir and Estragon fail to understand theirs, while Winnie keeps any realisation of absurdity carefully (even desperately) at bay. Victor's final act is to turn his back on humanity, achieving freedom of a kind in the deliberate act of opting out. It is an act Beckett had noted with appreciation (though in a very different context) in his early dialogue *Che Sciagura*: 'Can you not understand that the most extreme and passionate form of any act whatsoever, more so than actual participation, is an energetic, vehement, and self-conscious abstention?'[17]

Looking back on *En attendant Godot* from the vantage point of Beckett's later drama, it is interesting to find that the exchange between Vladimir and Estragon quoted so often for its lyrical quality, heralds the world of the later plays in a surprisingly literal manner:

Estragon: All the dead voices.
Vladimir: They make a noise like wings.
Estragon: Like leaves.
Vladimir: Like sand.
Estragon: Like leaves.
Silence.
Vladimir: They all speak together.
Estragon: Each one to itself.
Silence.
Vladimir: Rather they whisper.
Estragon: They rustle.
Vladimir: They murmur.
Estragon: They rustle.
Silence.
Vladimir: What do they say?
Estragon: They talk about their lives.
Vladimir: To have lived is not enough for them.
Estragon: They have to talk about it.
Vladimir: To be dead is not enough for them.
Estragon: It is not sufficient.

Here, it may be said, is a foretaste of the posthumous world of Beckett's later drama where, beyond the grave, his protagonists are still waiting — no longer for Godot, but for the silence of annihilation. After experiencing the kind of living death that is seen in *Happy Days*, where Winnie is embedded to the waist in a mound of earth in Act 1, which rises in Act 2 to clasp her about the neck, some of the protagonists in Beckett's subsequent plays seem to have passed beyond the grave. In *Play*, for example, three heads emerge from funerary urns, while in *Not I* there is simply a mouth gabbling in space, skewered by a spotlight. Instead of the peace of darkness and oblivion these characters seem to be experiencing a hideous kind of life in death, in which the human consciousness is condemned to an endless recapitulation of the circumstances of a barren existence, in a fruitless search for an event or phrase that would somehow give it meaning and thus perhaps enable the spate of words to cease. The repetitive language implies that there is nothing to be found, nothing to be said, nothing to be done. In an infinite cycle of experience the quest for an end is itself the only reality.

This study both defines and takes as its subject the middle period of Beckett's drama, the years 1956-76. It seeks to increase understanding of his writing for the theatre by studying not only the structure of the plays but the gestation of each one, leading to the emergence of the final text. The study of structure in Chapters 2-5 is placed before that of the manuscript drafts, since I believe that an appreciation of the patterning of the plays is a useful preparation for the detailed work on the drafts, a means of getting to know each play better before attempting to examine its origins. The evolution of the text thus becomes the second perspective from which the plays are explored in Chapters 6-9. Each play is followed from the first germ of an idea, through its various manuscript and typescript drafts, until the final text is arrived at. The craftsmanship with which Beckett customarily shapes his plays and develops their linguistic style is examined in Chapter 10, leading in Chapter 11, to a detailed analysis of the effectiveness of the plays in the media for which they were created, since no exploration of a play can be regarded as complete without considering its stagecraft, the dimension that gives it life. The radical simplicity of Beckett's dramatic imagination is one of his greatest strengths.

For a perspective view of Beckett's middle period it is important to be able to see the plays of 1956–1976 not only in the context of his earlier drama, but of the latest plays also. This study thus ends with commentaries on Beckett's work for television and theatre, from *Ghost Trio* to *What Where*. Looked at as a group the plays that follow *Footfalls* may be seen as marking a new direction in Beckett's drama, a movement towards largely visual communication. In his two most recent plays for television, for example, *Quad* and *Nacht und Träume*, Beckett dispenses with the spoken word altogether, relying on percussion, footsteps and song, combined with the dramatic image. Shape is accorded particular visual importance in the latest television plays. In *Ghost Trio* rectangles are deliberately isolated by the camera for audience inspection, while a narrator comments coldly on the uniformity of the image: 'Having seen that specimen of floor you have seen it all.' In *. . . but the clouds . . .* the playing area is a circle of light, in *Quad* light forms a square, while in both the latter plays a particular pattern of movement is rigorously followed. Other art forms also act as stimuli to Beckett's dramatic imagination in the latest plays. Music embodies the core of the protagonists's experience in *Ghost Trio* and a poem by Yeats performs the same function in *. . . but the clouds . . .* . In *Nacht und Träume* a poem by the German poet von Collin set to music by Schubert, combines both forms of expression. Thus an interesting fusion of poetry, music, image and movement is achieved in the latest television works. Beckett has, moreover, been greatly stimulated by the ability of film both to freeze and to recreate a series of images. Such recreation is the visual counterpart of the verbal repetition and cyclic action that has, throughout his drama, been Beckett's customary means of suggesting infinity. Television now demonstrates an added advantage, the ability to freeze time, to capture the moment and to recreate it at will.

The detailed examination of the middle period of Beckett's drama in Chapters 4-12 establishes particular perspectives from which to view the plays. These perspectives can also prove helpful in exploring the most recent work. Beckett's plays continually develop from and stimulate each other and the commentaries in the epilogue point to where and how his latest plays fit into the pattern of the earlier work. Beckett's dramatic imagination is seen to be still actively forging ahead into new areas, indeed *Quad* may be regarded as the fulfilment onstage of the goal he had set himself in 1937 in the letter to Axel Kaun, the achieving of an entirely new means of expression through the elimination of language.

CHAPTER 2
PATTERN

'It is the shape that matters' Beckett once said, enthusing over the proportion of a sentence of St. Augustine's: '"Do not despair: one of the thieves was saved. Do not presume: one of the thieves was damned." That sentence has a wonderful shape'.[1] Vladimir in *Waiting for Godot* bears the sentence in mind: 'One of the thieves was saved. (*Pause.*) It's a reasonable percentage.'

Shape is of enormous importance throughout the Beckett canon. As Molloy says 'I always had a mania for symmetry'.[2] To explore their structure is perhaps the best means of beginning to understand Beckett's plays. Beckett uses the shape of his work as part of his meaning, as he observed when discussing the work of James Joyce: 'His writing is not *about* something; *it is that something itself*'.[3]

John Pilling has revealed the precision with which the novels are structured,[4] however diffuse and uncontrolled a work like *The Unnamable* may seem. They abound in so-called 'closed systems' for comic effect, such as the ginger biscuit 'routine' in *Murphy*, or the sucking stones in Molloy, while in *Watt* we find the complexities of feeding the dog or exhaustive calculation of the ways in which five committee members may contemplate each other. These are painstaking but fruitless attempts to cover all possibilities, to structure experience into manageable proportions, and serve to illustrate the futility of attempting to impose order on living. It is only in art that any appearance of order may be achieved, through the artificiality of selection and arrangement.

Turning to the drama, two unpublished fragments (one in the possession of Trinity College, Dublin, the other owned by the author) show Beckett's planning of a work in the very early stages and reveal extraordinary exactitude. The Trinity College fragment is headed 'J M Mime' and was clearly planned for

Beckett's friend, the actor Jack Macgowran. It is intended as a mime for two players (son and father or mother) who are described as naked under their coats. The stage is plotted out in a square, the four corners of which (lettered A-D) are to be marked either by two boots and two hats or by four boots, recalling the boots and hat found onstage in *Godot*. Centre stage is also marked and lettered O.

There follow instructions for the action of the mime, revealing Beckett's unusual preoccupation with detail. The manuscript, which bears a startling resemblance to his recent play *Quad*,[5] runs into three pages of calculation. Part of 'J M Mime' is reproduced here as an illustration of Beckett's structural method. Rather in the manner of the moves in a game of chess, 'solutions' and 'errors' are worked out painstakingly, thus:

Action: starting from O return to O by greatest number of paths
(one way)
Maximum = 6 (out of 8)

e.g. OB, BD, DO, OA, AC, CO)
)
or) solutions
)
OB, BA, AO, OC, CD, DO)

e.g. OB, BD, DO, OA, AB —)
)
or) errors
)
OB, BA, AO, OC, CA —)

Ditto. 2 ways
Max = 16 (out of 16)

e.g. OB, BA, AO, AB, BO, OC, CA, AC, CO, OD, DC, CD, DB, BD, DO

(solution)

e.g. OB, BO, OA, AO, OC, CO, OD, DO,)

OB, BA, AB, BO, OA, AC, CO, OC, CD, DO, OD, DB, BD, DO) errors
)
OC, CO, CD, DO, OD, DC, CA, AC)

Complicate if necessary by

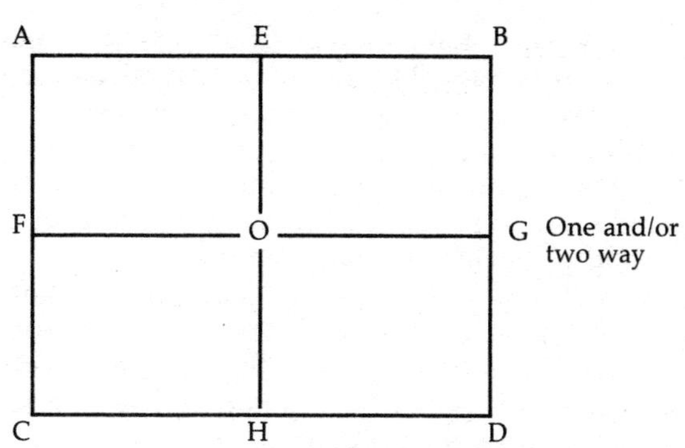

The idea of 'error' here may be compared with *Acte sans paroles I*, where all the actions of the protagonist in his efforts to reach his goal are frustrated, a variation of the Tantalus myth. The routes to the centre may well represent a further metaphor for living, though the fact that 'solutions' are possible is surprising in a Beckett universe.

The second fragment containing interesting evidence of Beckett's early dramatic planning is an unfinished play for two characters written in 1967-8, a page of which is reproduced in *Samuel Beckett : an exhibition*.[6] The reproduction shows Beckett to have jotted down the structure of the play, with the number of minutes each section is to take already decided. There are four sections. The first (consisting of arrivals and dialogue) is to last ten minutes, the second, central section (a female solo) twenty minutes. The third section (a male solo) and fourth (in which both characters leave the stage) are to take five and ten minutes respectively. It is not unknown for Beckett to time his plays. The drafts of *Cascando*, for example, are timed so as to make it clear he has a particularly swift delivery in mind. But to time sections before they are written and to a precise forty-five minutes, is another matter and involves a writing to order not unlike nineteenth century novel writing for serialisation. That Beckett was preparing the play in this manner is evident from subsequent jottings in which he repeats the 1-4 numbering, with hesitations as to how each section should be composed:

1. quel dialogue?
3. que fait l'homme seul?
4. quel dialogue? Et pourquoi décision l'en finir?
2. essentiellement explication de méthode, xxx calculs, maniement des seringues et bocaux.

Although it has already been stated that Beckett does not accept commissions, it seems likely that he had a 45 minute radio or television production in mind for this play.

Such a page of structural jottings could be seen as standard authorial practice, but the careful timing and a list of 'possible thèmes' (also present on the page reproduced in *Samuel Beckett : an exhibition*) seem more akin to musical composition. Beckett comes of a musical family; he is a competent pianist himself and married to a pianist, and his closest living relatives (his brother's son, Edward Beckett, and his first cousin John Beckett) are both professional musicians. The relation between Beckett's plays and musical structure is a fascinating subject, which will be further discussed in Chapter 11.[7]

The evidence of these plans for plays reveals the importance of pattern in the early stages of Beckett's creative process. We shall now go on to look at one of the most precisely patterned of Beckett's finished works in some detail.

CHAPTER 3
LESSNESS: A STUDY IN STRUCTURE

Of all the works in the Beckett canon, the one for which we have the most revealing evidence of the importance of structure in the initial act of creation is not a play, but a piece of prose, first written in French and published in 1969 as *Sans*, then translated into English as *Lessness* (1970). The work is unique, since in no other has Beckett provided a mathematical 'key' to demonstrate exactly how it was shaped. *Lessness* thus becomes important 'evidence' in a study of Beckett's patterning and may be seen as a prototype for an examination of his method. The work has, moreover, received both radio and stage performances and may therefore appropriately be considered in conjunction with the plays.

Establishing the precision of structure revealed in *Lessness* makes it possible to analyse the plays in a similarly detailed fashion. There follow in Chapter 4 analyses of six plays in which, although no authorial 'key' exists for consultation, extreme precision is, nonetheless, established as Beckett's typical method of procedure when shaping a text. A study of *Lessness* thus becomes an essential preliminary to a detailed exploration of the structure of the plays and an integral part of the ensuing discussion of pattern.

Lessness is composed of sixty sentences, divided into six sections of ten sentences each. These are lettered by Beckett A 1-10, B 1-10, C 1-10, D 1-10, E 1-10 and F 1-10, but they do not appear in the text in this order. Instead the sentences are shuffled into a completely different order and formed into twelve paragraphs containing varying numbers of sentences. The entire process is then repeated. Each sentence appears once more in a different order and paragraph sequence which forms the second half of the text. The complete work thus consists of 120 sentences divided into 24 paragraphs[1]. Beckett's scheme for the arrangement of sentences may be seen in Appendix II.

Ruby Cohn relates that Beckett described to her how the final arrangement of sentences was achieved:

> Beckett wrote each of these sixty sentences on a separate piece of paper, mixed them all in a container, and then drew them out in random order twice. This became the order of the hundred twenty sentences in *Sans*. Beckett then wrote the number 3 on four separate pieces of paper, the number 4 on six pieces of paper, the number 5 on four pieces, the number 6 on six pieces, and the number 7 on four pieces of paper. Again drawing randomly, he ordered the sentences into paragraphs according to the number drawn, finally totalling one hundred twenty.[2]

Beckett told Cohn this was 'the only honest thing to do'. The random method, known as aleatory technique (dependent on the throw of a dice) has been used by composers to establish the order in which numbered bars of music should be placed. It is illustrated, for example, in *Musikalisches Würfelspiel*, attributed to Mozart (K.Anh.C.30.01) which shows how an unlimited number of waltzes, rondos, hornpipes and reels could be composed according to the throw of a dice, and a similar principle governs John Cage's *Music of Changes* for piano (1951).

That Beckett placed his highly formal, carefully patterned work at hazard in this way aptly illustrates his view of the human condition. Beyond the man-made or imposed order, Beckett seems to be saying, lies an arbitrary and capricious world of chance. The same kind of statement occurs at the beginning of *Murphy*, where the novelist spends some time enumerating the knots tying Murphy to his chair, but the unpredictable happens and the result of his calculations is wrong. Although Beckett may well be enjoying a joke here at the expense of the Cartesian faith in mathematical truth, he is also demonstrating the fallibility of supposed certainties. Murphy might be assumed to have no head for figures but it may be observed that in *All That Fall*, Mr. Rooney, who is devoted to mathematics ('one of the few satisfactions in life!') encounters the same difficulty. He attempts to count the station steps, but can never arrive at a fixed number: 'Sometimes I wonder if they do not change them in the night.' Behind the world of apparently logical relations Beckett shows us a state of things so arbitrary that man's continued strivings towards order are no more than a mockery, yet he cannot stop: 'you must go on, I can't go on, I'll go on.'[3] It is his blinkered presence in the cosmos, his steadfast refusal to confront the facts of his condition squarely (as with Winnie in *Happy Days*) that marks the peculiar irony of his existence.

There are three parts to the key to *Lessness*. Beckett writes out each sentence of the piece labelling it with a particular letter and number from A 1 - F 10. A separate sheet shows these sentences twice arranged in paragraph order. He finally includes an explanation (headed 'Key') of the elements common to each group of sentences.[4] Although Beckett's key is necessary in order to establish any progression of thought in *Sans/Lessness*, the shuffled arrangement of sentences makes its own points by introducing the element of chance into formal patterning and, by emphasizing the cyclic nature of the piece, gives it its particular quality of endlessness. Instead of a prose statement in which certain themes evolve and some kind of progression from A 1 - F 10 may be deduced, the themes become linked in paragraphs that lead nowhere. Each paragraph of interleaved statements forms its own small circle of thought and is thus held static. These circles in turn revolve round each other, within the circle formed by linked phrases in the first and last paragraphs, thus forming a tight, verse-like structure.

When read consecutively from A 1 — F 10, *Lessness* may be seen to be concerned with recurring time cycles. Beckett's choice of a cyclic mode of expression to state a circular idea thus seems to be an example of the union of form and content that we have noticed him approving in the work of Joyce. In *Lessness*, the fact that the circles of words have been described as coming about fortuitously, comments upon the nature of time itself. Time is endless (hence the circles) but structured human time is arbitrary (hence the accidental arrangement of these circles.) Cohn sums it up as follows:

> Though the text is almost bare of figures, it compels calculation, and the resultant numbers serve to call attention to human time. The number of sentences per paragraph stops at seven, the number of days in a week. The number of paragraphs reaches twenty-four, the number of hours in a day. The number of different sentences is sixty, the number of seconds in a minute, of minutes in an hour. But the repetition of the sixty sentences in a different order suggests the capricious arrangement of passing time.[5]

Given that the arrangement of sentences is arbitrary, they seem almost uncannily well-dispersed. Not only do the sentences appear deftly interwoven, but each paragraph seems complete in itself, and aptly to fit into the pattern of the whole. The statement in each paragraph can either stand alone, or be seen as part of a pattern of recurring statements. This dual quality is partly due to the structure of each sentence, for there is no syntax apart from full stops. Each phrase, unpinned by commas, has the capacity to be part of the whole or to stand alone. As in *Ping*, from which, Beckett states in the key, *Lessness* 'proceeds', there are no verbs. Thus phrases may be linked in the reader's mind by, for example, the present tense, as:

B 1 (It is) Ash Grey (on) all sides earth sky (are) as one
(on) all sides (there is) endlessness.

Such an exercise loses the poetic quality of the prose. It was precisely Beckett's intention to free the language from the weight of tense and make all the sentences multi-dimensional, thus:

A 8 (There were
(There are Scattered ruins ash grey all sides true refuge
(There will be long last issueless

Repetition permeates *Lessness*; not only repetition of phrases that, because of the shuffled arrangement, reverberate through the text, but onomatopoeic repetition, as in words echoing the title (endlessness, changelessness) or words approximating towards the title (timeless, issueless). The sounds 'less' and 'ness' thus become distinctly recognised notes as the text unfolds. Alliterative repetition of this kind is also an integral part of the original French text. 'Sans' is echoed, for example, in 'sanctuaire', 'temps', 'en', 'blanc', 'passant', 'encore' and 'silence'.

Despite the element of chance in its construction *Lessness* appears precisely balanced. There is, for example, exact polarisation in the language, in phrases such as old love/new love, other nights/better days, light white/ blacked out. Colour values themselves are balanced. Light and darkness is a recurring theme in Beckett's work, as James Knowlson has pointed out;[6] in *Lessness* the predominant colour is grey, a combination of white and black that reflects the sameness and uniformity of the repetitive language and the blank world it describes:

A 9 Scattered ruins same grey as the sand ash grey true refuge.
B 6 No sound not a breath same grey all sides earth sky body ruins.

When, in this grey world, the colour blue appears, the surprise effect parallels that of the 'little body heart beating' that stands out the more sharply for its background of blank planes.

The effectiveness of *Lessness* rests on keeping a balance between similarity (repetition, alliteration) and the difference inherent in the particular theme that distinguishes each family of sentences. As Beckett reveals in the key, the ten sentences of each section are ' 'signed' by certain elements common to them all.' The signature of *Section A*, for example, is 'true refuge'. This phrase appears in each sentence, though its position is not fixed. It is found once at the beginning of a sentence, once at the end, and at different points in between in the remaining sentences. Were all ten sentences to be read consecutively, however, the effect would be less harmonious than balancing the phrase against some quite different image in another group of sentences, such as the 'little body' in Section C. The shuffling of sentences, in other words, though arbitrary, has the definite function of balancing a text which, when read consecutively, is over-repetitious. If all the like sentences come together, the balance is lost.

Certain phrases do recur from section to section. 'No sound', for example, occurs at A 4 A 5 A 6, B 4 B 6 B 8 B 9, E 6 and E 9. When shuffled, there is an exceptional concentration of the phrase at the beginning of the piece, in both Part I and Part II. It occurs in paragraphs 1, 2, 4, 5, 6 and 7 in Part I and paragraphs 1, 2 and 3 of the repeat. Effects of this nature can make it hard to believe that Beckett did not have his tongue in his cheek when describing his method of structuring the piece to Ruby Cohn. On the other hand each sentence, has as we have observed, the ability to stand alone, and a further arbitrary rearrangement of the text, though resulting in a different combination of sentences, would still produce basically the same effect of thought circles. And precisely because each sentence can stand alone, the new form would appear as inevitable as the present arrangement. To test this hypothesis I followed the directions quoted earlier and produced a new version of *Lessness*, which may be seen at Appendix III.[7]

Provided with Beckett's key, it is possible to discern a progression of thought in *Lessness*, a more ample version of the statement made in *Breath* (written apparently at much the same time)[8] of a continuing human life cycle. Each section contains certain key themes and emphasises particular words or phrases. 'True refuge', as has been observed, is the recurring phrase in *Section A*, although others (such as 'four walls over backwards' and 'scattered ruins') are repeated several times. Ruins dominate the imagery in this section. It is reminiscent of the ruined world seen from the window in *Endgame*, where all is 'grey' or at least 'Light black. From pole to pole.' In *Lessness* (A 2) physical structure is described as 'Blacked out fallen open four walls over backwards' while later in the section repetition reinforces the impression of devastation:

A 7 ... scattered ruins same grey as the sand.
A 8 Scattered ruins ash grey all sides ...
A 9 Scattered ruins same grey as the sand ash grey ...

While not wishing to restrict Beckett to a single interpretation, it may be observed that references to 'ash' and 'smouldering' close the first section of an earlier work, *Play*. They occur immediately before the three heads describe their changed state of being, inhabiting the urns to which they make no reference. With *Play* as a starting point, it is a short step from the 'blacked out fallen open four walls' of A 2 to the 'Scattered ruins ash grey all sides' of A 8 — from the coffin to the crematorium, perhaps. 'Dust to dust' could well be seen as the theme of A 9:

Scattered ruins same grey as the sand ash grey true refuge.

Beckett notes in his key that the common theme of *Section A* is the 'collapse of refuge'. Whatever refuge was represented by the 'four walls' has 'split asunder' and 'fallen open', leaving only 'scattered ruins'; yet the recurring phrase or signature for the section 'true refuge' has positive implications.

Section B describes some kind of limbo world in which images of earth and sky are indistinguishable from each other ('earth sky as one') and infinity is deliberately called to mind in six repetitions of the words 'endless' or 'endlessness'. Once more there is 'no sound' (four times repeated) and a new concept 'no stir' also occurs four times. Beckett notes in the key that the 'outer world' represented by 'earth ... sky juxtaposed or apart' is the common factor in all ten sentences of this section. The most startling image in *Section B* is, however, that of the 'little body only upright' that suddenly appears in an otherwise horizontal world in B 3:

Flatness endless little body only upright same grey all sides
earth sky body ruins

The image recurs in B 7:

. . . all sides endlessness little body only upright.

It seems impossible for life to exist in this void. Life, in this ash grey universe, might be seen in terms of 'in my end is my beginning' as in Eliot's *East Coker*. But Eliot's was a spiritual progression, paralleling the natural cycle, whereas Beckett's thought seems to tend here towards physical regeneration, in the manner of the phoenix. Compare *The Unnamable*:

It will be the same silence, the same as ever, murmurous with muted lamentation, panting and exhaling of impossible sorrow, like distant laughter, and brief spells of hush, as of one buried before his time. Long or short, the same silence. Then I resurrect and begin again.[9]

Section C, according to Beckett, represents 'body exposed', identified by the repetition of 'little body' in all ten sentences. The little body 'heart beating' (a new image) seems to be locked inescapably into a cyclic progression, its 'face to endlessness'. This section is full of shock imagery. The 'heart beating' calls to mind the end of Yeats's play *The Resurrection*, where 'The heart of a phantom is beating!'[10] The effect is also similar to George Herbert's poem 'Easter', where an apparently simple account of gathering an Easter posy suddenly presents us with a lurid glimpse of the risen Christ, scented as for the grave, in his embalming oils and spices:

I got me flowers to straw thy way;
I got me boughs off many a tree:
But thou wast up by break of day,
And brought'st thy sweets along with thee.[11]

In *Lessness*, although the little body is 'locked rigid' (C 1) its heart is beating. In C 2 the imagery suggests a corpse: 'Legs a single block arms fast to sides little body face to endlessness'. But C3 reminds us that the body is not horizontal: 'Heart beating little body only upright. . .'. Yeats again comes to mind with his poem 'The Black Tower':

There in the tomb stand the dead upright.[12]

C 3 continues:

. . . grey face features overrun two pale blue.

The new and striking colour image combined with the 'overrun' features has a real shock effect, as though live eyes are staring from a rotting face. In C 6 the body is further described as having a:

> . . . grey face features slit and little holes two pale blue.

The separate references to 'holes' and 'two pale blue' are disturbing images, as though the eyes in this body have somehow become divorced from their sockets. In C 8 we learn:

> . . . genitals overrun arse a single block grey crack overrun.

Decomposition, it appears, may have set in. But, horrifyingly, C 9 reveals the heart still beating and in C 10 the body is still upright, though almost skeleton-like:

> . . . Only upright little body grey smooth no relief a few holes.

References to ash are noticeably absent from *Section C*. Dust to dust imagery has been replaced by that of the little body 'legs a single block arms fast to sides'. But, if the undertones of the crematorium have disappeared, here there seems to be coffined decomposition, features gradually merging into each other, until all that is left is a 'few holes'. Yet, always undercutting and coexisting with the death imagery are life images, the upright body, its heart beating and the 'two pale blue' belying its 'grey face'.

Section D brings a structural change to the language. The phrase 'all gone from mind' is repeated ten times in an unchanging position in the sentence structure. It comes like a refrain at the end of each sentence and serves to emphasise the sense of being wiped clean that dominates this section, reinforced by phrases such as 'sheer white blank planes' and by such words as 'void'. The 'little body' of the previous section has become, in the first phrase of *Section D*, 'little void'. It appears that the little void has been purged in this section by a 'mighty light' until 'all gone from mind'.

It will be remembered that in *Play* three heads in their respective urns face a probing light beam. In *Section D* of *Lessness* physical imagery also concentrates upon the head and face. D 2, for example, has 'head through' and D 4 'face to calm eye', while, in each case, the phrase 'touch close' clearly associates the head with the light. It is contact with the light, the 'calm eye', that appears to erase 'all' from the mind:

D 2 Light white touch close head through calm eye light of reason all gone from mind.
D 4 Face to calm eye touch close all calm all white all gone from mind.

In both D 2 and D 5 the phrase 'light of reason' occurs following the phrase 'calm eye' and thus associated with it. As in *Play* it appears that light, 'the calm eye', performs a purging function. Towards the end of this section there is a particular sense of obliteration:

D 8 Blank planes sheer white eye calm long last all gone from mind.
D 9 Head through calm eye all light white calm all gone from mind.

In D 10 the idea of a 'refuge' appears, as in *Section A*, only here it is associated with light:

> Light refuge sheer white blank planes all gone from mind.

A refuge from the light, perhaps, recalling the wish of the heads in *Play*; or is the light itself a refuge, an agent bringing about the desired state of oblivion? The statement as it stands can be seen both ways. Beckett's key, however, shows him to have had a further possibility in mind, it reads:

Group D — Refuge forgotten — sign: 'all gone from mind'.

By the end of *Section D* there is not so much as a trace on the memory of the refuge that had collapsed in *Section A*.

In *Section E* all previous experience is denied:

E 1 Never was but grey air timeless no stir not a breath.

'The passing hour' is said to have occurred 'in vanished dream' alone. Beckett describes this section as:

Group E — Past and future denied — sign: 'never' — except in the one sentence 'figment dawn . . . etc.'

The idea of the past as merely a 'vanished dream' links with a theme Beckett has presented in earlier works such as *Play*. It is a theme to which we shall return in connexion with Yeats and concerns what Yeats termed the 'dreaming back' after death over one's past life, until a state of innocence or purification is achieved. In *Section D* of *Lessness* the fact that all has gone from mind could be seen as indicating that purification has been attained, so that life seems merely a 'vanished dream'. Yeats believed that after the state of innocence had been reached a further life or lives would be required from the human spirit, until it was freed from the cycle of creation. The statement in E 4 is of interest here:

never but in dream the happy dream only one time to serve.

The idea of servitude to a wheel of regeneration and the longing to be freed from it is one of the chief preoccupations of *The Unnamable* as we have seen in *Section B* or again in the following example:

. . . Then the breath fails, the end begins, you go silent, it's the end, short-lived, you begin again.[13]

Section E consists of a series of fictional propositions: that 'the days and nights' were dreams, that there 'never was' another state of being, that light itself is a 'figment'. It is the same kind of fiction that occurs in *Not I*, where the voice's 'vehement refusal to relinquish third person', to acknowledge that 'she' is 'I', is the core of the dramatic situation. The 'narrator' in *Lessness* relegates all manifestations of life (such as 'this wild laughter these cries', and blue, the only life-giving colour in this blank world) to 'wild imagining'. The imagination 'the blue celeste of poesy' has conjured up these ideas. It is as though what purports to be reason (though 'light of reason' was said to have vanished in *Section D*) is attempting to discredit romanticism. But we recognise the veracity of the imagination, which alone recalls the vanished past that the mind refuses to countenance as other than a 'figment'. The words that echo in *Section E* are determined negatives, 'never was' and 'never but', which occur nine times. The final sentence (also the closing sentence of the piece in the shuffled arrangement) stands alone:

E 10 Figment dawn dispeller of figments and the other called dusk.

In *Section F* dream gives place to reality and an affirmation of life takes place, with the introduction of verbs in the future tense: 'he will make it', 'he will stir in the sand', 'he will live again', 'it will be day and night again over him', 'the air heart will beat again'. The auxiliary verb occurs in every sentence, rejuvenating the earlier sterility, while the section (and indeed work as a whole) draws to a close with life-giving images of rain:

F8 On him will rain again as in the blessed days of blue the passing cloud.

F9 Old love new love as in the blessed days unhappiness will reign again.

F10 He will curse God again as in the blessed days face to the open sky the passing deluge.

Beckett describes the final section thus:

Group F — Past and future affirmed — sign: future tense.

The final impression when *Lessness* is read through consecutively is one of transitoriness within the eternal cycle. The fleeting nature of human existence (implied in the repetition of 'passing') contrasts with the 'endlessness' stressed earlier and is contained by it. Existence is an endless succession of passing moments, in which both past and future are continually affirmed. Love will again become part of the experience of he who denied the reality of dawn and dusk. But the experience is not to be wholly positive. Love, in Beckett's terms, means unhappiness, and 'unhappiness will reign again'. Regeneration will lead him to 'curse God again', recalling Hamm's attack on his father in *Endgame*: 'Accursed progenitor!'.

With such an interpretation in mind, the repetition of 'passing' becomes almost hopeful, implying at least a cessation of suffering. The particular irony of Beckett's vision is that *nothing* lasts, but the inescapable fact of 'being' itself. The way ahead is only 'one step more in the endlessness', like Zeno's never completed millet heap.[14] Within the 'passing' of the rainshower in the natural order is contained its future recurrence. Similarly, 'being' consists of an endless series of fleeting existences, each bringing its own unhappiness and ending in a temporary and thus delusive silence. The most that can be hoped for in such a vision is to pass the time not too unpleasantly, as in *Godot*:

Vladimir: That passed the time.
Estragon: It would have passed in any case.
Vladimir: Yes, but not so rapidly.

The fact that Beckett's personae throughout his work long to escape the cycle of being is not seen as perverse. Because their view of life is negative, the state of negation, of having been, is the one that appeals to them. The state described in *Section D* of *Lessness* of 'all gone from mind' is the desirable one, and the return, in *Section F,* a mockery.

For the life-giving rainshower (the 'gentle rain from heaven' of God's mercy, perhaps) to be described as a 'passing deluge' could be seen as the ultimate pessimism in *Lessness*. 'He will curse God again' since such rain is a mockery of mercy, bringing only temporary relief to one trapped in the cycle of creation. There are similarities here with the situation in *Play*, where the light gradually fades as the text unfolds, bringing possible implications of mercy and freedom for the trapped voices, only to return to full strength as the play closes. Any hope of help from divine intervention is thus seen to be ill-founded.

F 10 is not the end but part of the 'endlessness' of *Lessness*. The cycle that may be discerned with the aid of Beckett's key remains, however, for the general reader, intricately enmeshed in sentences that turn back upon themselves, creating a limbo world of their own. A search for meaning in this void seems to parallel the enigma of the human situation — the use of the future tense hinting at positives ('he will make it') but each such usage trapped in its own paragraph cycle. The text is thus doubly poised: there is both the original scheme which, when read consecutively, helps us to understand the work, and the published reading of the interleaved arrangement, which makes its own comment on the human predicament, and, by breaking up the repetitious sentence groups, balances the text. The cycle of being or content of the work is thus brilliantly fused with its form, in the cyclic structure of the language.

CHAPTER 4
FORM AND CONTENT; THE CIRCLE

The fusion of form and content we have noticed in *Lessness* is precisely of the kind to which Beckett drew attention in his early critical writings. His essay on Joyce (1929) contains the statement 'Here form *is* content, content *is* form',[1] while of Proust he said:

> Proust does not share the superstition that form is nothing and content everything ... For Proust the quality of language is more important than any system of ethics or aesthetics. Indeed he makes no attempt to dissociate form from content. The one is a concretion of the other, the revelation of a world.[2]

This chapter takes Beckett's observations on form as the starting point for analyses of six plays in which the essential role of shape in establishing meaning is discovered in his own work. The selection of plays is not chronological, since the group of plays under discussion (*Play, That Time, Breath, Acte sans Paroles II, Come and Go* and *Not I*) is chosen in order to reveal the precision of Beckett's structural method and to demonstrate his characteristic use of cyclic patterning. *Play*, a major example of Beckett's cyclic patterning, is taken first, because the symmetry of this play makes an interesting comparison with the mathematical exactitude of *Lessness*.

Play

At the end of his article on Joyce Beckett considers in some detail the patterning in Joyce and Dante, contrasting Dante's conical view of purgatory with Joyce's spherical one. Since *Play* also takes the purgatorial theme and makes use of both motifs, this is of especial interest. Beckett interprets Joyce as depicting the 'vicious circle of humanity', whereas Dante describes a spiral, implying culmination. An implicit parallel is made between the Joycean concept and Vico's division of human history, in the

Scienza Nuova, into recurring cycles, each followed by a *ricorso* or return. Vico's *ricorso* may also be seen in relation to *Play*, where the text is repeated once in its entirety and is beginning for a third time as the play ends.

Certain affinities between the plays of Beckett and those of W. B. Yeats should be taken into consideration here. We have already noticed Beckett's admiration for the play *At The Hawk's Well*, which he saw, among 'other Yeats' plays' when in Dublin.[3] In *Happy Days* he quotes the first line of *At The Hawk's Well* — 'I call to the eye of the mind' — as part of the sweep of English poetry in which he sets Winnie, her head full of half-remembered lines. Furthermore the title of one of Beckett's latest plays for television *. . . but the clouds . . .* is taken from the last verse of Yeats's poem 'The Tower'.[4] It would be strange indeed if Beckett, born and brought up in Ireland, had not been interested in the growing reputation of Yeats. As a young man, moreover, Beckett formed a close friendship with the poet's younger brother, Jack B. Yeats, and published reviews of his work as both writer and painter.[5] Parallels between Jack Yeats's writing and Beckett's own work have been observed by Roger Angus.[6]

In the winter of 1913-14, Ezra Pound introduced W. B. Yeats to the Japanese Noh play, bringing to his attention Ernest Fenollosa's work on the subject. Yeats subsequently took a great deal from the Noh tradition although he evolved his own style of dramatic writing, so that his plays are very much 'Yeats Noh'.[7] He particularly liked the stylised form of the Noh play, its dialogue counterpointed by linked opening, central and closing choruses, and his later and most successful plays (from *At The Hawk's Well* onwards) are similarly shaped. Beckett also uses the technique of the chorus in *Play*, where the three voices all speak together at certain points, before emerging singly, compelled by the light.

From ideas gained in a wide reading of philosophers from Plato to Swedenborg, Yeats in *A Vision* formed the view mentioned earlier that, after death, the human spirit was destined to dream back through its life.[8] Gradually the skein of life would be unwound until a state of innocence was reached — after which the spirit would either be given a new life, or, if it were fortunate, freed from the necessity of 'becoming' and allowed to remain at rest in the intuitive centre of the world, or *anima mundi*. In *The Only Jealousy of Emer*, for instance, we see the Goddess Fand offering to free Cuchulain from the burden of future incarnations, if he will only enter the state of eternity by kissing her.

Yeats stressed the fact that if a life had contained some unresolved emotional 'knot' the spirit would be forced to stay at that point until the knot were untied, when it could continue the process of purification. This is the situation in his *Purgatory* and *The Dreaming of the Bones* — where the spirits are trapped and compelled to relive their unhappy experience, like a record stuck in a groove. This also is the starting point for Beckett's *Play*, where voices issue from three human heads surmounting three urns centrally placed onstage.

Although nowhere specifically stated, the implication is that the voices (which belong to a man and two women) are reliving an emotional experience likely to have taken place immediately before death, since each moves from thoughts of the experience to a consideration of his/her changed state of being. When elicited by a probing light-beam which moves from urn to urn, each voice intones a monologue, apparently into a vacuum. Although the occupant of each urn is unaware of the presence of the other two, the audience gradually becomes aware that all three voices have been involved in the same emotional situation. This is achieved by a process of echo and counterpoint, so that one voice may repeat a phrase or apparently answer a question asked by another. The earlier statement is thus extended and the whole picture is built up fragmentarily, in the manner of Cubist art.[9]

As if to emphasise this point, the entire play is then repeated, so that the audience, at first unaware that the action has ended, begins to recognise phrases, finally with a sense of *déjà vu*, registering the *da capo* effect. Immediate recognition is made more difficult by the fact that the repeat may be conducted at a slower pace and with a decreased intensity of light and sound. The word picture builds itself up again in the way that a figure is suddenly recognised within a mass of Cubist shapes. The method is similar to that described by Dorothy Sayers in a letter to John Curnos in 1925, discussing the 'craft' of writing mystery stories. 'It is rather like laying a mosaic — putting each piece — apparently meaningless and detached — into its place, until one suddenly sees the thing as a consistent picture.'[10] Beckett achieves a dual Cubist effect in *Play*: the initial picture is built up fragmentarily and the audience forms a concept as to its meaning. The repeat then gradually re-exposes the same picture and the audience is forced to readjust to the realisation that it has heard it all before.

For convenience I have referred to a building up of 'the whole' picture. This, of course, is not the case. Beckett is always ambiguous and no sooner has he metaphorically revealed a minus, than he demonstrates the corresponding plus. For example, the nihilistic view of existence he is often said to demonstrate can emerge as a positive quality, that of endlessness. Beckett always balances his extremes, 'I take no sides . . .' he has said.[11] Thus, while we are enabled to get a fairly clear idea of the stresses of the emotional tangle in which the three voices in *Play* were involved, we cannot state when or how their deaths occurred — or even, with absolute certainty, that they are dead — although, given the urns, this would seem to be a logical starting point for our understanding of the play.

The relationship in which the voices are still trapped is what is often called the 'eternal triangle'. Beckett here seems to be playing upon the fullest possibilities of the word 'eternal', just as the whole play puns upon its title: *Play* is a play in which a beam of light seems to be playing a game with three urns. The male voice refers to the past as 'just . . . play' and wonders how long it will be before he can see his present situation in the same way. The final question, which echoes beyond the play, considers whether his presence in the universe is perhaps no more than an appalling joke. This question is emphasised by the ensuing repetition of the play, which reveals Beckett to have been playing an elaborate game with his audience. Is our supposedly God-given existence no more than the artifice of a supreme dramatic craftsman?

Beckett's play cannot be dismissed as mere trickery, however, for it can be seen to have developed structurally from the initial idea of the triangle: not only are there three voices issuing from the three urns, but each voice in its monologue makes nine basic statements or the square of three — making the total statement three cubed. Further, the concept of one person excluded implicit in a triangular relationship is carried through into the language: two voices continually echo each other, while the third makes an unrelated remark, yet still maintains its connexion with the other monologues, emphasising the complexity of the human situation. As the man's allegiance shifted between the two women, so the pattern of linked voices fluctuates. At the beginning, however, the intrusive comment comes from W II — who emerges as the 'other woman', threatening M's marriage with W I. As M says at one point: 'Adulterers, take warning, never admit'.

It will be remembered that Dante's *Divine Comedy* is in *terza rima*. This form works by introducing between a couplet an unrhymed line, which takes over the rhyme in the ensuing verse and is, in its turn, supplanted. This in effect is what W II has done to the relationship of M and W I, although the parallel should not be taken to excess. Interesting too is the fact that Beckett's prose both echoes the *terza rima* effect, and, by making an implicit link with Dante, strengthens the view that the three voices in *Play* are trapped in an after life.

A closer look at the alleged *terza rima* patterning reveals, in the opening chorus for example, both M and W I contemplating their obliteration and using the same words at the same points in their statements: 'It will come' and 'all over'. W II's statement, punning on the word 'shade', is sandwiched between them in the text. When the voices first divide into their separate accounts, that of W II is again placed between the others. All three voices make a similar remark, but the first and last relate to the other woman ('give her up' and 'give up that whore') while the central one relates to the man – 'give him up'. Moreover the first and third remarks refer to an oath which is not found in the central one and could be an oblique reference to the marriage bond. W I says: 'I swore by all I held most sacred' while M recalls her as having said 'So help me God'. The phrase emerges through repetition as M's own *cri de coeur*.

In the next group of three speeches the two guilty figures are linked by their common pretences to W I, who now becomes the central figure: 'What are you talking about?' says W II – and M: 'What have you to complain of?' In the series following the two women are linked by their common use of the verb 'confess', but perhaps rather more tenuously with a phrase similar in meaning 'there was no denying' at the centre of the previous series.

A *W1:* I said to him, *Give her up. I swore by all I held most sacred* –
(Spot from W1 to W2.)

W2: One morning as I was sitting stitching by the open
B window she burst in and flew at me. Give him up, she screamed, he's mine. Her photographs were kind to her. Seeing her now for the first time full length in the flesh I understood why he preferred me.
(Spot from W2 to M.)

A *M:* We were not long together when she smelled the rat. *Give up that whore* she said, or I'll cut my throat – (hiccup) pardon – *so help me God*. I knew she could have no proof. So I told her I did not know what she was talking about.
(Spot from M to W2.)

BII B	*W2:*	**What are you talking about?** I said, stitching away. Someone yours? Give up whom? I smell you off him she screamed, he stinks of bitch.
		(Spot from W2 to W1.)
C	*W1:*	Though I had him dogged for months by a first-rate man, no shadow of proof was forthcoming. And there was no denying that he continued as . . . assiduous as ever. This, and his horror of the merely Platonic thing, made me sometimes wonder if I were not accusing him unjustly. Yes.
		(Spot from W1 to M.)
BII	*M:*	**What have you to complain of?** I said. Have I been neglecting you? How could we be together in the way we are if there were someone else? Loving her as I did with all my heart, I could not but feel sorry for her.
		(Spot from M to W2.)
C	*W2:*	Fearing she was about to offer me violence I rang for Erskine and had her shown out. Her parting words, as he could testify, if he is still living, and has not forgotten, coming and going on the earth, letting people in, showing people out, were to the effect that she would settle my hash. I confess this did alarm me a little, at the time.
		(Spot from M to W1.)
D	*M:*	She was not convinced. I might have known. I smell her off you, she kept saying. There was no answer to this. So I took her in my arms and swore I could not live without her. I meant it, what is more. Yes, I am sure I did. She did not repulse me.
		(Spot from M to W1.)
C	*W1:*	Judge then of my astoundment when one fine morning, as I was sitting stricken in the morning room, he slunk in, fell on his knees before me, buried his face in my lap and . . . confessed.

It is obviously important not to be dogmatic here, because other verbal connexions between the speeches may be made. An abrupt break in the triads (or series of three speeches) is created by a blackout following W2's line: 'All night I smelt them smouldering'. By leaving the final triad incomplete, the apparent intervention of death in the narrative is paralleled. Had it been completed, there would have been 33 speeches to this point, paralleling Dante's usual practice of having 33 Canti to a book in the *Divine Comedy*. It is noticeable that there are 33 speeches (excluding choruses) in the final section of the play (which follows the blackout after W2's 'momentum coming'.)[12] Thus *Play* has a tripartite structure, divided by blackouts, with precisely balanced first and third sections and a long central section.

Returning to the article on Joyce, we find Beckett specifically noting Dante's emphasis on the number three:

> The death of Beatrice inspired nothing less than a highly complicated poem dealing with the importance of the number 3 in her life. Dante never ceased to be obsessed by this number. Thus the poem is divided into three Cantiche, each composed of 33 Canti, and written in terza rima.[13]

Beckett compares this emphasis with Joyce's preoccupation with the significance of numbers, ending: 'he is conscious that things with a common numerical characteristic tend towards a very significant interrelationship'. It is just such a 'significant interrelationship' that we find in *Play*.[14]

M's monologue may be taken as the type for the other two, in that each voice passes through similar stages of thought. Following M through his series of nine statements, we find the opening statement presenting what might be called the 'thesis' — to which the voice returns in more detail as the monologue progresses. M's thesis consists of a consideration of his new state. The second phase comprises the history of the triangular relationship — in M's case of being hag-ridden by two women. He speaks of them alternately, sometimes hiccuping, which serves to emphasise the dichotomy of his situation; his request for 'pardon' is clearly doubly meant. The climax comes with: 'Finally it was all too much. I simply could no longer —', the latter phrase being repeated just before the blackout. This time the strain has not merely held up the narrative, but apparently separated him from life. The third statement is a renewed consideration of his present state, leading to a questioning of the future (4th statement). In the fifth statement he fantasises about the two women and a realisation of pity for them both develops (6th). In the seventh statement he addresses the light, relapsing into fantasies about the women in the eighth. Finally he returns to questioning the light (9th) as a prelude to repeating the entire text.

This formula is paralleled exactly by the two women; since they are telling their own versions of the same story, it is obvious that some correlation will occur — but Beckett gives their statements a precise balance. In the initial expository phase, for example, the first woman speaks of the man then the second woman consecutively twice — while the second woman in the same manner speaks of the first woman then the man.

As each square of statements progresses, certain variations of theme occur; while, for example, the man and the second woman both spend phase four in questions, the first woman considers the possibility that there are no more questions to ask or answer: 'No-one asking me for anything at all'. In the fifth phase they all think of each other in various ways, leading, in the sixth phase, to pity. It is possible that this learning of pity — which may be compared with the auditor's 'helpless compassion' in *Not I* — is the 'truth' that is needed from each of them in order to unravel the emotional knot, before they can be freed for the downward spiral towards oblivion. It certainly marks a great change from the cat-like qualities the women had exhibited in their previous state, when, for example, W II was sharpening her claws with a nail-file as W I entered, spoiling for a brawl.

All three voices are conscious that the light is making demands of them — demands they are unable to fulfil, since they do not know what is being asked:

> *W I* Is it that I do not tell the truth, is that it, that some day somehow I may tell the truth at last and then no more light at last, for the truth?

By the end of her monologue W I seems to be challenging the light to register that it has had all it can from her — all she is able to give: 'Yes, and the whole thing there, all there, staring you in the face. You'll see it'. With his usual ambiguity Beckett has allowed this hint of possible discovery to apply to the woman herself; one day *she* may register the truth, which is perhaps no more than an acceptance of her situation. Since, however, Beckett sometimes leaves a way open to Christian interpretation (generally undercut by contrary information, such as M. Godot favouring the goatherd at the expense of the shepherd) there could be a link between the light and the opening of St. John's Gospel: 'And the light shineth in darkness; and the darkness comprehended it not'. The light is both friend and enemy to the voices, who each sense, with a mixture of relief and apprehension, that the time will come for it to leave them:

> *W 2* Some day you will tire of me and go out . . . for good.[ ] Give me up, as a bad job. Go away and start poking and pecking at someone else.[ ] On the other hand things may disimprove, there is that danger.

Although the voices are unaware of having uttered any liberating truths, the light may be less brilliant, less apparently demanding in the repeat and the reaction of the voices correspondingly slower and more hesitant, as if they were finding it increasingly difficult to remember, and had been dragged by the light from a greater distance. In this interpretation the energy which had stimulated the investigation seems to be becoming exhausted and the light appears as the victim of its own inquisition. On releasing the voices into darkness it must cease, a kind of *hara-kiri* effect that might also have religious implications; the voices are enabled to continue their dreaming back, but the light itself is extinguished.

That this was not Beckett's original concept is clear from the first English text of 1964, which lacks stage directions for the repeat. In the 1968 text there are detailed suggestions for its possible variation. The choice between playing the repeat as 'an exact replica', or with variations in speed, light, sound and speech order is left to the director. In his letter to George Devine, director of the first English performance in 1964, Beckett discusses the evolution of the repeat, which he describes as the *da capo*. The idea of variation arose in the 1964 Paris production, at which Beckett assisted:

> According to the text it is rigorously identical with the first statement. We now think it would be dramatically more effective to have it express a slight weakening, both of question and response, by means of less and perhaps slower light and correspondingly less volume and speed of voice.[ ] The impression of falling off which this would give, with suggestion of conceivable dark and silence in the end, or of an indefinite approximating towards it, would be reinforced if we obtained also, in the repeat, a quality of hesitancy, of both question and answer, perhaps not so much in a slowing down of actual débit as in a less confident movement of spot from one face to another and less immediate reaction of the voices.[15]

These new ideas were incorporated as possibilities into the stage directions of subsequent editions of *Play*. The original cyclic concept is still present, because the play ends just after the opening of a *second* repeat, where the voices are once more at 'normal strength'. Nevertheless, the possibility of eventual release from the cyclic experience is present in Yeats's plays, and Beckett seems to have played upon a similar concept when rehearsing *Play*, until a linear appearance developed. Stage directions for light intensity give a reduction to half strength at the first blackout the first time round, so that further reductions for the repeat produce an impression of continuous fading, heightened by the slowing down of the voices and their diminished sound. The light is in fact being used as a conductor's baton, to elicit tone and speed effects from the voices. It becomes virtually a fourth character — generating the 'action' — a kind of celestial ventriloquist, the heads its dummies.[16] The idea of a controlling but unseen presence operating the light is reminiscent of *Endgame*, where Hamm plays out his final game of chess against an unseen King.

The fact that *Play* ends on a third repeat makes a strong parallel with the end of Yeats's *Purgatory*: just as the old man is congratulating himself on having freed his mother from 'all that consequence', he hears his father's approaching hoof-beats, preluding the re-enactment of his parents' copulation - during which he himself will be beaten into being once more and his mother compelled yet again to repent. In *Play* just as it seems that the voices are to be freed, the needle sticks — and they are forced to start again at the beginning of the record.

The linear pattern that evolved in production is seriously offset by the return to cyclic action, when the light at the end of the play resumes 'normal strength'. In terms of pattern it is as though Beckett were toying with the idea of the Dantean cone or spiral and its implied culmination, only to find that there is no escape from the circle — Joyce's 'vicious circle of humanity'. Replying to an enquiry of my own about the repeat, Beckett wrote 'exact repeat preferable', and he recommended this approach in the 1976 production of the play at the Royal Court Theatre, directed by Donald McWhinnie.

Even should the light be extinguished and the enquiry prove linear, oblivion is not guaranteed for the voices. There could be other (later) lights impeding their 'dreaming back' and, on arrival at the state of innocence, a new life might immediately be required of them, a new upward spiral. We have already noticed that Beckett may have such an idea in mind. Towards the end of *The Unnamable*, for example, Mahood says:

> But say I succeed in dying, to adopt the most comfortable hypothesis, without having been able to believe I ever lived, I know to my cost it is not that they wish for me. For it has happened to me many times already, without their having granted me as much as a brief sick-leave among the worms, before resurrecting me.[17]

At the end of the book, the 'I' *persona* feels that release from the necessity of being can only be achieved through saying the thing unknown — which is exactly W I's preoccupation in *Play* and that of the Mouth in *Not I*: 'Perhaps I've said the thing that had to be said, that gives me the right to be done with speech, done with listening, done with hearing, without my knowing it.'[18]

It is important not to reduce Beckett's work to a single interpretation, since its particular delight is its richness of possibility. In *Play*, since it would be alien to Beckett to state the existence of so positive a condition as an 'after life', it remains an implication, gathering weight from the play's links with Dante and Yeats.

That Time

The triangular relationship in *Play* becomes the starting point for a complex structure of triple patterning. A later play, *That Time* (1974)[19] makes use of a tripartite structure very similar to that of *Play*. In this case the triangular theme is used to express the three main stages of a human lifespan: childhood, adulthood and old age. We shall look briefly at each stage, before seeing how the three are interwoven in a structure of extraordinary precision.

The protagonist of *That Time*, an old man, is never seen to utter. His head alone is visible, hanging in mid-air 'about ten feet above stage level'. He has an: 'old white face, long flaring white hair as if seen from above outspread'. The head seems to be suspended in space as though resting on an invisible pillow — which indeed, as will be seen later from the drafts, was Beckett's original concept. The old man listens to his recorded voice coming to him from both sides of the stage and above his head. The voice is labelled A B and C and each, as in *Play*, speaks a separate monologue. The first monologue (A) tells the tale of a lonely child hiding in a ruin 'where none ever came', 'talking to yourself who else'. On returning in old age to try to take a tram or train to the same spot, the voice describes finding the tram lines 'all rust' and the station 'closed down' so that he 'gave up' and never got there.

Monologue B relates a relationship of a kind, but: 'never turned to each other . . . no touching or anything of that nature always space between . . .'. The relationship seems to involve the duty increasingly to avow mutual love, so that the reiteration becomes not only a mockery of the marriage vow, but has perhaps implications of punishment for lovelessness. The two are 'always parallel like an axle-tree', recalling the Noh play *Nishikigi*, and Yeats's treatment of the same theme in *The*

Dreaming of the Bones, where two lovers are condemned to eternal separation. Voice B describes them as 'stretched out parallel in the sand ... stock still side by side', a graveyard situation that compares with the parallel urns in *Play*. The sense of negation is reinforced by the emphasis on stone in the play. All three voices are continually described as sitting on stone of some kind, or 'in the sand'.

The essential sterility of Voice B's approach to love is summed up in the reference to a dead rat 'caught in the reeds'. Throughout Beckett's drama an experience of love lost is remembered with nostalgic regret. In each case, from Krapp to Winnie, the experience is associated with water: a boat on a lake in *Endgame* and *Krapp*; a fantasy of 'a little dinghy, on the river' in *Play*; 'watching the ducks ... Holding hands exchanging vows ...' in *Eh Joe*; Winnie recalling 'that day ... the lake ... the reeds' in *Happy Days* or Words in *Words and Music*, describing the 'flare of the black disordered hair as though spread wide on water'. Effective living for Krapp and Croak seems to have been arrested at this point and in old age the memory holds them in a masochistic embrace.

It is in *Krapp's Last Tape* that we find what may be called the archetypal image of love in the Beckett canon, of which the other versions are merely echoes. A romantic river setting is the frame, with sexual undertones of reeds bowing 'before the stem' when the boat drifts over them, and the gentle rocking motion of the water; the girl is lying on the floorboards, eyes closed. The moment of vision Krapp experiences in later life is the memory of these eyes opening as he bent over her. In subsequent works the stimulus 'love' produces in Beckett the response of similar imagery, though abbreviated, (as with Winnie's 'that day ... the lake ... the reeds'). The memory is always poignant, a recollection of love lost. But in *That Time* there is no girl, no lost love in a boat caught in the reeds, but a 'dead rat it looked like'. Love is not only lost here, but dead and putrid. Nostalgia has become a horrifying cynicism. This is particularly ironic since *That Time* is very close in concept to *Krapp's Last Tape*. Both plays were written for Patrick Magee and have as protagonist an old man reviewing his life, either through voices in the head, or on tape. But in *That Time* there is not even the transcendent memory of love that gives Krapp insight, however masochistic, in old age. The vision has shrunk.

The third monologue, C, describes the old man, now a Beckettian tramp, haunting public places: the Portrait Gallery or the Public Library ('free culture') or the Post Office, for warmth and somewhere to sit. He has Mouth's reluctance to accept his identity: 'could you ever say I to yourself in your life . . .' and is always having 'turning points', experiences he will 'never be the same after'. He is also confused: 'was that the time or was that another time?' The question is rhetorical. Each voice suggests that his so-called experiences are merely words and life itself a fiction.

Recalling the solitary child turning himself 'into children' in *Endgame,* Voice A describes 'making it all up on the doorstep as you went along making yourself all up again for the millionth time forgetting it all where you were and what for . . .'. Beckett's protagonists all pass the time in story telling, a situation that aptly parallels the authorial creative process, indeed much of the irony of his work rests on the tension between actual author and protagonist author, and the difficulties experienced by both.[20] In *That Time* Voice B describes why it feels the necessity to tell stories: 'just one of those things you kept making up to keep the void out just another of those old tales to keep the void from pouring in on top of you the shroud.' Voice C, on the other hand, deals with the problem of potential void by attempting a story in which he has never existed: 'trying making it up that way as you went along how it would work that way for a change never having been how never having been would work the old rounds trying to wangle you into it . . .'.

Voice B finally abandons his attempt to keep out the void:

> no words left to keep it out so gave it up there by the window in the dark or moonlight gave up for good and let it in and nothing the worse a great shroud billowing in all over you on top of you and little or nothing the worse

The 'shroud' seems to link with the dust of Voice C's final vision. The sense of aging is extreme. The old man finds the library peopled by 'a bevy of old ones' soundlessly turning 'the leaves' and then, in ultimate irony for the protagonist author, men and books alike, all human endeavour, is suddenly reduced to nothing: 'whole place suddenly full of dust when you opened your eyes from floor to ceiling nothing only dust and not a sound.' There seems to be an echo here of Beckett's remark, quoted in the Shenker article (*New York Times* , 6 May 1956) 'At the end of my work there's nothing but dust . . .'. The stages of human life described by the three voices in *That Time* are soon passed. C's final words make an explicit link with *Come and Go*:

'come and gone no one come and gone in no time gone in no time.' The end of *That Time* also has something in common with the grey world described in *Lessness*, and again the idea of an endless cycle of life and time is implicit in 'the old rounds'. There is, however, a possibility of release at the end of the play, unlike the other works so far discussed.

Structurally the three main stages of the human lifespan are presented in the form of interleaved monologues in *That Time*, as we have seen in *Play*, though the threefold patterning is even more precise. *That Time* consists of thirty-six paragraphs in all. The play is divided into three sections of twelve speeches each and each voice speaks four times in each section, thus having one third of the total text. Unlike the random ordering we have observed in *Lessness*, the speeches are precisely interleaved, so that the play opens with the first speech from Voice A and closes with the last speech from Voice C.

In Section I Voice A begins and Voice B closes the section;
in Section II Voice C begins and Voice A closes the section;
in Section III Voice B begins and Voice C closes the section.

The balance is perfect. The division into sections or scenes is marked not with blackouts as in *Play*, but with silences, an appropriate device for a play in which the possibility of silence is always elusively present. The pattern made as each voice speaks its twelve paragraphs emerges thus:

	I			II			III	
1	A C B		5	C B A		9	B A C	
2	A C B		6	C B A		10	B A C	
3	A C B		7	C B A		11	B A C	
4	C A B	*silence*	8	B C A	*silence*	12	B A C	*silence*

It will be noticed that the rhythm established in sequences 1-3 in Scene 1 and sequences 5-7 in Scene 2 changes (in sequences 4 and 8 respectively) in each case just before silence interrupts the narrative. It thus becomes strikingly apparent that there is no such disturbance to the pattern established in Scene 3, which remains regular. The precision of patterning in *That Time* is such that the question of why Scene 3 should differ from the earlier scenes inevitably arises and an answer appears to be suggested in the stage directions. Throughout the play Listener's eyes open soon after silence interrupts the narrative, so that it appears to be cause and effect:

Silence. 10 seconds. Breath audible. After 3 seconds eyes open.

Following Scenes 1 and 2, however, his eyes close again shortly after the narrative is resumed, again suggesting cause and effect. At the end of the play Listener's eyes open as usual but no voice resumes speaking, so that it appears to be delight in the unbroken silence that stimulates his smile. The smile is held '5 seconds till fade out and curtain.' The apparently endless narrative seems finally to have ceased after culminating in a vision of dust, thus freeing Listener from the burden of hearing. Unlike *Play, That Time* has a linear ending — silence is finally achieved and the pattern of voices works out.

The language of the interior monologue is Beckett's natural mode of expression, a stream of consciousness made up of phrases only. In *That Time* phrases are strung together without breaks, without even the dots between them that mark the frenetic pace of *Not I*. There is no punctuation at all in *That Time* and not even capital letters at the beginning of each paragraph. The paragraphs are merely a convenience for breaking up and interleaving the monologues, which is done with a mathematical precision that recalls the shaping of *Lessness*. The different voices and series of interwoven images have an impact that would be lost were each monologue spoken separately. In a prefatory note to *That Time* Beckett states that 'the switch from one (voice) to another must be clearly faintly perceptible', and that such an effect should be 'assisted mechanically (e.g. three-fold pitch)' if necessary. But he also stresses that A B and C are essentially 'moments of one and the same voice'. It was such an effect of sameness with difference that Beckett hoped would be achieved in the radio presentation of *Lessness* but found disappointing because the voices were too individual.[21]

All three works discussed so far express their meaning through a fusion of content with form. In *Lessness* the human life cycle is fused with the word circles in which it is expressed. *Play* and *That Time* both use a tripartite structure to express different kinds of triangular theme. The so-called 'eternal triangle' in *Play* is expressed appropriately in an endless cyclic structure, while *That Time* looks at three stages of a human life cycle with implications of a final culmination, thus developing a linear structure. Nonetheless the extreme symmetry of *That Time* and the very close relation between its triple monologue structure and that of *Play*, make it necessary to include this one linear play in a chapter otherwise concerned with cyclic form. The circle is, moreover, apparent throughout *That Time* in the constant repetition of language.

Breath

Beckett's archetypal use of cyclic form is to be found in *Breath*. *Breath* is a sigh lasting thirty seconds. It begins and ends with an identical birth cry, and encompasses between the two the pangs of birth, followed by the death rattle. The play is often dismissed as a mere joke or gimmick, not least because it first appeared as a preface to the American production of Kenneth Tynan's sexual farce *Oh Calcutta*! in 1969. *Breath* is, however, the ultimate reduction of Beckett's life-cycle theme. Moreover the stress laid in the stage directions on the two cries ('important that the two cries be identical') reinforces the view of existence as endless repetition that we have noticed in *The Unnamable*, *Lessness* and *Play*.

The cry in *Breath* is often linked with Pozzo's famous line in *Waiting for Godot*:

> They give birth astride of a grave, the light gleams an instant, then it's night once more.

But as a statement of Beckett's vision of the human situation, these lines are incomplete. The transitory nature of human life seems bad enough to Pozzo, but the vision of life that emerges in the later plays goes further. Human existence, Beckett seems to be saying, is an issueless predicament, Joyce's 'vicious circle of humanity' in fact, from which there is no way out because a 'step forward is, by definition, a step back'.[22] Nightfall (in Pozzo's terms) would be a release from such a situation, if it brought with it a cessation of consciousness. But it does not. Night brings no darkness in *Play* (nor later in *Not I*) instead it appears that Beckett's protagonists must continue endlessly to narrate.

Acte sans paroles II

Three further plays where cyclic form is of particular importance are considered in this chapter. The earliest is the mime *Acte sans paroles II* written in French in 1956.[23] It is a mime for two players, who are a typical Beckett 'pseudo couple' of complementary types. A is slow, lethargic and awkward, B 'brisk, rapid, precise'. The contrast is not unlike the pre-war laxative advertisement portraying Mr. Can and Mr. Can't!

When the mime opens, both men are in sacks onstage and beside each sack is a pile of clothes. A phallic-looking goad enters stage right and eventually succeeds in rousing A from his womb-like refuge. He dresses, performs various actions with reluctance, takes pills, prays, moves both sacks towards centre stage, undresses and crawls back into his refuge. The second sack is now nearer the re-entering goad. A single prod produces B, bustling with energy, briskly consulting watch, mirror, map and compass, getting through far more action than A and once more moving the sacks before returning to a recumbent posture. When the goad reappears at the end of the mime, it again prods A, so that the seemingly infinite routine is just starting once more as the mime closes.

The cyclic action could hardly be more explicit. The tools of living, the toothbrush, comb, watch and mirror that occupy B's time presage Winnie's handbag in *Happy Days*. Even the wheels of the goad are given a symbolic function. At the first prod (of A) no wheel is visible; a single wheel appears when B is prodded and two wheels when A is attacked once more. At the same time the sacks move from stage right to stage left, in what is evidently an infinite progression of the wheel of life.

Come and Go

With the exception of *Breath*, no Beckett play is more clearly structured in circles than the 'dramaticule' *Come and Go*. Together these two stage pieces mark Beckett's most concise statement of the cyclic theme. *Come and Go* is the stage play immediately preceding *Breath* in the Beckett canon and the linguistic reduction is from 121 words to none at all. The drafts of *Come and Go*, in which the play evolves to its 121 words, are discussed later in this study, but from the point of view of patterning it may be observed that the cyclic quality of the play emerges in greater relief as the language decreases.

Beckett's diagram of 'successive positions' in his notes to the published text emphasises the pattern of movement. By the end of the play each woman has progressed in rotation, thus:

1.	FLO	VI	RU
2.	(FLO		RU
	(	FLO	RU
3.	VI	FLO	RU

4.	(VI		RU
	(VI	RU	
5.	VI	RU	FLO
6.	(VI		FLO
	(	VI	FLO
7.	RU	VI	FLO

The progression is plotted with extreme precision. In stage 7, Vi has returned to the centre position again and Flo and Ru have circumambulated the stage and changed places. It is Vi's turn to exit left as the curtain falls, thus setting in motion a further turn of the wheel that would bring the women back to their positions in stage 1 above, ready to begin a further series:

8.	(RU		FLO
	(RU	FLO	
9	RU	FLO	VI
10.	(RU		VI
	(	RU	VI
11.	FLO	RU	VI
12.	(FLO		VI
	(FLO	VI	
13.	FLO	VI	RU

As in *Breath* and *Acte sans paroles II,* the progression seems infinite. When the play ends each woman has made an entrance and an exit, sat in the central position to gossip and been gossiped about in her turn. These gossips form the main 'action' of *Come and Go,* contributing to the structural balance and circularity of the piece, as the following diagram reveals:

FLO already knows VI is ill, tells RU
RU already knows FLO is ill, tells VI whom she now knows to be ill also
VI already knows RU is ill, tells FLO whom she now knows to be ill also.

The cyclic patterning of movement and action in *Come and Go* is echoed in the repetitive language. Speeches are not identical throughout, but variations on a theme:

Ru Does she not realize?
Vi Has she not been told?
Flo Does she not know?

or

Flo God grant not.
Ru God forbid.
Vi Please God not.

Such variations are carried out further in the floral-cum-herbal names of the women; in the colours they wear (different yet all muted); and in their voices, 'colourless' throughout, except during the gossips, when 'three very different sounds' are allowed to break the uniformity. This effect of similarity with difference was magnificently achieved in the 1966 Schiller Theater production of the play, where the three women each appeared in clothes of essentially the same style, though the colours were different, as if they were, Proustian-fashion, facets of a single personality.[24]

Not I

If *Acte sans paroles II* presents cyclic action and *Come and Go* combines circles of language and action, *Not I*, a third example of precise patterning, is primarily concerned with linguistic circularity. The play is a spate of words, structured into recurring patterns or circles expressive of Mouth's predicament. She is stuck in a mental groove beyond which she is unable (or unwilling) to progress. Once again in Beckett's writing, theme and form coalesce. The text is composed around five pauses, triggered off by the utterance of a particular phrase. During these pauses the lips cease to move, but the hitherto motionless figure of an auditor, a dimly-lit cowled figure at one side of the stage, stretches out his arms. The pause is a recurring part of the action and therefore cyclic, but the diminishing gestures of the auditor present a linear pattern. By the end of the play he has ceased to respond to Mouth's repeated denials of selfhood.

Beckett's 'analysis' of *Not I* (to be discussed in Chapter 7) reveals the care with which the text is built up from certain themes, some expanding, some contracting as the play progresses.[25] As in *Play* there are nine basic statements in *Not I*: birth, the April morning when 'all went out', buzzing and light, God, punishment, words and mouth, speechlessness, Croker's Acres and the unknown thing that must be told. These are interlinked throughout and all reappear in the last one and a quarter pages of the text – except the Croker's Acres episode, which is never repeated. But 'face in the grass' could be taken as a substitute here, since this phrase does not appear in the text until after the incident at Croker's Acres.

Certain episodes which occur once only can be seen as landmarks in a bleak cycle of existence: the gathering of cowslips to make a ball, the eye on a distant bell, the supermart visit, the arrival one evening at Croker's Acres, and the court scene with its implication of judgement. The Croker's Acres episode alone forms a brief life cycle:

> . . . Just the birth cry to get her going . . . then no more till this . . . home! . . . a little mound in Croker's Acres . . .

These cycles fall within a framework of cyclic word patterns which both echo and reecho what appears to be the life cycle of the voice and form part of the complete circle the text may be taken to describe. There is no closing full stop, but an implication of rebirth, so that reading from the last line to the first is both syntactically and thematically possible. It should be emphasised that nowhere is it stated that the April morning blackout was the time of death, although the idea is perhaps suggested in subsequent references to the body:

> . . . more likely the machine . . . so disconnected . . . never got the message . . . or powerless to respond . . . like numbed . . .

Beckett's lack of syntactical definition allows statements to fold at least two ways throughout the play. This can be seen in the contraction of the birth theme, occurring on its repetition: 'Before its time', for example, could mean either premature birth or that the world is unready for the child; 'Godforsaken hole' could refer equally to the womb or the world and 'no love' to the parents for each other, or for their child, or that the child has entered a loveless world. As the birth theme contracts, so the April morning theme gathers momentum — with additional images such as 'larks', 'face in the grass' and 'pick it up'.

The linking of the buzzing and light themes appears to tie *Not I* closely to the subject of *Play*. It is not only a pun that links the thought 'flashes' with the light. The light, which is said to be 'ferreting' and 'poking around', may be seen as stimulating thought. It is always mentioned in conjunction with the buzzing in the skull — to which, by the question '. . . what? . . . the buzzing? . . .', attention is repeatedly drawn.

With the idea of purgatory in mind, the early laughter at the mention of God is interesting; it develops into '. . . God is love . . . she'll be purged . . .', the first positive mention of love in the play. Earlier 'she' had experienced 'no love of any kind', but the idea of purgation heralds her hope of a merciful God, replacing her early thoughts of punishment. Self- questioning about her lack of suffering ('. . . so far . . . ha! . . . so far . . .') is sandwiched between her changing attitude to God. His name at first produces laughter but '. . . God is love . . . tender mercies . . .' are among the last words spoken and contribute to the irony of the play. There is no 'mercy' for Mouth; her compassionate auditor is 'helpless'.

In a play where a mouth is the central image, words and mouth appropriately form the longest theme and contrast with narrated memories of speechlessness. She who was 'practically speechless all her days' except for an occasional '. . . sudden urge to . . . tell' is compared with the numb body from which words now pour in an uncontrollable stream, the brain all the while begging the mouth to stop. As the words come 'quicker and quicker' they are paralleled by the brain 'flickering away like mad' and the probing light. The remembered urge to tell links with the voice's realisation that there may be '. . . something she had to tell . . . something she didn't know herself . . . wouldn't know if she heard . . .'. This theme is the last to develop and emerges as the crucial question of the play. As with Woman I in *Play,* the voice does not know what is being demanded of her, but is determined to find out: 'Keep on . . . hit on it in the end . . .'. The implication is that if this something is told, all will become clear. It may be no more than an obligation for the voice to accept the story as her own. Throughout the play the gigantic self-deception that 'she' is *not* 'I' links ironically with the fact that, when trying to simulate suffering, 'she' is said to be 'incapable of deceit'; nor is she able to deny responsibility for the voice: 'then finally had to admit . . . could be none other . . . than her own.'

The structure of repeated themes is composed around an underlying structure of pauses, each time preceded by the phrase 'What? . . . who? . . . no! . . . she!' It is the 'vehement refusal to relinquish third person' that provokes gestures 'of helpless compassion' from the auditor. As Mouth's denials increase in strength, so the gestures diminish, until the final pause where the word 'she', emphatically repeated, elicits no gesture at all. Mouth has carefully avoided accepting the story as her own, but until she does so there can be no progress. As the curtain falls on her determination to 'keep on', the voice can still be heard, recalling the 'largely unintelligible' chorus in *Play,* before each voice is singled out by the light.

In terms of pattern although, as in *Play,* the cyclic element is omnipresent, the monologue takes place at such speed that the impression is of a whirlwind of words. The total effect is not unlike a Francis Bacon painting of a screaming mouth — vocalised. The whole desperate spate of words may be seen to be pinpointed by the two screams as a cry of pain.

Beckett once said in conversation with Tom Driver:

> What I am saying does not mean that there will henceforth be no form in art. It only means that there will be a new form, and that this form will be of such a type that it admits the chaos and does not try to say that the chaos is really something else.[ ] To find a form that accommodates the mess, that is the task of the artist now.[26]

In *Not I* Beckett appears to have found such a form. He holds 'the mess' in a tight geometry, so that the image of the frantic mouth repeating word patterns becomes a visual and oral symbol of the human predicament.

CHAPTER 5
CYCLIC AND LINEAR PATTERNING

The circle has been a constant motif in the works so far discussed; we shall now widen the focus to see whether the same motif occurs throughout Beckett's plays, and whether any other kinds of patterning are evident in them. The remaining plays are looked at chronologically, beginning with *Godot* and *Fin de partie*. Although as discussed in the introduction it is not the purpose of this study to explore the early plays in detail, it is useful to be able to look at the plays as a body in order to gain a perspective view of Beckett's structural patterning.

En attendant Godot

In *En attendant Godot*, Beckett's first published play, we find a clear example of cyclic action, in that the events of Act 2 largely repeat those of Act 1.[1] Although Pozzo and Lucky have changed between the acts, Vladimir and Estragon remain the same. This is emphasised linguistically by the identical repetition of the final lines of each act, though the speakers are reversed in Act 2. The two acts in *Godot* appear to be part of an endless series. As Ihab Hassan points out:

> The inaction of the play is cyclical, and its events are endlessly repetitious; its two acts are symmetric, both equal images of an absence. Two acts, as Samuel Beckett knew, are enough to represent a sequence stretching to infinity...[2]

In the later plays (with the exception of the repeat of *Play*) the idea of a series is implied rather than actual. In *Not I*, for example, Mouth continues speaking after the fall of the curtain and, since there is no final full stop in the text, merely a hyphen, the actress naturally returns to the opening lines of the play.

Beckett's 1975 Schiller Theater production of *Godot* (seen at the Royal Court Theatre, London, in April 1976) was remarkable for its structural balance. Beckett emphasised not only the cyclic nature of the play in the repetitions of language and action, but brought out the visual-aural balance within the contrasting comic routines and language rhythms of which the play is composed. Words were liberally invaded by silence, periods of movement by stillness, yet the production went at a tremendous pace. Language rhythms sprang to life as speeches were rattled off like a comedian's patter, while comic action routines constantly called to mind the circus clown. James Knowlson said of the production that Beckett had emphasised the 'sense of form in movement, shaping speech, gestures and movements into a precisely organised, musically balanced and aesthetically satisfying work'.[3] Knowlson is here echoing Beckett's remark to Charles Marowitz in 1962:

> Producers don't seem to have any sense of form in movement. The kind of form one finds in music, for instance, where themes keep recurring. When in a text, actions are repeated, they ought to be made unusual the first time, so that when they happen again — in exactly the same way — an audience will recognise them from before. In the revival of *Godot* (in Paris) I tried to get at something of that stylised movement that's in the play.[4]

The following extract from the account of rehearsals for the 1975 Berlin production given in the programme by Beckett's production assistant, Walter Asmus, reveals Beckett's approach to the play to have remained unchanged:

> It should be done very simply, without long passages. To give confusion shape, he says,[5] a shape through repetition, repetition of themes. Not only themes in the script, but also themes of the body. When at the beginning Estragon is asleep leaning on the stone, that is a theme that repeats itself a few times. There are fixed points of writing, where everything stands completely still, where silence threatens to swallow everything up. Then the action starts again.[6]

Achieving 'a shape through repetition of themes' is precisely what we have also noticed in the structuring of *Not I*.

Fin de partie

Beckett's second published play, *Fin de partie*, is no less patterned than *Godot*. Certain limited actions recur, with a deliberation which has caused them to be compared with the moves in a game of chess. Hamm's position enthroned, kinglike, centre stage and

Clov's admission that he used to inspect Hamm's 'paupers' like a knight 'on horse', together with the English title 'Endgame' (as in chess) reinforce the view that chess is part of the experience of the play. It appears, moreover, that an early French title for the play, 'La Fin du Jeu' had the same connotations.[7] The parallel should not be taken too far, although it is interesting to compare the unseen king against whom Hamm's endgame must be played, with the hostile forces offstage in the mimes (*Actes sans paroles I and II*) written the same year as *Fin de partie*.

In a production notebook prepared for a Schiller Theater production of *Endspiel* in September 1967,[8] Beckett structures the play as follows, for rehearsal purposes:

1		xxxx Clov	1	— 1st inspection
2	30	Hamm 〃	2	
3		Nagg — Nell	3	
4		1st Runde	4	
5		2nd inspection	5	
6	42	Flea	6	
7		Dog	7	
8		Pegg — Boathook — Madman — alarm	8	
(9)	6	Hamm	9	
10		Nagg's Curse	10	
11	20	Order — Hamm's Story — Nell dead	11	
12		2nd Runde	12	
13		Rug — Clov's refusal to touch	13	
14		Hamm	14	
15	28	Rat escaped — no more paint.		— 3rd inspection
16		Hamm		

Ruby Cohn in 'Beckett directs Happy Days'[9] states categorically that such divisions are not structural but 'a matter of mechanical convenience for rehearsal purposes only'. However Stanley Gontarski rightly points out that they cannot be called entirely arbitrary because they 'reveal points at which the author-director thought shifts in the play occurred.'[10] The latter is obviously an important caveat, but both views should be borne in mind when considering Beckett's production notebooks. The divisions *are* partly for convenience, but the points at which breaks occur also help to reveal the rhythms and action routines in the play.

Looking at Beckett's divisions for the German *Endspiel* it is particularly interesting to find that the left-hand brackets build the play up to a focal point, that of Hamm's story, which stands alone. There are three sections bracketed together at the opening and close and five and four sections respectively on each side of Hamm's story. This seems to produce a pyramidal structure, a building up to and away from a central point, Hamm's objectification into narrative form of personal experience. The figures to the right of each left-hand bracket probably refer to the number of actions in each section, but are not identified precisely in the notebook.

The end of *Endgame* is often seen as cyclic, in that Hamm's face is once more covered, the bin lids are replaced and Clov, though prepared for departure, does not leave. Such a view would compare Clov's continued presence with the immobility of Vladimir and Estragon at the end of *Godot*. This reading of the play is possible, but so is the view that the play marks the closing stages of a game of chess. There has been an advancement of action during the space of the play. Nell appears at last to have died (see section 11 of Beckett's production diagram: 'Nell dead') while the final section is subsequently referrred to in the production notebook as 'Hamm's last monologue'. Both may be regarded as repeated events in a continuing series, but *Fin de partie* may also be seen as the forerunner of certain plays in which a linear structure is not eclipsed by the circle, although, as we shall see, generally contained by it. Ihab Hassan points to a dwindling, spiralling motion even in the circularity of *Godot*:

> 'And yet the force of entropy may be felt even in a cyclical system: the world of the play tends to run down.'[11]

Acte sans paroles I

The mime *Acte sans paroles I* is perhaps Beckett's clearest example of linear structure. It was to have had its première with *Fin de partie*, at the Marseilles Festival in August 1956, but the arrangements foundered.[12] The mime is a nightmare vision of life as an arena from which there is no exit and no reward for endeavour beyond the realisation, on which it closes, that there is no point in trying again. The protagonist undergoes a process of conditioning throughout the mime, during which he learns that though a whistle may urge him to strive, he can never achieve. It is the myth of Sisyphus told in mime, combined with the tale of

Tantalus. No matter how hard the man tries to reach his goal (a carafe of water above his head) and no matter how nearly he succeeds, it remains always just out of reach.

Conditioning begins with the protagonist's realisation that he cannot leave the stage. He is flung on from the wings at the outset and, each time he tries to leave, attracted by a whistle offstage, he is catapulted back again. On the third occasion he has learned his lesson and makes no attempt to leave. His attitude here is paralleled by the situation at the end of the mime, when water is dangled before his nose but he makes no attempt to take it. He 'does not move' (as at the end of *Godot*) having learned there is 'nothing to be done'. Any effort to reach the water would result in its disappearance, so he might at least save energy. The situation has something in common with Yeats's *At The Hawk's Well*, where again the water is always out of reach. The protagonist's gradual learning of acceptance and stoicism is hard to take in *Acte sans paroles I* because it is so explicit and lacks the leaven of ambiguity. The circus clown comic routines with which the failures are cumulatively performed do not really lighten the piece. Rather do they produce a cynical laughter, a cynicism eventually learned by the protagonist. The fact that suicide is denied him has no positive implications. He cannot even die; the bough on which he was about to hang himself collapses and the scissors, for which he finally bares his throat, are whisked into the flies. All he can do is perform unnecessary actions, such as *neatly* coiling the useless rope when the tree has failed him.

The pattern is that of:

(1) Stimulus; (2) Response; (3) Barrier;

repeated throughout until each lesson is learned. Finally, repeated stimuli produce no response at all. He remains contemplating the hands that have proved such ineffectual tools. The linear pattern has been completed.

Linear patterning of some description is present in all the remaining plays in this study, but in almost every case the line is seen to be contained by the circle. In *Happy Days*, for example, although we see the earth encroaching in linear fashion upon Winnie, the heap can never be completed in a finite universe, as Richard Coe points out: 'for the nearer it gets to the totality, the slower it increases'.[13] Even were the mound to cover Winnie in some future Act 3, the implication, in the context of Beckett's later drama, is that she would still be there, under the soil, contemplating her causes for happiness. It should be remembered in this connexion that *Play* is Beckett's next stage play after *Happy Days*.

All That Fall

All That Fall, the first of the radio plays, is circular in form in that the action returns more or less to its starting point. We first meet Mrs. Rooney on the road en route to the station and leave her on her way home at the end of the play. The difficulty of the journey is emphasised by her dragging feet and the hazards of travelling in general by the hinny that will not move, the flat bicycle tyre, the car that will not start until it is choked ('she was getting too much air!') and the train that has stopped on the line. Maddy's hopes of returning 'safe to haven' with her husband have perhaps implications of a final end to journeying, which, given their age and state of health, cannot be far off.

In musical terms the journey out rises to a crescendo as the train arrives, and repeated themes pattern the route home. A certain amount of correlation between the two journeys must be expected, in that Mrs. Rooney is retracing her steps. But more oblique echoes (such as the reference to Hardy in both sections) could suggest conscious patterning. In order to register these parallels it is simplest to see the 'events' of each journey in diagram form. The diagram relates only to parallels occurring between the outward and return journeys. Repeated patterns that occur within one journey alone are excluded. Mrs. Rooney's getting stuck in the car *and* on the station steps, for example, occurs only on the outward journey. Moreover one stage direction only has been taken where several are present in each journey, as with the footsteps. To some extent, then, the following shape is controlled by selection, but the paralleled elements in each journey occur in a very similar sequence:

	Outward Journey	*Return Journey*	
1	Footsteps	Footsteps	12
2	'Death and the Maiden'	Dead child — killed by train	11
3	Hinny	Wild laughter	10
4	Dung	Hardy	9
5	Mrs. Rooney's language	'Death and the Maiden'	8
6	Laburnum	Dung	7
7	Hardy	Hinnies	6
8	Rural sounds	Laburnum	5

	Outward Journey		*Return Journey*	
9	Wild laughter		Mrs. Rooney's language	4
10	Dead hen — killed by car		Rural sounds	3
11	Up station steps		Down station steps	2
12	Up mail passes	→	Down train draws in	1

The above scheme brings out the play's cyclic qualities, though of course the play ends in linear fashion, in the climax of suspicion that occurs on the news of the child's death.

Theatre I

Although this play was not published until 1974 (under the title *Fragment de théâtre*) its chronological place in Beckett's dramatic writing is between *All that Fall* and *Krapp's Last Tape*, since the first version of the play is dated December 1956.[14] Not surprisingly the play has strong echoes of both *En attendant Godot* and *Fin de partie*, the two stage plays that preceded it. The action consists of the meeting and interaction between two tramps, recalling Vladimir and Estragon. They are, however, variously disabled, thus also bringing *Fin de partie* strongly to mind — indeed they share Hamm's disabilities between them, since A is blind and B is confined to a wheelchair. The two men are interdependent, another Beckett 'pseudo couple'. The possibility of B acting as A's eyes, while A pushes the wheelchair thus emerges. If they help each other, they can function as one. 'If you ask me we were made for each other' B comments sardonically. Their predicament is also strongly reminiscent of the blind beggar and the lame beggar in Yeats's comic play *The Cat and The Moon*.

When the play begins A is playing his fiddle on a street corner and B enters propelling his wheelchair with a pole. B at first addresses A with familiarity, as 'Billy', as though A were known to him, but this is subsequently undercut by B's question: 'May I call you Billy, like my son?' The possibility that this is one in a series of meetings between the tramps, as in *Godot* is never clarified. The action of the play is linear, in that the balance of power between the two men suddenly shifts after the final line has been spoken, resulting in an unexpected climax. Cyclic action cannot, however, be ruled out, since further interaction between the two men is implicit in the ending.

There are four main sequences of action leading to the final climax. The first of these, a conversation between the two men, culminates in B proposing a partnership between them, with himself as the eyes and A as the legs pushing the wheelchair. To demonstrate his potential usefulness B spots possible food — a tin in the gutter. This initiates the second sequence of action, for A at once puts down his violin, gropes his way to B's chair and starts pushing it blindly. Instead of guiding him to the tin B panics and, when A continues pushing, strikes him with the pole. A halts, stranded, uncertain of where he left his violin and starts groping about in the dark.

B begins the third sequence of action by asking A to tuck in his rug. A moves towards the voice and B takes his hand. After dealing with the rug, A's hands explore B's body from the feet upwards (as in Yeats's *The Death of Cuchulain*): 'A: Have you only one leg? B: Just the one'. A further note of grotesque comedy is struck when A's hands encounter B's face: 'A: Is that your face? B: I confess it is. (*Pause*). What else could it be? (*A's fingers stray, stay*) That? My wen.' A remains kneeling at B's feet and the tone darkens, in dialogue that would not be out of place in either *Godot* or *Fin de partie*:

> *A:* Will it not soon be night?
> (*B looks at sky*)
> *B:* Day . . . night . . . (*Looks*) It seems to me sometimes the earth must have got stuck, one sunless day, in the heart of winter, in the grey of evening.

B finally pushes A away so that he falls on all fours and in the final sequence of action A tries to return to his initial position. B taunts him, saying maliciously that he might steal A's violin. Getting no response from A, he pokes him in the back with his pole. But he has gone too far. The final direction states:

> *A whirls round, seizes the end of the pole and wrenches it from B's grasp.*

This renders B powerless to move and thus even more helpless than A had been when groping blindly in the dark. Co-operation between the two men is seen to be essential to their survival, but cannot be guaranteed. The outcome remains ambiguous. Implicit in the pattern of the linear ending is the realisation that only an acceptance of their interdependence can resolve the stalemate and result in progress. There is no indication in the text, however, that they are capable of more than cyclic action, a ceaseless sparring, with one trying to dominate the other.

Krapp's Last Tape

The linear implications of *Krapp's Last Tape* are apparent from the title. It is Krapp's LAST tape and death lurks in the shadows close at hand. Beckett, when preparing the German actor Martin Held for the part[15] explained: 'Old Nick's there. Death is standing behind him and unconsciously he's looking for it.'[16] Beckett requested Held to glance over his shoulder from time to time, as though aware of someone behind him, like the old man in the portrait gallery in *That Time*:

> as you peered trying to make it out gradually of all things a face appeared had you swivel on the slab to see who it was was thère at your elbow...

Structurally, therefore, *Krapp's Last Tape* must be seen as a linear play, although once again the line is modified by the circle. There is constant repetition of action, for example Krapp's drinking bouts. Above all, however, there is the linguistic repetition of the episode in the boat, recorded on spool five box three. The constant replaying of this extract reflects the mental groove or 'deeper coil' of memory in which Krapp remains trapped, as in *Murphy*:

> Scraps of bodies, of landscapes, hands, eyes, lines and colours evoking nothing, rose and climbed out of sight before him, as though reeled upward off a spool level with his throat. It was his experience that this should be stopped, whenever possible, before the deeper coils were reached.[17]

By externalising Krapp's overriding memory on the spool of tape that provides the recurring action in *Krapp's Last Tape*, Beckett is once again fusing form with content. Krapp's tape may also be compared with the spools of life the characters in *Play* are attempting posthumously to unravel. In *Krapp*, the earlier play (1958) we see the life line actualised in the spools of tape, whereas in *Play* (1963), it is simply implied. Beckett told the actor Pierre Chabert of Krapp 'The spool is his whole life.'[18] Krapp throws away the present in favour of a moment in the past beyond which he is unable, mentally, to progress. In both plays the progress of the line is impeded by an emotional knot, the problem of sex, which entraps the characters in a recurring experience.

Theatre II

Theatre II, written a few months after *Krapp's Last Tape*, is ostensibly linear in structure, in that two of its three characters (A and B) are expecting to leave just before the play closes, having completed their investigation of C's papers. A even says, somewhat self-consciously: 'How end?' In fact, however, neither leaves the stage, reminiscent of the ending of each act of *Godot*. Nor does C, (who has stood beside an open window upstage centre throughout the play, his back to the audience) actually jump. The play's structure is perhaps best appreciated in schematised form, delineating the seven main sequences of action:

1. A and B (seated at desks downstage left and right 'forming symmetry') discuss C's papers. C is at window upstage centre, his back to the audience.
2. B's desk lamp keeps going out when he tries to read C's 'confidences'.
3. Further problem with B's lamp. He joins A.
4. A goes to the window and inspects C's face.
5. The investigation is completed and C's 'record, closed and final'. 'Let him jump,' says B.
6. A bird cage is discovered and returned to its place.
7. B returns to his own desk and remains motionless. A goes to the window, looks at C in surprise and raises his handkerchief to C's face.

The play ends on a linear note by coming to an unexpected climax after the last words have been spoken, in a surprise ending typical of Beckett. C appears to be weeping, although the question of whether he will finally leap remains ambiguous.

Embers

Beckett's second radio play, *Embers*, is structured on a similar kind of continuum to *All That Fall*. The progression of sounds and voices recurs regularly:

		Sea	15
1	Sea	Sea (*a little louder*)	14
2	Boots	Boots	13
3	Sea (*louder*)	Sea (*a little louder*)	12
		Boots	11
4	Henry's Monologue	Henry's Monologue	10
5	Ada and Henry	Ada and Henry	9
6	Addie and Music Master	Addie and Riding Master	8

Ada and Henry
7

All That Fall built up to the event of the arrival of the train, but the central 'event' (No. 7) in *Embers* is merely a three-line exchange between Ada and Henry, concerning their daughter's education, and cannot be regarded as a climax. The cyclic element in the play is, however, conspicuously present in the repetition of themes.

Happy Days

Beckett's notebook for the 1971 production of *Glückliche Tage* (*Happy Days*)[19] at the Schiller Theater, Berlin divides the text into sections for rehearsal purposes. Act I has eight sections and Act II, four. Astonishingly detailed lists of the repetition, variation and interruption of both text and action are also made. Beckett notes, for example, '31 smiles' and 17 'turns to bag'. These turns are, moreover, subdivided according to type:

3 kinds of turn

1. Unbroken — 8
2. Head and on — 3
3. Head and back — 6

Correspondences in language and action between the two acts are also noted, showing that Beckett was making such parallels deliberately:

Happy Expressions

I	4 after glücklicher Tag pp.104 111 127 134
II	1 after glücklicher Tag p.148 (no smile with 2 other GT)

The intensity of the second act is thus increased by omitting the accompanying smile on the last two occasions that the phrase is repeated.

The list of properties in the notebook (minutely itemised under the heading *bag*) contains not only those we see on the mound, but two (the comb and hairbrush) that are never shown, merely understood to be present by Winnie's reference to brushing her hair. The notebook lists 'Known contents in order of appearance'. Item 12 ('Miscellaneous Not Shown') refers presumably to other odds and ends that could be present in the handbag but are not produced for inspection. Perhaps the most startling note as to detail occurs after Willie's also largely *unseen* actions in Act I have been listed:

WILLIE *Bref*

1 Sleeping behind mound
2 Waked. Struck by bottle. Sits up. Reads paper.
3 Stops reading. Fans face with paper. Inspects card. Blows nose.
4 Collapses. Crawls into hole.
5 In hole.
6 In hole. Raises 5 fingers.
7 In hole. Sings. Picks nose. Eats pickings.
8 Leaves hole. Sits up. Reads paper. Stops reading.

In all 17 sentences 45 words

The list of actions might have been made by another director, but the final comment is peculiarly Beckettian.

Such extreme care in breaking down a text for production implies at least equal care in creating it. Introducing his study of the drafts of *Happy Days*, Gontarski points out that 'The shaping of themes, tone, the pattern of literary allusions, and the overall structure of the play, ostensibly different categories, are all, fundamentally, matters of form.'[20] *Happy Days* has a visually linear appearance in that the mound grows, but it is an 'impossible heap', like Zeno's heap of millet.[21] Linear progression is, moreover, modified by the circle, as the days spiral by for Winnie, bringing a little more earth but no end to the cycle. As we have come to expect of Beckett the visual image of *Happy Days* is carried out linguistically, in that many themes are presented and actions performed in Act I that are repeated in a reduced form in Act 2, thus forming a diminishing circle or spiral. We have observed that Beckett divides Act 1 into eight sections and Act 2 into precisely half that number for rehearsal purposes and that his production notebook specifically points to repetitions from act to act. Act 2, in its reduction of language, may be seen as a climbing towards silence that parallels the rising mound.

Various kinds of pattern are revealed in Act 1 of *Happy Days*. In the first place Beckett's requirements for the set are the 'maximum of simplicity and symmetry'. The action is cyclic in form — in that things end as they began, though the 'bell for sleep' has not yet rung when the curtain falls. The objects extracted from the handbag are replaced with the first (i.e. the toothbrush) last; Willie returns to the newspaper he had at the outset, and prayer is again referred to in connexion with Winnie. Whether or not she prays is ambiguous; there is a perfunctory prayer at the opening, but at the end of the act, merely a long pause. The toothbrush action both contributes to the cyclic effect and provides the climax to the theme that begins almost with her monologue. Willie finally defines a hog as a 'castrated male swine' or, it seems, himself.

Act 2 shows Winnie much the same, still mercifully unable fully to appreciate her predicament. Now embedded to the neck, her possibilities for action are restricted to facial expression, and she has to rely more on language to pass the time, introducing, for example, the story of Mildred. Again two bells rouse her to consciousness. In Act 1 she had remarked 'Another heavenly day', on waking to her merciless exposure to 'blazing light'; the remark, in relation to her obvious plight, seeming to imply a malign divinity. In Act 2 the irony is intensified: 'Hail, holy light!' is the opening line of *Paradise Lost* (Book 3) and Winnie, despite her positive thinking, is now reduced to a head.

Winnie refers to the bag in Act 2 but cannot inspect its contents, nor can she see Willie. Her subsequent attempt to see her nostrils, lips, etc. recalls the facial inspection of Act 1. Compressing two more early themes she thinks of the sunshade and revolver, both of which are evident on the mound beside her. She also wonders once more whether to sing, and repeats the Shower/Cooker narration. There are more bells in Act 2, as though time is at last getting shorter for Winnie, and because there is less text, there also appear to be more unremembered quotations; (indeed the introduction of a minor Irish poet like Charles Wolfe (with 'Go forget me')[22] might well suggest a weakening in the standard of literature!). Even the smallest of details may become part of the patterning of the whole, such as Winnie's complaint of a painful neck in Act 2 that recalls the crick in her neck suffered when admiring Willie's antics in Act 1.

Willie's appearance at the end of Act 2 may be compared with his verbal presentation of himself at the end of Act 1. In the latter, the physical separation between husband and wife points to the mental distance between them. In Act 2 the 'reunion' is marked by the fact that Willie cannot reach his wife and, as they look at each other, Winnie's happy smile disappears. The final confrontation between husband and wife produces a dramatic climax, a linear movement, that closes an otherwise cyclic play.

Words and Music, Esquisse radiophonique, Cascando

A group of radio plays follows *Happy Days* and the first of these, *Words and Music*, uses the concept of arrival and departure as a structural device, as in Beckett's first works for radio. In *All*

That Fall it is the journey itself that takes up most of the action, whereas *Words and Music* follows the structural pattern of *Embers* and uses the protagonist's arrival and departure as a frame. Croak's coming and going merely occupy the opening and close of *Words and Music*, however, and the substance of the play is his encounter with Joe (Words) and Bob (Music).

Over half the brief text of *Words and Music* is spent in the struggle for unity of expression between Joe and Bob and it is not until two thirds of the way through the play that the first verse of the lyric appears. The second verse emerges hesitantly, after which the play ends abruptly in Croak's departure, with a brief reprise from Music. The themes of love and age proposed by Croak have come to fruition in the culminating lyric. Offsetting the linear movement, however, is the fact that Croak appears trapped in memory by the experience the lyric records and will thus at some stage demand its repetition. The cyclic theme cannot therefore be excluded. *Words and Music* makes a strong parallel with *Krapp's Last Tape* here. Croak's 'anguish', as the lyric comes nearer to pinning down an experience that appears to be connected with 'the face' that delayed him on the stairs, compares forcibly with Krapp's masochistic replaying of spool five box three, the experience to which he has remained emotionally bound. The two old men with the unattractive names are in a similar state of physical decrepitude; Krapp's may be seen onstage, Croak's deduced from the sound of his voice and his shuffling gait.

The face is the catalyst that unites Croak's two themes and brings about the union of Words and Music. When Words introduces 'the face in the ashes' into the lyric, the theme of love that Croak had demanded on arrival, after seeing the face on the stairs, is at last expressed. Now old, love for Croak is no more than a memory, hence his ironic proposal of age as the theme to follow love. When a union between the two themes is achieved, it proves too much for him, and he drops his club and shuffles off. Words and Music have managed to unite, but Croak and his love can unite only in memory. In *Krapp's Last Tape* the memory that holds Krapp captive to his past is also that of a face, the face below him in the rowing boat and the eyes that finally opened. In *Words and Music* also the emphasis is on the eyes:

> the brows uncloud, the lips part and the eyes... (*pause*) ... a little colour comes back into the cheeks and the eyes... (*reverently*) ...open.

The two experiences are essentially the same, and, as we have seen, recurring.

Words and Music was written late in November 1961 and two days after its completion Beckett wrote the French *Esquisse radiophonique.*[23] A union between Voice and Music (both controlled by a 'click' suggesting a radio switch) is again the theme. As the two unite they become fainter and the protagonist, to whom they have become 'needs', is in terror of losing them altogether. The situation resembles an advanced state of mental illness, where the fear is not of hearing voices in the head, but of their disappearance. As he tells the doctor on the telephone:

. . . I tell you they're ending . . . ENDING . . . I can't stay like that after . . .

When he switches on again after this conversation, Voice and Music are described as 'failing.'

The protagonist's final shock (received by telephone) concerns a double confinement. The word 'confinement' embraces both imprisonment and birth. It is further left ambiguous whether the doctor is merely prevented by two confinements from visiting him until noon the following day, or whether the double birth is scheduled for that hour, and bears any relation to the dwindling into silence of Voice and Music, on which the play ends. In the 'long pause' that follows their extinction, the protagonist is left in agonised expectation:

He: (*Whisper.*) Tomorrow . . . noon . . .

Once again in Beckett the implications of birth follow on the heels of extinction, but, despite this cyclic theme, the *Esquisse* is clearly linear in conception, since it leads to the blotting out of Music and Voice.

Cascando, written just after the *Esquisse,* also has a linear construction, and again the characterisation of Voice and Music objectifies the difficulty of turning into words an imaginative idea. Beckett first used the title 'Cascando' for a poem written in 1936. Towards the end of verse two the problem of creation is beautifully stated:

the churn of stale words in the heart again
love love love thud of the old plunger
pestling the unalterable
whey of words.[24]

In the play *Cascando* the same compulsion to tell stories is present, combined with a longing for freedom:

Voice: - this time... it's the right one ...finish...no more stories
(*together*)
Music: --

Opener's task is to release Voice, Music, or both 'at will'. But, as the play progresses, they seem to appear without him, or else he has stopped informing us of his actions. Opener, however, maintains he has a definite function:

Opener: They say, It's in his head.
No. I open.

No enmity exists between Voice and Music in this play. It seems to be partly their fusion that gives them the impression they have found the right story at last, the story of stories that will free them from the necessity of telling more. This is the 'Woburn' story.[25] The implication seems to be that if they can catch up with Woburn, pinpoint him somehow, they will be able to achieve full self-realisation.

Woburn ...it's him ...see him...say him...to the end...don't let go--

Woburn seems to be the missing link, for which the Unnamable also searches:

...you must say words, as long as there are any, until they find me, until they say me.[26]

Whether Woburn is finally caught remains ambiguous. Teller and tale are on the verge of achieving some kind of fusion (Opener's last speech is a fervent 'good!') but the final words belong to Voice and Music and are non-committal:

Voice: ... don't let go...Woburn...he clings on... come on...
(*together*)
Music: --
come on —

Silence.

CURTAIN.

As Clas Zilliacus points out, 'The play . . . does not end. It is cut off.'[27] Silence could represent Woburn's final evasion or the release of achievement, what the Unnamable calls 'the true silence'[28] that extinguishes further words. Rare though it is in Beckett, the weight of *Cascando* lies with the latter. We have already noticed a comparable linear movement at the end of *Esquisse radiophonique* and in the later play *That Time*. But a Beckett play never wholly escapes the circle and a circular movement is also present in *Cascando*. Certain phrases, such as 'the month of May', recur like a refrain, for example, and Opener's function is cyclic:

Opener: I open the door . . . . . . And I close.
(*Silence.*)
I open both . . . . . . And I close.
(*Silence.*)
I start again.

Film and Eh Joe

In *Film*, Beckett's only venture into writing for the cinema, instead of an attempt to pinpoint his identity, we find the protagonist in headlong flight from himself. The progression is again linear, in that E (the eye following the object, O) gains ground gradually, until the final inescapable confrontation. There is, however, a circular pattern of movement as the piece unfolds, in the repetition of O entering 'perceivedness'. In the street and on the stairs O becomes paralysed by his awareness of E, who twice withdraws and lets him move on, only to catch up with him irrevocably in the room. The piece thus falls into three sections, each with its confrontation. Beckett's description is as follows:

The film is divided into three parts. 1. The street (about eight minutes.) 2. The stairs (about five minutes.) 3. The room (about 17 minutes.)[29]

Inside the room there is a further three-part structure, comprising the preparation of the room, the inspection of the room, the inspection and destruction of the photographs and the confrontation between E and O.

In *Eh Joe*, Beckett's first play for television, the situation of a man haunted by memories alone in a room recalls both *Krapp's Last Tape* and *Words and Music*, while the image is an extension of *Film*. The play opens with a brief section of preparing the room and ascertaining that there are no intruders (as in the first part of the room sequence in *Film*). The bulk of *Eh Joe* is then concerned with Joe 'relaxed' as, in part three of the room sequence in *Film*, O dozes before the confrontation with E. Joe's eyes, however, are wide open and intent as he listens to a voice in his head. It is that of the woman whom he betrayed into suicide by loving her too little. Each time the voice gains a point, the camera moves a little nearer Joe's face. As in *Film*, he never utters. Both protagonists attempt to escape self-knowledge by shutting themselves in a room away from observation. O in *Film* is afraid of the self that is observing him, Joe of the voice in his head that is forcing him to face the implications of the woman's death.

The camera has nine moves in towards a close-up of Joe's face, but, despite this, the pattern is cyclic rather than linear. By the last move, the camera has gone as far as it can and holds Joe firmly in its eye, but there is no indication in the text that it will release him. Voice and image both fade out *together* at the end of the play. It is possible that Joe may succeed in achieving 'mental thuggee' and that the voice will leave him eventually, as have other voices in his head in the past. But what we are shown in the play is Joe trapped in a cycle of past experience, as are so many Beckett protagonists.

Footfalls

Footfalls seems to combine line and circle in a similar manner to *Eh Joe*. The play is structured into four sections. Each section is separated by a blackout and silence and there is a marked impression of the passage of time between them. Each blackout is distinguished by the gradually softening chime of a bell and is followed by a diminished level of light. Since both levels were 'faint' and 'dim' at the outset, there is minimal sound and light by the end of the play. The technique recalls the dwindling procedure for the repeat of *Play* that evolved in rehearsal in Paris in 1964.[30] Similarly the footsteps get slower from scene to scene and fewer lengths are paced — until, in the final length, as Beckett told me, 'the energy just runs out'. May must wait, rather like a wind-up gramophone, until enough impetus has returned to allow her to reach stage right.

At the beginning of *Footfalls* May is said to be 'in (her) forties' and her mother still needing the attentions required by the old and infirm. But as the play progresses, an extreme distancing effect occurs, so that we begin to doubt the physical presence of either woman. The two lives appear to have set up echoes which reverberate ever more faintly from section to section. Beckett suggested that Rose Hill (who played the mother's voice) for the première at the Royal Court Theatre, London, in May 1976 should play it 'like one ghost speaking to another.'

Light gleams faintly on a strip of bare stage at the end of the play. May/Amy has apparently stopped her pacing and disappeared. To this extent the play is linear. But, in the cyclic context of language and action, the likelihood seems to be that beyond the hearing of the theatre audience, the protagonist's feet still pace[31] and May has *not* done:

> . . . revolving it all [] (*Pause.*) It all. (*Pause.*) It all.

The very repetition of these words at the end of each section suggests an infinite cycle.[32] The echoes of her restless feet seem to have widened out beyond our hearing, as seven days spiral into endlessness:

> one two three four five six seven wheel one two three four five six seven wheel.[33]

Footfalls is the story of a woman who, as in *Not I*, seems to be trying to come to terms with her life. It may be observed here that Beckett has referred actresses playing May to Carl Jung's description of a child who, though living, had never fully come to life: 'She was never born.'[34] May's existence, as described by her mother, has largely been spent in pacing up and down a strip of floor, listening to her footfalls, in an apparent attempt to perceive the passage of her life, and, by extension, to give it meaning. In death (if we take Beckett's remark that it is a ghost play) she still seeks to understand.

May's urge to perceive brings the C18 philosopher, Bishop Berkeley, to mind. In particular his dictum which so fascinated Beckett that he used it as the epigraph to *Film*: 'Esse est percipi' (to be is to be perceived). May, however, is the direct opposite of the protagonist in *Film*, who is in full flight from self-perception. Her whole being is concentrated on the attempt to perceive. 'The motion alone is not enough?' enquires her mother. 'No, mother' she replies: 'the motion alone is not enough, I must hear the feet however faint they fall.'

Although there is no reason to suppose that Beckett had Shakespeare in mind when he wrote *Footfalls*, the whole play is extraordinarily realised in these lines from *Macbeth*:

Tomorrow, and tomorrow, and tomorrow,
Creeps in this petty pace from day to day
To the last syllable of recorded time,
And all our yesterdays have lighted fools
The way to dusty death. Out, out, brief candle!
Life's but a walking shadow, a poor player,
That struts and frets his hour upon the stage
And then is heard no more; it is a tale
Told by an idiot, full of sound and fury
Signifying nothing.

We see, in May, the 'walking shadow', the 'brief candle' of her life over, pacing out her 'yesterdays' on her strip of stage — apparently bent on telling her tale of no significance 'To the last syllable of recorded time'. At the same time May is merely a 'player' pacing the stage. The extreme bitterness of the final phrase 'signifying nothing' is an ironical comment on May's fruitless search for meaning in her endless recapitulation of the same 'tale'.

In *Footfalls* there seems to be especial irony surrounding the lyrical reference to the candelabrum. May's passage up and down the North transept of the Church ('his poor arm') is reflected in the candelabrum. In many Roman Catholic churches the bank of candles lit continually by those at prayer is found in the North transept.[35] If those lighted candles are seen as prayers for the dead (as they often are) the irony that it is an *unquiet* spirit whose passage makes them waver becomes extreme. Prayer, in such a context, is seen as essentially ineffectual. The beauty of the lines draws attention to them, as in the Shakespeare passage, but (again as in *Macbeth*) they leave a bitter taste.

From a structural point of view the movement of *Footfalls* is indeed linear, in so far as May has vanished at the end of play; but her vanishing seems to be contained by the circle like an echo, so that one is left with an overriding impression of repetition.

Thus at the end of this discussion of Beckett's use of pattern we still find him fusing form and content, circle and life cycle, as in his earlier plays; still using the circle or spiral as motifs with which to express the unending cycle of being. Although in a few plays linear progression may be said to have escaped the circle, in most cases it is contained by it and a circular movement is present in every play. We have seen Beckett making his circles in different ways, while employing largely the same themes. The later plays have been remarkable for the ever-narrowing focus and growing brevity of the scale, until circle and life-cycle join in the *reductio ad absurdum, Breath*.

In his inaugural lecture as Merton Professor of English Literature at Oxford, John Carey remarked on the 'relatively modern consciousness of the indissoluble fusion of form and content in a work of literature'.[36] He went on to say that 'It is a fusion, we now take it for granted, so subtle and profound that the terms 'form' and'content' have themselves come to seem coarse and obsolete — no longer acceptable elements in a critic's vocabulary, since they insist upon a separation in which we no longer believe.' But, when Beckett pointed to the form/content fusion in his early essays on Joyce and Proust, he was helping to create the 'modern consciousness' of their indissolubility, and subsequently structured his own works on the same principle. In so doing Beckett achieves what Walter Pater already in the nineteenth century regarded as the desirable condition for a work of art:

> ... that this form, this mode of handling, should become an end in itself, should penetrate every part of the matter: this is what all art constantly strives after.[37]

CHAPTER 6
DRAFTING THE TEXT

The meticulous craftsmanship we have come to expect in the structuring of Beckett's plays is equally evident in his manuscript drafts. The growth of the plays, from the germ of an idea to the completed text, is the subject of the next four chapters. A considerable body of draft material for most of Beckett's plays and prose works is to be found in university libraries in both Europe and America. A chart of the extent and whereabouts of known draft material for the plays under discussion in these chapters, from *All That Fall* to *Footfalls* (1956-1976), is included at Appendix I.

Even for a small text the volume of reworking is immense. There are, for example, no less than six manuscript and ten typescript drafts of the French prose text *Bing* as well as several further drafts for *Ping*, its English translation.[1] Preliminary drafts of the plays are often widely scattered and material is continually coming to light. Ohio State University, for example, has drafts of *Fin de partie* and *Happy Days* so extensive that they would seem to be complete, but an alternative version of part of *Fin de partie* is to be found at Trinity College, Dublin[2] and additional fragments of the play may be seen in a notebook at Reading University. The same notebook also contains the first signs of *Happy Days*.[3] Moreover the Reading library has a further typescript (with author's MS. corrections) of an abandoned play inscribed by Beckett as 'avant *Fin de partie*'.[4] It may well be that more drafts of both these plays remain to be found. Thus, in the absence of definite authorial information to the contrary, no set of preliminary drafts should be regarded as complete.

Before embarking on a discussion of the drafts of the plays in English, beginning with *All That Fall*, we should look briefly at the genesis of the plays in French, in order to ascertain whether there are common features in the creation of all Beckett's dramatic works.

En attendant Godot

Few have seen the manuscript of *En attendant Godot*, which is still in Beckett's possession. One of these, Colin Duckworth, was informed by Beckett that 'There were no preliminary drafts of *GODOT*. I still have the original MS. which you are welcome to see.'[5] The MS. was begun on 9 October 1948 and completed on 29 January 1949. Duckworth's account of his two-hour examination of it describes an exercise book in which 'Beckett wrote on each right-hand page to the end of the book, then continued on each left-hand page beginning at the beginning of the book again.'[6] This is unusual. Beckett's normal practice is to write on the right-hand pages of an exercise book, leaving the left-hand pages blank for notes, second thoughts, alterations and (in the first stages of a work particularly) complicated and grotesque doodles, created apparently while wrestling with the dialogue. Beckett, however, told Duckworth that the composition of *Godot* had come about with little struggle: 'I didn't have too much trouble with it.' Duckworth comments: 'I found out when I studied the manuscript months later, he was telling nothing less than the truth.'[7]

The fact that the play came so fluently and easily to the page may have been partly because Beckett wrote it as deliberate relaxation for a mind tired by the *trilogy*. The way had, moreover, been prepared in earlier works, as Beckett himself suggested to Duckworth: 'If you want to find the origins of *En attendant Godot*, look at *Murphy*.'[8] Duckworth looked further, at the then discarded novel *Mercier et Camier*, tracing 'many coincidences of style and theme' between it and *Godot*.[9] He also observed echoes of the Glazier's conversation with his son in *Éleuthéria*, in Vladimir's conversation with the boy in *Godot*.[10] Thus, although we have no drafts of *Godot*, we can to some extent see its evolution from earlier works. It may be observed here that another holograph version of the play in the manuscript library of the University of Texas at Austin (listed in the Beckett bibliography as the 'original French MS')[11] is not a further stage in the evolution of the text, but what Beckett described to me as 'merely a fair copy made in a foul moment for the sake of a few quid.'[12]

Perhaps Duckworth's most interesting discoveries in the original manuscript concern the withholding of information from the final text. Noting, for example, a particular debt to Dante's *Purgatorio*, he remarks:

Certain 'clues', then, have been progressively suppressed — clues which the reader of Dante will follow without hesitation (hence, no doubt, their suppression).[13]

In the MS. version, moreover, M. Godot exists, in proof of which he sends a letter to Vladimir and Estragon.[14] Beckett himself drew Duckworth's attention to a note in the MS. about the identity of Godot, remarking that he had subsequently 'completely forgotten about it':

> Suggérer que Pozzo est peut-être Godot après tout, venu au rendez-vous, et qu'il ne sait pas que Vladimir et Estragon sont Vladimir et Estragon. Mais le messager?[15]

Duckworth comments that the above cannot be a preliminary note, since none of the characters are distinguished by name at their first appearance in the manuscript; 'proof enough', he continues, 'that it is the original draft.'[16]

The suppression of the written message from *Godot* gives the play an extra dimension, balancing it on the resultant ambiguity. Duckworth, after observing various linguistic transformations (that, for instance, Lucky's 'quaqua' was initially 'quoique' and that the reference to 'la divine Miranda' was originally more overtly literary: 'à la façon de la Miranda du divin Shakespeare') concludes:

> We can see, therefore, that part of the process of mystification through the disintegration of language originates from post- manuscript stages in composition. Repeated, deformed, and nonsensical words replace some earlier coherent expressions.[17]

Here then, in the manuscript of Beckett's first published play, we have evidence of a 'process of mystification' taking place in the drafts. Beckett completed *En attendant Godot* in January 1949 but it was not until more than four years later that he began another play.

Fin de partie

The 'struggle' Beckett had in writing *Fin de partie* is detailed in a series of letters to his friend the American director, Alan Schneider.[18] Among the most significant of these is one dated 12 April 1956, where he outlines a structural problem:

> It has turned out a three-legged giraffe, to mention only the

architectonics, and leaves me in doubt whether to take a leg off or add one on.

A subsequent letter (dated 21 June 1956) shows him to have taken the former course; 'one act' has emerged, but 'longish, hour and a quarter I fancy'. Beckett describes the play as 'Rather difficult and elliptic, mostly depending on the power of the text to claw, more inhuman than *Godot*'.

The bulk of the drafts of *Fin de partie*, a holograph and three successive typescripts, are held by The Ohio State University Libraries.[19] The first, as John Fletcher points out 'represents to all intents and purposes a fair copy of the manuscript, and the second does not differ substantially from the published text.' The important reduction to a single act thus took place 'between these two typewritten drafts (both made by Beckett himself)'.[20] Beckett indeed informed me in 1978 that he does 'all his own typing'.[21]

All three of the Ohio typescripts are much altered by hand. Typescript 1 consists of 65 pages, while the text is cut virtually by half in Typescript 2, to 35 pages. Typescript 3 has 38 pages. A note on the first page of Typescript 1 states '75 minutes'. On the first page of Act 2 another '35 minutes' is added, thus making the first draft almost two hours long. Beckett's estimate of an 'hour and a quarter' for the one-act play (a reduction of only 35 minutes, despite the greatly reduced text) seems to indicate the speed of delivery required. A later letter to Schneider describes the play as 'A very long one act, over an hour and a half I shd. think.'[22]

A MS. note described by Fletcher as preceding Typescript 1 reads: 'Act 1. Hilare. Acte 2. Mortellement triste.'[23] Act 1 closes with the death of Nell; her bin has been removed from the stage when Act 2 opens. The three men wear black headgear in Act 2 and their formerly red faces are white. Nagg too appears to be nearing extinction, and, in his final speech, tells Clov not to bother to renew his sawdust. There is no major alteration in the shaping of the play; Beckett simply amalgamated the two acts. But in so doing he removed the specific from the text, so that a study of the early draft makes explicit what is merely implied in the finished play.

The most substantial changes in the later play are the omission of three scenes interestingly outlined by Ruby Cohn.[24] Two of these concern Clov disguised. In Act 1 Clov turns himself into a woman because Hamm, after listening to a passage from the Old

Testament, decides that he should be begetting. Should a child be conceived, however, the disguised Clov tells Hamm they will drown it ('Nip some young doom in the bud' as Mr. Rooney muses in Beckett's next play, *All That Fall*.) In Act 2 Clov disguises himself as a schoolboy and Hamm teaches the 'boy' to carry out the duties Clov used to perform. But, despite Hamm's pleas, the boy finally leaves the stage. He appears to be a foreshadowing of the child sighted by Clov from the window in the final version, while his hunger links with the famished child in Hamm's 'chronicle'. Thus in the repetition of the element of disguise in the embryo *Fin de partie*, Act 2 deliberately parallels Act 1, which, as we have observed in Chapter 5, is Beckett's usual practice with two act structures.

In the third scene which is also later omitted Hamm requires Nagg's head to be placed in a pillory, obliging his father both to listen to him and then to recount his life story. Nagg refuses, but is finally bludgeoned into speech (reminiscent, as we shall see, of Fox being whipped into narration in *Radio II*). The pillory scene takes place in Act 2, after the death of Nell. However, Beckett's reworking of *Fin de partie* does not consist entirely of excisions. Two passages in the published text are entirely missing from the Ohio drafts. The first of these is Nagg's comic tale about the tailor and his trousers; the second is Clov's speech 'from (the) heart' just before the play closes, that recalls Lucky's outburst in *Godot*. It is Clov's longest and most significant utterance.

We have observed that the death of Nell in Typescript 1 is implied rather than stated in the published text. A similar removal of the specific is introduced into the stage properties. A large Bible on a stand in the MS., for example, is replaced in Typescript 2 by an anonymous painting, face to the wall. Similarly the relationships between the characters are much more clearly stated in early versions of the play. Final names do not appear until a MS. note in the margin of Typescript 2; in the first three drafts of *Fin de partie*, as Fletcher observes:

> the characters are simply designated as A, B, P and M. In the dialogue, however, A is addressed as Guillaume, B as James, P as Pépé (by A) and Walther (by M), and M as Mémé. It is clear that P and M are A's parents, and there is a suggestion (which survives in the final version) that B is his son; but the holograph notes preceding T1 speak only of a 'père adoptif' and 'fils adoptif'.[25]

Typescript 3 bears the following MS. note on the first page:

NAGG, un homme
NELL, sa femme
HAMM, leur fils
CLOV, un factotum

These precise identifications are, however, removed from the published text, the technique we have already noticed Beckett employing in *Godot*.

A resumé of the content of the French drafts is a necessary introduction to a study of the English ones. Having noticed a consistent trend towards developing ambiguity as the French drafts progress, we are now in a position to establish whether Beckett's creative method has remained constant. We shall look in particular at alterations in the presentation of theme in the English drafts and the bearing of any such alterations on the interpretation of the final text.

Discussion of the drafts is not at first chronological, as with the investigation of Beckett's structural patterning. The analysis of structure opened with the clearest examples of cyclic patterning, thus enabling the reader to appreciate Beckett's characteristic method and to recognise it subsequently when looking at the remaining plays. Similarly, this study of Beckett's drafts in English begins with the most striking examples — three plays in which the final text differs markedly from the initial stages. Once the development of these plays has been recognised as characteristic of Beckett's method, it becomes possible to study the development of the remaining plays chronologically in the light of insights gained, and to establish whether similarities in his creative process are apparent throughout the plays under discussion.

CHAPTER 7
DEVELOPING AMBIGUITY

Come and Go

What appears to be a preliminary scene among the early drafts of *Come and Go* bears virtually no relation to the published text, except that it concerns three women. The women have floral names and seem to be on the fringe of life, in that they hear about sex (from a book read aloud) rather than participate in it.

The remainder of the early drafts are Beckett's first attempts at achieving the cyclic form of entrance and exit that we recognise from the published version, but they contain two themes absent in the final text. The first of these, the question of sex, recalls the preliminary scene. But there has been a development. Active participation now occurs and each of the women rejoices in a lover. The second theme states explicitly that all three women are in the last stages of terminal illness, whereas the published text merely implies that this may be so.

The beauty of the final version is its brevity: movement stylised, dialogue pared to 121 words, but perfectly patterned and proportioned. The more concise, the more highly stylised Beckett's 'dramaticule' becomes, the more telling it is, until the final point is wordless. 'I can feel the rings' says Flo, as the three women sit, hands linked, staring into space. But it is on three pairs of ringless hands that the light focuses just before the curtain falls.

The early drafts of *Come and Go*, a holograph and two typescripts, are at Reading University.[1] They are all undated. Two further holograph versions, the second dated at the close 'Ussy 16.1.65.' were published in facsimile by the Manus Presse, Stuttgart in a limited edition of *Kommen und Gehen* in 1968.[2] Four minimally altered pre-publication typescripts are held at Washington University, St. Louis. These are undated, but the manuscript of the French translation (also held at Washington) is dated 'Ussy 21.3.65', showing Beckett to have been composing in English and translating into French almost simultaneously.

The version of *Come and Go* bearing the least relation to the published text is not the Reading holograph, but a typescript headed 'Scene 1'.[3] Its title suggests that it is the first scene of a sketch. Since the scene stands very much alone in the play's development, it will be considered first; (here and elsewhere in this volume Beckett's alterations are indicated in **bold**.) There are three characters, Viola, Poppy and Rose. Poppy reads aloud from a titillating book, interrupted at intervals by the others. She is required to re-read an earlier passage, in order to establish the whereabouts of Aubrey, whose habits recall those of Willie in *Happy Days*:

Poppy '. . . Aubrey stretched out to the flames his long hairy legs, took a sip of his ~~brandy~~ **Sandeman** relit his cigar and resumed alone his collection of obscene postcards.'

Literal-minded Viola, having established Aubrey's current occupation, is not prepared to hear more until she has ascertained the level of his trousers:

Viola Are his trousers off already then?
Rose Not in my recollection — why?
Viola His long hairy legs.
Rose ~~A lover's~~ **The** legs may be hairy and ~~his~~ **the** trousers still **be** on. Poppy.
Poppy (who has been checking the text) When last seen his trousers were still on.

Poppy continues reading, a parody of pornographic writing that arouses Viola's critical faculties:

Poppy '. . . then falling to her knees plunged them between her thighs in an exstasy of anticipation.'
Viola This is ~~careless~~ **slipshod** writing.
Rose You mean one cannot plunge one's knees between one's thighs?

The sketch ends with Poppy, apparently overcome by her text, leaving the room:

Poppy '. . . Finally she sprang to her feet and, still moist, entered the ~~darkened~~ bedroom.' Excuse me just one moment.
Poppy gets up, lays down the book and goes out laboriously.

I have quoted liberally from this typescript to indicate how little connects its hilarious revue-like style with the disturbing short text finally printed. Beckett must have realised its inappropriateness as a first scene and the entire script is crossed out in his hand.

In the holograph, headed by Beckett 'Before *Come and Go*' two separate attempts at a text much nearer to the final version appear.[4] According to current placing at Reading University Library, the first of these is entitled *Good Heavens* and the second *Type of Confidence*. It appears, however, that the latter is the first attempt and *Good Heavens* a rewrite. The following linguistic comparison shows *Good Heavens* improving upon the vocabulary in *Type of Confidence*:

	Type of Confidence		*Good Heavens*
B	(*appalled*) No!	*B*	(*appalled*) ~~No!~~ **Good heavens!**
A	. . . she thinks it is acidity	*A*	. . . she thinks it is ~~acidity~~ **heartburn**
A	. . . so as to make my peace with God in the time that remained.	*A*	. . . so as to make my peace with my maker in the time that remained.

Although the last example has no words crossed out, the alliterative change (from 'God' to 'my maker') is the kind of alteration typically made by Beckett as drafts progress. Furthermore C's sister, referred to in both sections, is nameless in *Type of Confidence*, but becomes 'Mrs. Flower' in *Good Heavens*. Thus it appears that the sheet containing *Type of Confidence* should be placed first rather than last in the collection of holograph sheets at Reading University. The error arose because Beckett himself wrote 'Before *Come and Go*' beside the *Good Heavens* title, thus making it appear the first page. If the misplacement hypothesis is correct, an interesting corollary ensues. The *Type of Confidence* heading appears on a clean sheet, as would be expected of a new draft. But, at the top of the sheet, preceding the title, is a diagram that reveals Beckett to have plotted the entire play before writing any dialogue. The diagram schematizes what is known to whom throughout:

	1	ABC.	
B knows about C	2	~~AB~~ ***Exit C***	
" " " ***A***	3	A to B about C ~~B to C~~	***A knows about C***
	4	Enter C.	***A*** " " ***B***

	5	Exit A.
C knows about A	6	B to C about A ~~C to B~~
″ ″ ″ ***B***	7	Enter A.
	8	Exit B.
	9	C to A about B ~~A to C~~
	10	Enter B.

Beckett thus began the play with the structure of three confidential gossips clearly in mind; after jotting down the structure, he sketched a ''type'' (or illustration) of the kind of confidence he envisaged, before going on to draft the play in full. As would be expected were this so, *Type of Confidence* is a fragment, and consists solely of dialogue between A and B, ending on the entrance of C; *Good Heavens* is almost complete, apart from the final conversation between C and A.

In both versions conversation centres upon two secrets: first the recipe each woman has for her apparently flawless complexion and secondly the terminal illness of the absent member of the trio. The diagram reveals it to be Beckett's intention that all three women should both gossip and be gossiped about. The difference between what is said face to face and what is said behind the back of the missing person reveals both a devastating feminine hypocrisy and the irony that the secret is told by one whom the hearer already knows (or soon discovers) to be doomed also. And while each woman muses upon the fate of the other two, she remains supremely unaware of her own. In *Good Heavens*, each expresses admiration for the complexion of that other with whom she is left alone, while silently appalled by how ill she looks. A merciful lie (A: 'You do look wonderful'; B: 'You look so fresh') in each case succeeds in drawing from the other the secret behind the radiant skin. It is not beauty creams but, in A's case a discharged prisoner, in C's 'the croquet champion' and in B's, what appears to be a visit to a brothel:

A Good heavens! Is that place going still?
B Oh very much so. (*Complacent laugh.*)[5] Very much so indeed.

B makes a further self-revelation, capable of even broader interpretation, not to mention a side-swipe at the university:

~~*B*~~ ***C*** . . .Have you been using something on your skin?
(~~*C*~~***B*** *whispers in* ~~*B*~~ ***C's*** *ear.*)
~~*B*~~ Good heavens! ~~Is he up again~~?
B Oh very much so. (*Complacent laugh.*) Very much so indeed!

B No cream to touch it.
~~*B*~~ *C* I did not know he was up.

The alterations reveal that when writing the holograph dialogue Beckett at times became confused as to what dialogue belonged to which letter. This shows him to have been thinking in terms of what had to be said, rather than who should say it. The voices are mouthpieces, letters rather than characters, and Beckett is merely working out the pattern he set himself on Page One. Even when names appear the personalities are indistinguishable, as if the three were one. Indeed the costume note in the published text reads:

Apart from colour differentiation, three figures as alike as possible.

That all three women are aspects of a single personality is of course an attractive explanation for their extraordinary resemblance and mutual mortal illness. It is more likely, however, that Beckett is once again developing his constant theme of birth 'astride of a grave'.

The precise nature of the secret concerning each woman in the published text remains undisclosed. Those in the holograph, however, though also whispered, are at once clarified for the audience by the recipient's responses. The first open secret is comic, a complexion cure. The second secret both reminds us of the published text (in the 'appalled' response it elicits) and is unlike it, in that serious illness is not implied, but explicit and fatal:

A. She told me she was condemned.
(*She whispers in B's ear.*)
B. (*Appalled.*) ~~No!~~ **Good heavens!**
A. The worst kind. (*Pause.*) Three months. (*Pause.*) At the outside.

The second typescript at Reading University is also headed 'Before *Come and Go* in Beckett's hand.[6] It is a further attempt to shape the conversations taking place between two of the women in the absence of the third. Each dualogue is typed on a separate sheet and the women are named, Rose, Vi and Poppy. This is both an extension of the holograph (in which the only name mentioned was 'Mrs. Flower') and an abbreviation of the first typescript, which has 'Viola' rather than 'Vi'. The conversations are tightened by the removal of an exchange of skin secrets between the women. In each dualogue, instead of a mutual exchange of sexual confidences, one woman only discloses her complexion recipe, and discussion of the imminent demise of the absentee ensues. The pattern of utterance is highlighted by the reduction of words. The draft is, however, extended by a comic addition, the introduction of three sorrowing husbands, all conspicuously absent:

Rose (of Poppy). I ran into her husband at the Gaiety. He is half crazed with grief.

Poppy (of Vi). Her husband wrote me from Madeira. He is heartbroken.

Vi (of Rose). Her husband called **me** from Naples. He was weeping over the wire.

Typescript 2 is classified at Reading University by the same manuscript number as the 'Scene I' already discussed, thus suggesting it follows on from Scene I, as a second scene. The heading II on the first page of the three page typescript reinforces this view. However, the numerals IV and VI are typed at the head of the two remaining pages of text and it becomes apparent that these numerals denote the gossips between the women. The first gossip is headed II, the second IV and the third VI. The figures thus appear to represent stages II, IV and VI of Beckett's fully developed vision of the play. Stages I, III, V and VII would thus consist of the linking material that is found in the published text, before, between and after the three gossips, when all the women are present onstage. It is possible that 'Scene I' was Beckett's first attempt at drafting such linking material. That Beckett was shaping his text in this manner is evident from a diagram that follows the first dualogue:

I	V. R. P.
II	V. R.
III	V. R. P.
IV	P. R.
V	V. R. P.
VI	V. P.
VII	V. R. P.

Stages II, IV and VI are clearly identified here as the three dualogues noted above. Typescript 2 is thus not 'Scene 2' but Scenes 2, 4 and 6, or three separate stages in the development of the play that was envisaged in the *Type of Confidence* holograph. Beckett could not resist the introduction of sorrowing husbands into the second typescript, but a cutting and shaping of the gossips has already begun. Moreover the precise patterning of the final text is beginning to evolve. Stage directions for the rotation of each woman from seat to seat occur here for the first time. Each is to move to the seat of the absent woman while the gossip takes place. The entire typescript is crossed through, except for the diagram, which is hand written. On the back of the last sheet, a further note in Beckett's hand describes the piece as a 'dramaticule'.

The Manus Presse facsimiles of two further holographs reveal a text much nearer the final version than the Reading material. In the first (a single page) Beckett reverts to the ABC characterisation of the Reading holographs, but he has begun to work on the text that links together the three gossips. Thus the dialogue opens on a scene we recognise:

I

C When did we three last meet?
A Let us not speak.
B Just sit together as we used to, in the playground at Miss Wade's, on the log.
A Holding hands that way.

. . .

B Dreaming of ~~life and~~ love

Exit C.

Under the heading 'II' half way down the page, there is an attempt to restructure the gossips: B asks A how she finds C and A asks C how she finds B. Beckett is here trying out the pattern of repeated phrases evident in the final text. At the top of the page he lists various possibilities:

She may not
Who knows

God grant not.
God forbid.
Please God not.

He selects the second group of phrases. In the first gossip B says 'God grant not' and in the second, A says 'God forbid.'

The second Manus Presse facsimile reveals that the text as we know it has largely evolved. The conversation between the three women in the first facsimile has been spaced out and extended and the two brief dialogues have developed into the three gossips between the women, now named Ru (~~A~~), Vi (C) and Flo (B). The last line reads:

Flo: I can feel ~~your~~ **the** rings.

The advantage of making the reference to rings non-specific has occurred to Beckett here. The text is followed by the notes on 'Lighting', 'Costume', 'Seat', 'Exits' and 'Ohs', found in the published version, with the exception of the final note on voices. On the blank verso page opposite these notes Beckett has jotted a diagram of the final hand positions, which is of great interest in that it shows him to have been visualising the women as colours. He has described the costume colours in the notes, with Vi wearing 'dull red'. In the final tableau Vi sits in the central position once more, her arms, as Beckett notes on the blank page, above those of Ru and Flo. Underneath he draws the following diagram:

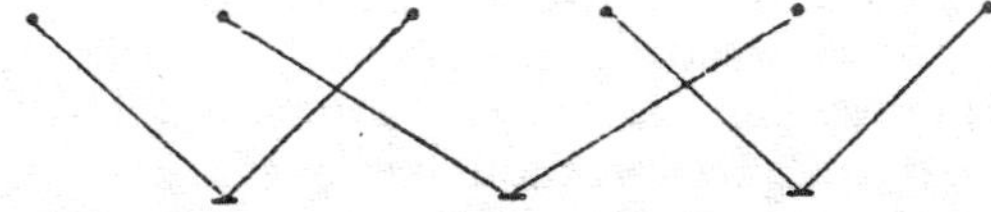

Red's top[7]

The remaining drafts are the four Washington typescripts, lettered 0-3. Typescript 0 appears to be a fair copy of the Manus Presse second facsimile, omitting the final notes. The title *Come and Go* is inked into this draft, but not in Beckett's hand; it is, however, typed into Typescript 1, which also contains the character note 'Age undeterminable' for the first time. Fuller notes than those in the second facsimile appear in this draft. Diagrams for 'Successive Positions' and for 'Hands' are included, together with the note on 'Voices' missing hitherto and a ponderous note on 'Colours':

Much duller in performance than samples herewith indicative only of relative values. If insufficiently dulled by nature of lighting they should be uniformly darkened.

This note remains in Typescript 2, but is omitted from 3, the final draft.

Typescript 1 contains the following manuscript additions to the text in Beckett's hand at the opening and close of the play:

opening:

Vi **Ru**
Ru **Yes**
Vi **Flo**
Flo **Yes**

Vi When did we three last meet?

close:

Flo **Ru.** (***silence***.) **Vi.** (***silence***.) I can feel the rings.

These additions are incorporated into Typescripts 2 and 3 and are present in part in the New York edition of the play,[8] but not in the Calder text.[9] The latter seems to be based on the unrevised Typescript 1, also omitting the note on colours.

In the drafts of *Come and Go* we see Beckett advancing towards an ever stricter patterning, cutting and shaping until, as with a poem, not a word can be lost. By the final text he is no longer relying on identical phraseology to achieve the effect of repetition, but employing more subtle and interesting variations on a theme. In the Reading holographs, for example, a stock response ('Oh very much so . . . very much so indeed!') is made by each woman to a question about her lover. This is reduced, in the ensuing typescript, to Rose alone making the full response, Vi contenting herself with 'Oh very much so', while Poppy does not use the phrase at all. By the final version, the two secrets have become one. The responses all concern God, as we have seen, but are linguistically varied (God grant not/God forbid/ Please God not); the three women invoke respectively a generous, a forbidding and a merciful God.

Visually the notes introduced into the Manus Presse holograph, particularly those on costume and movement ('Exits') emphasise the theme of similarity with difference. The colours worn are different, but all 'dulled', the faces are all shaded by hats and all three women move noiselessly into and out of the surrounding shadow. The addition of the vocal note in the Washington typescripts gives them all low 'colourless' voices, 'except for three "Ohs" and two lines following'. The sense of ritual in both language and movement is strengthened by the final joining of hands, while the carefully plotted hand positioning forms the shape of a Celtic 'endless' knot, symbolising infinity.

It is in the power and economy of the ending that the final version of *Come and Go* achieves its greatest effect. Not until after the last line has been spoken is a further dimension added to the play by the light, teasing the mind into additional speculation. The stage directions reveal it to be hands rather than faces that are 'made up to be as visible as possible' and that there are 'no rings apparent'. As soon as this point is registered, the full force of the play begins to emerge and the various hints fall into place. Three lifetimes are suggested in the 121 words of the final Calder text. Three faded flowers sit recalling the days of their freshness 'at Miss Wade's'. Their floral names have been abbreviated to single syllables, their colours are dulled. Ru is in violet — and both puns are intentional. There is nothing left to these women but rue for the love that has passed them by. Gone are the lovers and sorrowing husbands of the early drafts. The only reference to love in the published text is 'Dreaming' and the only sexual experience known to these women appears to have been in fantasy. The play indeed ends in fantasy as Flo asserts she can feel the rings that are not there.

The fact that the women see 'little change' in each other is significant. The overriding impression of the play is of lack of event. Precisely the tragedy of the women in *Come and Go* is that they appear perpetually to have been waiting for an event, possibly marriage, that never happens. And now, with death looming an unwanted lover in the shade, they seem to be about to die before having ever fully lived; 'never been properly born' as Beckett notes laconically in the Appendix to *Watt*.[10] In the nightmare vision of his later drama the three women may indeed have to endure permanent waiting, condemned to an after-life in which the perpetually active consciousness endlessly recounts its life. *Come and Go* is the waiting situation in Chekhov's *Three Sisters*, or in *Godot*, reduced to its essence. The brevity of the play makes us forcibly aware of impermanence, that 'Beauty's a flower'[11] and must fade. Death 'the invisible worm' in Blake's poem 'The Sick Rose'[12] is already at work. It seems likely that Beckett had this analogy in mind when writing *Come and Go*. 'How do you think Rose is looking?' enquires Poppy in the second Reading University typescript. 'Sick.' replies Vi.

Instead of the tangible lovers of the early drafts and the explicit discussions about mortality, the final text is ambiguous. The probability, given the horror with which each undisclosed secret is received, is that it is again Death who stretches out his arms to the three women in the surrounding darkness. 'Ich bin nicht wild!' says Death, the lover, in Matthias Claudius's poem 'Der Tod und das Mädchen'; 'Sollst sanft in meinen Armen schlafen!'[13] It was to this poem that Schubert composed his

Quartet in D Minor (D810 — 'Death and the Maiden') that lies at the heart of *All That Fall*.[14] The same poem, as James Knowlson has pointed out, lies behind Krapp's uneasy glances over his shoulder into the shadows in *Krapp's Last Tape*.[15] A similar weight of darkness surrounds the women in *Come and Go* and it seems likely that the poem forms part of the experience of this play also. The ambiguities in the final version fill out with surprising richness and depth this textually bare play. Beckett has achieved this effect by combining an obscure minimal text with precise and explicit stage directions, capable of directing audience attention to possibilities not verbally stated and making the play a *tour de force*.

Play

In the drafts of *Come and Go* we have noticed a movement away from the explicit, which gives the final text considerably more power 'to claw'. In *Play* a progression towards ambiguity may be discerned in the later drafts, but the embryo of the play has its own obscurities, notably at the close, where the apparently unfinished text breaks off. This early draft is an undated three page typescript which Beckett has headed 'Before *Play*' in manuscript.[16] The most startling difference between this text and the final version is that a woman and two men constitute the triangle. Three heads protrude from 'three white boxes, one yard high.' But there is no further visual resemblance to the final text. The heads in the early draft are not only named ('from left to right as seen from the auditorium... Syke, Nickie and Conk') but comically characterised: Syke is 'Bald, florid, plump, very long (18'') absolutely horizontal blond moustache', while Conk is his opposite: 'Blue-pale, sleek black hair, long profoundly drooping black moustache.' Nickie is a redhead with 'milky complexion, full red lips, green earrings.' The three heads are spotlit in turn, in order that they may introduce themselves by name — a more traditional but less effective opening than the muttered chorus from three urns 'simultaneously faintly lit' in the published text.

Although in this early draft the three figures are not in urns (and might thus be argued to be in a more ambiguous situation than in the play as we know it) the text is immediately more explicit. Instead of *Play*'s inaudible chorus, followed by a gradual unfolding of the triangular relationship, Nickie plunges into a monologue in which she begs mercy from the light, thus at once revealing the purgatorial aspect of the play:

Nickie: I am not ready. (*Pause. Spot off. Five seconds. Spot on.*) I am not ready. (*Pause.*) I need more dark. (*Pause.*) I say I need more dark. (*Pause.*) Please! (*Pause.*) What is this mercy that when I beg oh please not again so soon again gives me back my dark and then this no mercy that when I beg a moment's grace not even a moment's grace so that I keep on begging, yes, that must be it, to keep me begging on. (*Pause.*) Please! (*Pause.*)

In the published text such speculations take place in the central section of the play, after the blackout that follows the account of the man caught between two women. Throughout *Play*, moreover, the light moves swiftly from head to head, creating the necessary stage movement as it does so. Comic opportunities are also created by cutting off one speaker and juxtaposing another with a different point of view, whereas in the early draft, the comedy is largely visual. The text of the early draft is often amusing in its delineation of character, but loses tension because it is spoken in long monologue paragraphs, instead of being split up by the movement of the light. At the inception of the play, therefore, light is less likely to be seen as a character in the action.

Unlike Nickie, the two men in the early draft do not question their current situation at all. Their monologues are concerned entirely with self-description, culminating in their separate encounters with Nickie. Syke speaks first, briefly delineating his Oxford career: 'Jesus...Brasenose...you know [ ][17] midnight oil...all that'; his biological pursuits ('open air...bird lover ...ringing pipits') and his war: 'down in flames...usual show ...permanent limp'. Thence to a chicken farm in Dumfries, with nothing of moment to record until his meeting with Nickie. Towards her his reactions are still ambivalent: 'then this bitch ...wonder where she is now [ ] my sweet love...my one love ...my —'. Conk, by contrast, was a man of the world, with 'rank, looks, health, brains, charm, wit, French, humour, good humour, private means, a place in town, two outside...' combined with 'the power to please. Women I won unwooed weekly...'. He had in effect 'no complaints, until the day I met that carrot-haired slut.'

Nickie in turn recalls meeting the two men. Of Conk she says simply 'such male beauty I had never seen [ ] never encountered' but her meeting with Syke is described in more detail. It was at an auction, his extraordinary moustache tickling her cheek, as he gazed at a stuffed bird: 'Feeling the tickle of hair against my cheek, and assuming the usual low familiarity, I turned sharply to rebuke the offender, and then there was this hair against my lips.' Syke had only become aware of Nickie after feeling her eyes upon him, as later she was to feel Conk's eyes boring into her back one evening after Syke had seen her home:

Conk: . . . She was with a ~~lout~~ **clod**, a gross pink bald whiskered ~~lout~~ **clod** with a gammy leg. I hope she's gone back to him. She got rid of him at the door after the usual and stood watching him hobble away. Then she ran up the steps and put her key in the door. I asked her afterwards, what possessed you to turn, why in the name of God didn't you go straight in? She said she felt eyes boring into her . . .

The draft ends with Conk driving Nickie home and their looking at each other, while Nickie again holds her door key. Beckett is thus already patterning the action in the play's early stages. But long sections of autobiographical monologue are clearly more suited to a stream of consciousness novel or to solo performance, as in Beckett's latest plays. In the final text the action is tightened by the omission of all personal detail except the situation of jealousy between the two women. Concentration on this dramatic conflict causes Beckett to omit the realisation of love by both men in the early draft, that, despite the comic undercutting, reaches a depth not found in the later text. Until he met Nickie, love for Syke had been of the mechanical variety, later to be found in *Not I*:

love . . . all my arse . . . who could love me . . . ten minutes . . . button up and go home . . . sleep it off . . . then this . . . one look and all gone . . . nothing but her . . . new life . . .

He finds himself needed for the first time:

me wanted . . . holy God . . . darling Syke . . . never leave me . . . never done . . . getting . . . giving . . . all one . . . Grand Canary . . . down at noon . . . lie touching by the sea . . . mouths . . . like one . . . like one –

This is a far more sympathetic picture of love than Beckett usually allows himself. The two 'lovers' in *That Time*, for example, never touch. In the final version of *Play*, however, Syke's romantic idyll becomes distorted into Woman 1's attempt to celebrate her victory over Woman 2 by a trip to 'our darling Grand Canary'.

Conk's realisation of love is connected with the puzzling episode on which the first draft closes. While driving Nickie home she had suddenly commanded him to stop the car, leaped out and returned with a wounded bird that she cushioned in her breast:

Conk: A sparrow, she told me later, when it died. She put it down between her breasts and held it there from the outside, I mean she didn't put her hand down with it. What are your plans for that? I said. She turned and looked at me. (*Pause*.) Was it then I was — fleshed? (*Pause*.) In the end I put out the light and drove on. We stood together at the foot of the steps. The street lamps went out. She asked me to take the key ~~out of~~ **from** her bag and put it in her hand, then hang the bag on her arm. I stood waiting for her to go up. Let me see you drive off, she said. (*Pause*.) So a little — from her hand. In the grey of the morning.

Here the draft ends. Beckett has added in manuscript: 'dwindle in reflector.' Cutting off the narrative at this point is equivalent to the blackout on Page 15 of the Faber edition of *Play*. But the light in the Reading typescript is not yet the active participator in the action that it becomes in ensuing drafts, both in its role as inquisitor and in its power to frame and mark stages in the action by the use of blackouts. It is clear from the early version that a mere juxtaposition of image (three people in boxes) with text (monologue narration of past events) is not enough to hold audience attention. But Nickie's first speech in this version in which (as we have seen) she begs for dark, showed Beckett the way to progress and the ensuing drafts immediately increase the role of light.

The episode of the sparrow in the early version is capable of wide interpretation. There may be echoes of Skelton's 'Philip Sparrow' in the bird at the breast. Moreover the introduction of a bird into Nickie's relations with Conk at once recalls the abandoned bird-lover, Syke, while the bird's injury parallels Syke's war wound. Nestling the wounded sparrow in her breast both marks Nickie's divided allegiance and, paradoxically, is the cause of Conk's subjugation to her ('Was it then I was — fleshed?') The incident also has affinities with Clov's song in *Fin de partie*, omitted from the English text:

Joli oiseau, quitte ta cage,
Vole vers ma bien-aimée,
Niche-toi dans son corsage,
Dis-lui combien je suis emmerdé.[18]

There is more genuine sexual arousal in Nickie's description of Syke's moustache brushing her lips or Conk's feelings as Nickie cradles the bird in her bosom than in the man's comic exertions ('What a male!') of the final text. The omission of such episodes demonstrates the changed tone of the final version. Beckett is concerned in *Play* less with human affection (characterised in his more typical manner in the final text as grotesque folly) than with a more serious form of delusion, to which human nature is also subject. In the final version it is man's folly in believing in the possibility of divine mercy that is under examination. We are confronted by endless recapitulations of the past, with no reprieve. The change of emphasis marks an extension from man's personal preoccupations in a love affair, to concern for his position in the universe: 'Am I as much as being seen?'

Following the 'Before *Play*' typescript, ten further drafts chronicle the development of *Play*.[19] They are all typescripts and three of them are dated. Typescript 4 is dated 'August 1962' and Typescripts 8 and 10 'Ussy December 1963'. How far in advance of these 'Before *Play*' was written is unknown. The Washington University material chronicles a painstaking re-working throughout the ten drafts; liberal use of this large body of material is made in Appendix VII to demonstrate in detail the kinds of changes that occur in Beckett's development of a text. The general trend in the evolution of the later drafts of *Play* is once again towards ambiguity of expression. Richard Admussen comments:

> The general state of being and the attitudes of the characters were originally much more explicit — that all are dead, for instance, is considerably clearer at the outset; each wonders if the others feel sorry for him and someone speaks of reasoning 'in the old earthly way.' As work on the play progressed, one can see it become more hermetic as far as the dialogue is concerned, the author seeking to *evoke* the state of the characters rather than to *describe* it. So while the dialogue moves from the concrete to the vague, Beckett finds other means to make the spectator sense, and even experience, their state.[20]

We have now looked at very early material for two plays, 'Before *Come and Go*' and 'Before *Play*'. In each case a play of depth and insight has metamorphosed from an explicit situation of broad domestic comedy. There are serious undertones in the early drafts and, as we have observed, genuine feeling in the men's reactions to Nickie in 'Before *Play*'. But the plays at this stage are inward-looking, dealing with the particular rather than the universal and almost everything is unmemorably evident. In subsequent drafts Beckett sets about purging the concrete from his text, making a play that does not yield itself up entirely at first sight, but has to be thought about and worked at, and has the capacity, in so doing, to extend our experience of human nature.

He enlists our concern not with the characters in these plays (we have seen that characterisation in *Come and Go* is interchangeable) but with the predicament in which these characters find themselves, which becomes, by extension, man's predicament.

The final play to be considered in this chapter because of the explicit nature of its preliminary material is *Not I*. The seeds of the play are to be found in three fragments in a notebook at Trinity College Dublin.[21] They were written in December 1963, the month of the completion of *Play* and it is not difficult to imagine Beckett, bored with the latter after laborious re-working diverting himself by trying out a new theme. Immediately following these fragments in the notebook, however, is a plan for a further play on the triangular theme. Its strong resemblance to *Play* makes it worth quoting here — following our discussion of *Play* — though the likeness apparently prevented it from developing beyond the planning stage. The three characters are a man (A) and two women (B) and (C). The two women sit upstage centre and the man downstage right, their three chairs thus forming a triangle onstage. There is no dialogue, merely the following structural plan:

1. General light. All 3 seated. B & C plain chairs, A armchair. B & C bowed heads. A head up looking at them.
2. General light gradually down, all light on C's face, **her head lifts, rest darkness.**
3. ~~C's statement.~~ **C's statement**
4. XX Gradual return to general light, C's head down, B's still down — A's still up looking.
5. General light gradually down, all light on B's face, her head lifts, rest darkness.
6. B's statement.
7. Gradual return to general light, B's head down, C's still down, A's now down.

Curtain

A preliminary diagram of the stage considers a possible fourth character, D, sitting downstage left, opposite A. But since there is a question mark beside the letter D and it does not appear in the subsequent scheme, Beckett clearly had second thoughts about this. Following the scheme a note considers the possibility of A being female — and whether A's head should be bowed at stage 4 (after C's statement) and remain bowed at stage 7. It seems likely that the statements of C and B are intended to induce in A a feeling of remorse, which, with the emphasis on three heads and fluctuating light levels, links the scheme clearly with *Play*.

Not I

The first fragment related to *Not I* in the Trinity College notebook is headed *Kilcool*. Kilcoole is the name of a small resort south of Dublin, between Greystones and Wicklow; in the text Beckett reinstates the 'e' in Kilcoole. The fragment, a monologue for a female voice, centres upon childhood memories of Kilcoole and is dated 8 December 1963. It is followed by authorial aides-mémoire, in which Beckett decides how the play should be written and isolates certain themes. The second fragment (dated 23 December 1963) does not mention Kilcoole specifically, though repeating some of the material found in the earlier draft. Its main innovations are the memory of being abandoned by a lover and the use of two voices (normal and assumed). In the final fragment (dated 29 December 1963) the voice senses that there is 'someone in me, trying to get out', makes various calculations on the amount of silence that may be achieved in a year by judicious daily pausing and ends in an almost liturgical passage of repeated negatives.

The three dates do not, then, represent new beginnings to the work so much as continuations of a monologue. Each fragment consists of memories taken from largely different stages of life, the first recalling childhood, the second adulthood, the third old age and perhaps beyond, as, for example: 'Was I in someone once, and where is she now, if I was in her once, and she let me out —'. There are undoubted similarities here with the three strands of memory in *That Time*. Moreover the image envisaged in stage directions following the second fragment is:

Old woman's face, 4 ft. above stage level, slightly off centre, lit by strong steady light — Body not visible. Stage in darkness. Nothing visible but face.

Beckett has called *That Time* 'a brother to *Not I*.'[22] It appears that just as, having completed *Play*, he went on toying with the triangular theme in the scheme for a play quoted above, so, having written *Not I* (employing a more radical image than that envisaged in the Trinity College fragments) he subsequently returned to his original idea of a head suspended in space and wrote *That Time*. It is even possible that he had Kilcoole in mind ('this ruin in Kilcoole') when describing the ruin in *That Time* where the protagonist hid as a child.

What then are the particular resemblances between these fragments and *Not I* that justify considering them as early attempts to draft the play? The opening stage directions of the *Kilcool* fragment call for:

Woman's face alone in constant light.
Nothing but ~~fixed~~ ***lined*** *lit face and speech.*

The directions go on to note that a certain part of the text produces tears on the face '...near beginning, brief; towards middle, longer; and, longest, to close. Curtain down on **lit** weeping face.' The tears are to be followed each time by a pause for their abatement, recalling the pauses after Mouth's repeated denials of selfhood in *Not I*. But perhaps the most striking resemblance to the theme of *Not I* is the final direction:

Talks of herself in 3rd person.

The monologue describes, as with Mouth, an orphaned child ('...papa dead – we have seen and then mamma...') taken to the bosom of a widowed, childless aunt 'to go on living with her in her humble home in Kilcoole that is the time we are come to now.' Other memories of the voice have, it seems, been discarded before the text begins:

We have seen no more of that all has been weighed all that remained and tip tip now the one scale now the other so no more those other times other homes...

It seems possible that the voice is 'dreaming back' Yeatsian fashion, unravelling a life, while it is weighed in the purgatorial balance. But childhood memories appear to be its entire experience, since it moves immediately from thoughts of Kilcoole to:

When she so young so long ago was laid in Redford by the sea [ ] that short sickness when we come to that and then the dark where she was laid...'

It is difficult to equate the story of the young girl laid in the dark with the woman's face that provides the visual image. Yet that we are supposed to do so is evident from the direction 'Talks of herself in 3rd person.' It is as though the girl who was laid in the dark has gone on growing nonetheless, into the woman now speaking, whose face is seen held in the light from which she prays to be released:

this prayer giver of light and taker of it away this prayer again take it away. (*Pause. Weeps. Five seconds.*)

After one and a half pages the text is marked 'abandoned' and various aides-mémoire ensue before a further draft is attempted. Beckett appears to have taken a hard look at the preceding text and decided how best to develop it. The following passage is quoted in full for its insights into his working method:

Themes, lay down before writing.

to each theme a certain pause length.

" " " " different voice quality.
(speed, ~~high~~ **high or low** moved or cold etc.)

1 theme only leads to tears
" " " " smile
" " " " laugh

Details of above prayer to time for dark
as life is darkened. This is the tear-producer.
Three times, including curtain (light on weeping
face, prayer unanswered.)

Within given theme normal conversation
pauses. Only before text engaged put a full length pause.

Whole text spoken over soft rapid buzz only audible
in major pauses and during silent weeping.

'I' 'me' etc. never spoken outside assumed voice.

Identification by final prayer to time in assumed voice —

Beckett goes on to 'lay down' eight themes that, as in *Not I*, tell the story of a life:

Themes

1. Light — dark leading to prayer for dark & tears. ~~3 time~~ **three times:** opening, midway, end.
2. Voice imitated.
3. Thoughts.
4. Lover.
5. Age.

6. Never presumes seen, heard.
7. Her body.
8. Burial.

These themes compare interestingly with Beckett's holograph 'analysis' of his first full draft of *Not I* as such at Reading University, which is printed as Appendix IV of this study. Here again the analysis seems to have been made after writing the first draft and fifteen themes are isolated. Several passages are marked 'amplify', one 'mention earlier', one 'add to' and one 'another ex(ample)'. The analysis is thus a breakdown of the holograph text, with Beckett's memoranda regarding its alteration and expansion.

Returning to the Trinity College notebook, we find Beckett drafting new material in the second fragment, to give substance to some of the themes he had isolated after the first draft. Thus the second fragment opens with theme 4, the 'lover', leaving his mistress:

. . .leave her like that ~~without~~ **in** the state she was in —

Moreover the text is drafted in two voices 'normal' and 'assumed' to comply with theme 2 'voice imitated'. Beckett first tried out ideas for the two voices on a blank page facing the *Kilcool* fragment; as observed earlier it is Beckett's practice to write his text on the right hand pages of a notebook, leaving the left blank for notes and alterations to the text. But in this case it seems likely that, having already filled the left hand pages of the second fragment with mathematical calculations and notes on themes, he simply used the first blank page he came to, which happened to be the one facing the original (i.e. *Kilcool*) fragment. The notes for two voices bear little relation to the *Kilcool* text, but are incorporated almost verbatim into the text of the second fragment; indeed they seem from their content to be an attempt to begin drafting the text described under the heading *Themes* (above). The first paragraph is described as 'Ex(ample) of I' and tells of the young girl:

~~Neari~~ **coming up to** ~~her~~ **the** end **alone** quite still on her back. . .

leading into the prayer to 'time giver of light' and resulting tears that we have observed in the *Kilcool* fragment. The second paragraph is in deliberate contrast. The voice speaks in an assumed tone 'low, fast, breathless', and scolds the normal voice for challenging her to 'go out,live! (*Pause*.) Can't you. . .'

Ah you and your living, will you stop talking to me about living. (*Pause with panting*. (***Panting***) What else am I doing only living, what else do you call this I'm doing only living. (*Panting*.) Is it because I'm sitting here quiet with my thoughts — (*panting*) — not whining for anything and not fussing over anything — (*panting*) — that I amn't living. . .

The dichotomy in the woman is made more obvious than in the published text by the use of these two voices. Moreover the normal voice understands her predicament (hence the prayer to time for release) whereas the assumed voice, like Mouth in *Not I*, pushes such realisation away. When asked by the normal voice:

How is it that — (*pause*) How is it ~~you can't~~ **one cannot** see the — (*pause*) — ~~the~~ cause . . .

the assumed voice responds in terror:

. . .(*assumed voice, vehement*.) Take it away! Take it away! Go away! (*Panting*) XXXXX Turn it off!

Here, in explicit form, is the situation in *Not I*, where the self-questioning inner voice is unheard, but produces in Mouth a 'vehement refusal to relinquish third person'. In the Trinity College fragment the question is voiced — and equally forcibly rejected. But the assumed voice has been made to acknowledge its refusal to listen ('take it away!') whereas Mouth, more subtly, maintains her fiction ('she!. . .SHE!') until the end of the play. 'Take it away!' spoken by the assumed voice is also the 'identification by final prayer to time in assumed voice' that Beckett planned in the notes following *Kilcool*. The assumed voice has dropped her guard and joined in the plea from the normal voice to blot out her existence and take the light away.

There is a further difference from the published text in a reversal of roles. In the Trinity College fragment, the normal voice, who is aware of the reality of her situation, carries the bulk of the text. The assumed voice seems to be that in which she tries, unsuccessfully, to convince herself of a fiction. In *Not I* Mouth avoids the truth throughout, so that the text (apart from the 22 inner promptings noted by Beckett in Typescript 5 at Reading University) is entirely self-deception.

Immediately after the second fragment in the T.C.D. notebook Beckett began a rewrite, but got no further than a mere snatch of text ('. . . leave her like that in the state she was in — oh!') and the opening stage directions, the first directions since the *Kilcool* fragment. The first of these directions (quoted on Page 92 above) concerns the face. The remainder are as follows:

Grey hair drawn tightly back from forehead.
Shrill tremulous voice, bad enunciation.
Speech begins before rise of curtain.

According to Beckett's note '"I" "me" etc. never spoken outside assumed voice,' the final fragment at Trinity College is spoken entirely in the first person and thus by the assumed voice. In fact, however, this fragment seems to be spoken by the *normal* voice throughout, since the instruction 'assumed voice' is given specifically for six words of the text only. The fragment opens with paragraphs on two themes jotted down once more on earlier pages. The first theme insists that the voice has an audience:

I am not talking to myself, more than that I cannot say, I am not talking to myself . . .

The idea of speech as punishment is then raised for the first time:

. . . there is ~~nothing~~ **no more** I wish to say **every word is mild torture** I would give all I have to stop . . .

There follows a consideration of how much silence the voice can hope to achieve, including exhaustive calculations on the subject:

30 million seconds in a year
how many ~~pauses~~ **silences** of 3 seconds to
make total silence of 24 hrs.
=86.000 seconds.

The calculations mount up,in fragment 3, to the extraordinary total of a week's annual silence:

I have worked it out while going along, one second, two seconds, every now and ~~then~~ **again**, a week a year, ~~isn't~~ **it not** amazing . . .

The voice goes on to reflect on 'things said before' in contrast with 'virgin' remarks, calling herself in the process 'this old whore', the first direct equation between voice and visual image in the text. Her 'virgin' contribution to the ensuing passage is the feeling that:

~~There is~~ **Someone** in me, trying to get out, saying let me out...

'Let me out! let me out!' is subsequently repeated by the assumed voice as its sole contribution to fragment 3. It now appears that the assumed voice is no longer prepared to ignore her situation. Instead she joins with the normal voice in demanding to be released.

Though apparently understanding her situation in fragment 2, the normal voice in panic questions it again in fragment 3:

> Was I in someone once, and where is she now, if I was in her once, and she let me out –

And the implications of punishment increase:

> Oh I am wearied, if the impossible were being asked it would ~~not be so bad~~ **be less hellish.**

Reflections on the deficiencies of her memory ('memory gone') lead the voice into the moving litany of negation on which the fragment closes. The first half of this passage is quoted below:

> Nothing speaks of nothing
> XXX
> There is no me and there is noone else, there is noone at all, there never was anyone at all.
>
> My I's are nothing and my mes are nothing and my my's are nothing and so for all the other persons of the quartet or quintet or minuet and trio
>
> I am nothing speaking of nothing neither to myself nor to anyone else
>
> I have been speaking for ever and will go on speaking for ever.

The fragment ends, then, in some kind of Cartesian nightmare, in which the fact of 'cogito' brings no assurance of 'sum'.

The despairing nature of the vision does not change from first to last, but aspects of the Trinity College fragments are much more explicit than the final text. The fact that the voice is recounting memories from beyond the grave is the most striking example. We are informed in *Kilcool* that she 'talks of herself in 3rd person'. Thus when she describes 'the dark where *she* (my *underlining*) was laid so young so long ago' it is herself to whom the experience refers. Corroboration that 'the dark' means death is explicit. Burial is the eighth and final theme in the list made after writing *Kilcool*, though Beckett had second thoughts about stating it too bluntly in the text: '~~Neari~~ **coming up to** ~~her~~ **the** end'. By the published text the phrase has become much more subtle: 'coming up to sixty when — ...what?...seventy?...good God!'. 'Seventy' draws attention to man's allotted span of three score years and ten, so that the idea of death remains a strong possibility, but it is the more telling for not being stated. That Mouth, moreoever, can lie about her age, in her condition, sets a tone of grim humour in the final text that is lacking in the early fragments, where the tone is too often self-pitying.

Such refinements did not, however, come all at once. When Beckett came to write *Not I* in 1972, more than eight years after the Dublin fragments,[23] the play developed through two holograph and six typescript drafts. The jerky repetitious style of the final text is there from the start and the technique of self-questioning leading to further information being vouchsafed, rather than the two separate voices of the Dublin fragments. Some advance in technique on the earlier material is therefore present in the first holograph version of *Not I*,[24] but the content is still extremely explicit when compared with the final text. Some examples will indicate where this is so:

1. birth into the world — this world — of a ~~small~~ **tiny** baby boy or girl **in a small...**
2. The child was born 'in a small ~~place~~ **hole** ~~in the~~ **on the coast....**'
3. Walking in a field with ~~her~~ **my** youngest grandchild ~~looking~~ **searching** for cowslips...

The surprising change from third to first person occurs on page 1:

and ~~she~~ **I** found ~~her~~ **my** self in the dark — and:
for ~~she~~ **I** could still hear the buzzing in ~~her~~ **my** ears...

But Beckett thought better of this after about twenty lines, crossed out the first version and began to rewrite, with Mouth at once denying her selfhood.

...What?...I?...no...no!...she...

This phrase grows in importance during the second holograph. It is repeated twice and shaped each time, both to establish an echo and draw attention to the denial.

Stage directions are crammed into the margin beside holograph 1, but with an arrow indicating that they belong to holograph 2.

Beckett has decided that he wishes the image to be centred on Mouth, but has not yet envisaged that it can be completely isolated; the direction reads 'as little as possible of rest of face.' An auditor is present, but is to make only a 'single brief movement where indicated.' The idea of his gestures corresponding with Mouth's denials of selfhood only emerges at the end of various passages of addenda, drafted three weeks after the completion of the holograph.

The addenda passages were written in response to memoranda underlined in red, made by Beckett in his holograph 'analysis' of the text in which, as mentioned earlier, he broke down the text under fifteen themes or headings.[25] The analysis elucidates several points in the text. It refers, for example, to Mouth's 'fantasy of returning to the field where all went out' and calls its tale an 'enumeration of woes'. Under the heading 'speculations' there is reference to being 'denied by interrupter', while a further heading, 'interruptions', clarifies that the interrupter is that part of the consciousness continually trying to prod the voice into self-acceptance, signified by the question 'what?'. Beckett acknowledges a problem in 'reconciling' interruptions 'to propose 1st person' with interruptions 'to deny she had to ~~say~~ **tell** anything.'

The notes most revealing of technique in Beckett's analysis show him intentionally working towards ambiguity in the text. One reads:

> Tho not explicitly stated suffering begins with voice and thought w. buzzing.

Two other notes, both underlined in red, state '*not made clear*', meaning, presumably, intentionally ambiguous rather than requiring clarification:

> ***beam*** . . . . . .from beginning — moon image — moon denied — just part of punishment — but painless — so far — same spot at first (*notxxxxxxxx made clear*) — then flickering (*analogy with thought*) — ferreting — pain beginning — (*not made clear*.)

The series of six typescript drafts that follow the *Not I* holographs give a clear picture of the kinds of changes that Beckett makes customarily when revising and polishing a text. A chart of these has been attempted as the most economical means of demonstrating such changes, and is found in Appendix VII. Two developments in the direction of ambiguity may, however, be observed here: all reference to the first person is cancelled in

Typescript 2 (so that the question 'What?...I...' is altered to 'What?...Who?...) and in Typescript 5 the image is restricted to Mouth alone.

A comparison of the draft material at Reading University with the final text reveals one interesting omission. The final note regarding the auditor's 'gesture of helpless compassion' occurs nowhere in the drafts and appears suddenly in the Faber text. It must have occurred to Beckett that an explanatory note in the published text could prevent any serious misapprehension of his intention with regard to the gesture, described in the drafts hitherto simply as an arm movement. It is mentioned first in the addenda notes:

> This consists in simple **sideways** raising of **Listener's** arms clear of sides and their falling back with if possible just audible thud of hands on thighs.

The audible thud was omitted from the notes to Typescript 6, but the final 'compassion' note remains an authorial intervention in interpretation unique in Beckett's directions, though arguably necessary. The note is helpful in developing our understanding of the situation described and the play gains by this. The overall ambiguity is still present, moreover, in that the identity of the auditor remains uncertain.

A typed synopsis of the play is held with the drafts at Reading University.[26] It appears to be an abstract of the final text, in the same way that the analysis was made from an early draft. The synopsis, too, is uncharacteristically revealing since it lists five 'Life scenes' (field, shopping centre, Croker's Acres, courtroom and rushing out to tell) implying that the voice recalling these scenes is now in some sense beyond life. This pinpoints the play in a manner alien to Beckett's general practice of keeping his options open. But since it is found only in a University Library, it is not accessible to the average playgoer. There is, however, a fundamental problem here about the study of an author's discarded drafts and notes. In their introduction to *Fin de partie*, for example, John and Beryl Fletcher state firmly that:

> in pruning his work Beckett undoubtedly improved it, but sometimes he compressed things so drastically that the surviving statement is somewhat obscure.[27]

Fletcher therefore decided to indicate 'the original intention' in his notes.

Precisely the reason that Beckett suppresses the specific from his later drafts, however, is (as we have noticed in the three plays discussed in this chapter) to free the plays from limiting identifications. *This* is his intention; so to pin down the 'original intention' in a note, however illuminating, may have a destructive effect on the text, unless the full evolutionary process is stressed. It is like trying to place the husk of a seed on top of a flower, without explaining that, during the process of germination, one thing has become the other. On the other hand, as Fletcher points out, it is certainly useful to be able to clarify the origin of such obscure expressions as Hamm's reference to pardon near the end of the play, which 'is a survival from T(ypescript) 1, where Clov pleads 'Pardonne-moi!' for having struck Hamm with the dog, and provokes this reply on Hamm's part.'[28]

The obvious danger of such explanations is that Beckett may be accused either of careless cutting or of ambiguity *per se*. Beckett has no wish to produce an impenetrable text and has, on the contrary, a distinct vision of reality to communicate. But he is not prepared to compromise with that vision by pinning labels to his characters or making limiting identifications. It is profitless, for example, to attempt to ascertain the identity of Godot. When asked by Alan Schneider: 'Who or what does Godot mean?' Beckett replied: 'If I knew, I would have said so in the play.'[29] And of *Endgame* he wrote to Schneider:

> Hamm as stated, and Clov as stated, together as stated, nec tecum nec sine te, in such a place, and in such a world, that's all I can manage, more than I could.[30]

Beckett gives enough information to stimulate the imagination and the ambiguities in his plays are compelling because they force audiences to work, rather than sit back awaiting entertainment. As he once remarked in an interview with Tom Driver: '. . . the key word in my plays is 'perhaps'.'[31]

CHAPTER 8
GENESIS: SOUND AND SCREEN

The drafts of Beckett's remaining plays written during the period 1956-76 are looked at chronologically. The development of the stage works has been separated from those designed for other media. Since the radio plays form a natural group all Beckett's plays for the broadcast media are considered in a single chapter, which in turn allows us to look at the remaining stage plays together, in a subsequent chapter. The main focus throughout is the nature of the prefatory material for each play and its shaping towards the final text. As in the previous chapter we shall also observe a steady movement away from direct statement into ambiguity, as the drafts progress.

All That Fall

All That Fall, the first of Beckett's published plays to be written in English, was written as the result of an invitation to Beckett by the BBC Third Programme to write a piece for radio. Martin Esslin recounts the circumstances of the BBC suggestion in his article 'Samuel Beckett and the Art of Broadcasting'.[1] Beckett was first approached towards the end of June 1956 and the play was sent to the BBC on 27 September of the same year. 'J'ai écrit *All That Fall* très rapidement, en 56' Beckett wrote to Jean-Jacques Mayoux.[2]

Compared with most of the other plays under discussion *All That Fall* has very few drafts. A holograph and a single typescript are both held at the Humanities Research Center of the University of Texas at Austin. The holograph is dated at its close 'Ussy September 1956' and the completed text was sent to the BBC on 27 September. A later typescript, described by Beckett as 'TS for Grove..1957' is held at Washington University, St. Louis. This was the typescript used for the American publication and contains minor corrections only. There are, however, three pages of jottings concerning the play in a notebook at Reading University, headed 'Été 56'.[3] These jottings represent ideas for changes to the Texas holograph and are frequently incorporated into it as alterations. The altered holograph then becomes the basis for the Texas typescript, which in turn is amended by hand. Minor vocabulary differences apart, the BBC script is identical with the revised Texas typescript.

Despite the paucity of draft material, a movement towards ambiguity may be observed as the play evolves. Clas Zilliacus describes this process as 'the suppression of several "clues"'.[4] There are two main instances of such a development in the play, from holograph to typescript. The first is a case of extension rather than suppression and concerns the evolution of the title. The holograph is headed:

~~*Lovely Day for the Races*~~ ***ALL THAT FALL***

The alteration appears to stem from the Reading notebook, where Beckett identifies Psalm 145, from which he takes his title:

The Lord upholdeth all that fall and raiseth up all those that be bowed down. (Ps. 145 14)

It seems evident that the aptness of Psalm 145 to his theme only occurred to Beckett after completing the holograph. In the latter, at the point where an enquiry about the next day's sermon is made, Beckett refers to a different text:

Mr. K. Has he announced his text.

Mrs. K. (quote) 'sparrow text.'

Silence. They join in wild prolonged laughter.

Mr. and Mrs. Rooney were orginally Hugh and Emma Kennedy. The 'sparrow text' is not lost by the introduction of Psalm 145, however, as it is still incorporated into the typescript separately:

Mrs. Rooney: It is like the sparrows, than many of which we are of more value. . .

The ambiguities inherent in Beckett's final choice of title for the play afford him opportunities for the kinds of irony at which he excels. The fate of the child proves that the fallen are not upheld; it is Mr. Tyler, rather than the Lord who saved the preacher's life when they were climbing together; the Rooneys support each other as best they can on the treacherous station steps, but Mrs. Rooney's wish to be 'in atoms' and her spouse anticipating with relief the loss of further faculties, hardly holds out much hope for fallen humanity. Mr. Rooney comments on their situation:

> The perfect pair. Like Dante's damned, with their faces arsy-versy. Our tears will water our bottoms.[5]

The second development in the drafts of *All That Fall* introduces an ambiguity into the text. It occurs when Jerry runs up with the ball at the end of the play. In the holograph there is no doubt as to the ownership of the ball:

> *Mr. K.* Perhaps it is not mine at all.
> *Jerry.* It has your name on it, Sir.

Jerry's remark is curious. Mr. Kennedy's name on the ball makes it less likely to have been the child's toy. If, therefore, it was intended that the ball should link Mr. Rooney with the child's death, it is, to say the least, a heavy-handed method of establishing murderer and victim on a 'whodunnit' level. In the typescript Beckett strengthened the ending by omitting Jerry's remark, but leaving an implication of guilt in Mr. Rooney's reluctance to accept the ball as his property, or to discuss the matter further. Suspicion of Mr. Rooney is thus allowed to gather and cling because of the ambiguity.

Omitted from the typescript is an earlier remark of Mr. Rooney's that can, with hindsight, be seen to link directly with the death of the child announced at the end of the play. In the holograph Mr. Kennedy states:

> I should like to kill a child before I die. A little girl. (*Pause.*)

In the typescript, however, the wish has become capable of altruistic interpretation:

> *Mr. Rooney.* Did you ever wish to kill a child? (*Pause.*)
> Nip some young doom in the bud. (*Pause.*)

Had the holograph passage remained in the text, there would have been no ambiguity in the play's ending. But although direct reference to the death of a little girl is subsequently omitted from the text and we are never told the sex of the child who falls from the train, the final version is, nonetheless, permeated by the deaths of female children.

Once the play's ending has been registered, these deaths can be seen to contribute to a central theme, pinpointed by the music that introduces the play and is heard again just before its close. As already discussed in Chapter 7 Schubert's Quartet No. 14 in D Minor was inspired by the Matthias Claudius poem 'Der Tod und das Mädchen'.[6] The quartet is first mentioned on a blank left hand page towards the end of the holograph. On the following page of text it is identified by Mr. Kennedy:

Mr. K. (*Indistinctly.*) Death and the Maiden.
Silence
Mrs. K. You are crying.
Mr. K. Yes.

The music also illumines Mrs. Rooney's great sadness, to which her thoughts continually return in the published text, the death of her daughter Minnie:

Oh I am just a hysterical old hag I know, destroyed with sorrow and pining and gentility and church-going and fat and rheumatism and childlessness. (*Pause. Brokenly.*) Minnie! Little Minnie! (*Pause.*)

It is not only the death of Minnie but a series of dead or dying women who provide the context for Beckett's play: there is the 'poor woman' 'alone in that ruinous old house' who plays *Death and the maiden*; Mr. Tyler's daughter has had her 'whole — er — bag of tricks' removed, leaving him grandchildless. When, moreover, as if giving evidence, Mr. Rooney narrates his account of the train journey for Maddy's approval, Mrs. Rooney's sole response is to voice her musings on the 'mind doctor's' tale of a little girl:

The only thing wrong with her as far as he could see was that she was dying. And she did in fact die, shortly after he washed his hands of her.

The juxtaposition of husband and wife here not only highlights the spurious tale Mr. Rooney has unfolded, but nicely counterpoints his unspoken thoughts of the death of the child on the train by his wife's broodings on the death of a little girl. The climax of the psychiatrist's account, recalled by Maddy, is that the trouble with the child was that 'she had never been really born!' It is possible that the trouble with the Rooneys is that Minnie is merely a figment of Maddy's imagination. Such an interpretation makes sense of her obsession with hinnies (even, perhaps of her 'lifelong preoccupation with horses' buttocks'!) A hinny is the offspring of a she-ass by a stallion and hinnies populate the play, from Christy's beast at the opening, to the animal upon which Christ rode into Jerusalem. 'Can hinnies procreate, I wonder?' enquires Maddy. But hinnies are sterile, and it seems possible that Maddy also has failed to procreate, as later appears to have been the case with Winnie in *Happy Days*. However the reference to 'the mind doctor' refers to an actual event during a period of psychoanalysis that Beckett undertook in London in 1935 with Dr. Wilfred Bion. Beckett attended one or more of Jung's lectures at the Tavistock Clinic in October 1935 and especially remembers Jung's story of a little girl, a ten year old child who, though present in the flesh had, according to Jung 'never been born entirely.'[7] She was having dreams that Jung took to be intimations of her death, which indeed occurred within the year. Beckett mentioned this story to the actresses Billie Whitelaw and Hildegard Schmahl when rehearsing *Footfalls* in London and Berlin in 1976.

The Jung lecture is clearly the stimulus for Maddy's remarks about the child in *All That Fall*. Beckett also interweaves themes of sterility and childlessness as part of the experience of the play, culminating in the actual death of a child, with a deft lightness of touch that never does more than suggest. It is because apparently chance references accumulate for the audience in the final text, mounting up gradually in the mind and then moving sharply into focus against the ending that the play is so dramatically effective. Clumsy verbal underlining has been omitted and the audience is given the satisfaction of making its own judgements.

Embers

Fewer drafts have come to light for *Embers* than for any other Beckett play and Beckett has confirmed in a letter to me that he has no idea what has become of the early material. Bearing in mind his tendency to move away from the specific as the drafts develop, it is likely that access to the early material for this, his most baffling play, would prove illuminating. If the lack of drafts were to result in the exclusion of *Embers* from our discussion it would mean ignoring this play alone among those written between 1956-76. Moreover the extreme ambiguity of the final text would seem to make it both valid and relevant to explore *Embers* as far as possible in this chapter.

I have been able to trace only two typescripts for *Embers*. The earliest, at Trinity College Dublin, is a typescript with manuscript corrections.[8] The second is the typescript preceding the Faber proof of the text. Both typescript and proof are held by the University of Texas at Austin and inscribed by Beckett 'for Jake Schwartz, Paris, Feb. 1960.' Martin Esslin notes that 'copyright clearance' for the BBC script of the play ('this as yet untitled manuscript') was requested on 13 February 1959, that a subsequent BBC memorandum is headed *Ebb*, but that by April 1959, the title had become *Embers*.[9] This may help to date the Dublin typescript somewhere between February and April 1959, since it is headed *Ebb*, with *Embers* written underneath. Beside these alternative headings are four phrases from the text which seem also to have been under consideration as titles. These are: 'The Water's Edge'; 'Why life, Henry?'; 'Not a Soul' and 'All day all night'.

The Trinity College typescript shows Beckett toying with the idea of using several different voices to convey scenes in flashback during Henry's monologue, in addition to the scenes with Ada and Addie. Four separate voices are placed at one stage as afterthoughts in the stage directions: 'Henry then', 'Henry now' (as in Krapp then and now), 'Father' and 'Addie'. But a note in the Texas typescript reverses this decision: 'All his voice. Wail Addie's voice.' Beckett's final solution is thus for Henry to speak for the characters in his head, though occasionally (as with his daughter's 'wail' and the scenes with her instructors) they are so strongly present in his mind that they emerge as evocations, with no conscious effort on Henry's part. His power to evoke nonhuman sounds is underlined early in the text:

Hooves! (*Pause. Louder.*) Hooves! (*Sound of hooves walking on hard road. They die rapidly away. Pause.*) Again! (*Hooves as before. Pause. Excitedly.*) Train it to mark time!

The voice of Henry's wife Ada also appears to be an evocation. Beckett uses the technique again in *Eh Joe*, where the image dwindles to a man's face, listening intently to the voice of an unseen woman. That Ada is not present in the flesh in *Embers* is suggested in an addition to the stage directions of the Dublin typescript: 'no sound as she sits.' But ambiguity is introduced when, in a further addition, Beckett makes her remark 'Poor Addie', showing her to have heard the scenes in which her daughter is tortured by her teachers. Before this change Ada had merely remarked to her husband: 'you are silent today' and 'what are you thinking of?' thus proving, apparently, that she had not been privy to her daughter's miseries. It is not clear, however, whether she has not heard them simply because it is impossible to eavesdrop upon the thoughts of another person, or because she herself is an evocation and Henry, when thinking of Addie, has thus temporarily excluded his wife.

Beckett omits the more concrete proposition (that Ada did hear the Addie scenes) from the Texas version, with the resulting implication that she is an involuntary voice, passing in and out of her husband's head.[10] Ambiguity about her presence or absence is, however, central to the play and depends, for its effect, upon radio presentation. As Beckett remarked when discussing *Cendres*, the French translation, with Paul-Louis Mignon: '*Cendres* repose sur une ambiguïté: le personnage a-t-il une hallucination ou est-il en présence de la réalité? La réalisation scenique détruirait l'ambiguïté.'[11]

Both Addie scenes are appended to the Trinity College typescript and do not appear in context. They reveal the rigorous training to which the child's imaginative and physical nature are subjected. The riding scene is deliberately sexual in its language. Following Addie's cry from horseback comes her father's evocation of his first love-making with her mother. Here a rough sea takes over the action, heralding Ada's orgasmic cry. At the close of the scene, Beckett notes as an afterthought: **'End of evocation'.**

It is evident from such additions to the Trinity College typescript that Beckett was aiming to clarify certain aspects of his text, while leaving its main purport (and particularly the relevance of the Bolton and Holloway narration) open to speculation. The Texas typescript is little altered, apart from the minor modifications already mentioned; it is only after its completion that a manuscript note names Henry and Ada, who have been known hitherto simply as 'He' and 'She'.

Two interesting changes are made among several small alterations in the Faber proof of the text. One of these inserts the phrase 'little book' after Henry's anguished outburst 'Christ!' at the end of the play, thus apparently inviting the possibility of Christian interpretation. The second change marginally increases the ambiguity of Henry's final speech by replacing the pronouns 'him' and 'he' by 'you' in both cases:

. . . Left soon afterwards, passed ~~him~~ **you** on the road, didn't see her, looking out to... (*Pause.*) Can't have been looking out to *sea*. (*Pause*). Unless ~~he~~ **you** had gone round the other side...

The only way of making sense of this passage is to assume Henry to be mulling over what Ada had begun to tell him about his father, adding to her account, as if trying to reconstruct the events of that day. 'You' then becomes the father, to whom Henry speaks aloud.

Since all voices in the play are evocations, apart from Henry's own, only the sea may be said irrefutably to be present with him. All the pauses are filled with the sound of the sea and we hear Henry's footsteps crunching on the shingle. There is no silence. The play indeed ends on a contradiction worthy of the end of *Godot*: 'Not a sound' says Henry, but we still hear the sea. Ada, however, appears to have found silence beneath the waves:

Ada: Underneath all is as quiet as the grave. Not a sound.
All day all night, not a sound.

Whether such knowledge means that Ada, like Henry's father, has drowned is unimportant. For Henry she is still present in his head. His concern is to drown the sound of the sea by some means, even to the absurdity of carrying about his gramophone. But his reasons for this remain ambiguous. Perhaps in drowning the voice of the sea, he hopes also to drown the persistent voice of his wife, or to lessen his need to be with his father; for he both tries to evade the sea and yet is drawn to the shore, to try 'to get him to be with me.' The function of the sea appears to be to help Henry to come to terms with his father's death by drowning, even, perhaps, with the fact of death itself. The sea is an impersonal inescapable presence that, having claimed his father, is, like death, in the background until the time comes to absorb Henry into itself.

Henry may sit on the strand between life and death, but his life is a study in vacancy, a negation:

Saturday...nothing.Sunday...Sunday...nothing all day. (*Pause.*) Nothing, all day nothing. (*Pause.*) All day all night nothing. (*Pause.*) Not a sound.

A wholly unsentimental, uncompromising position is taken in *Embers*, in which the whole business of living is decried. This is emphasised by Henry dashing two large stones together, before throwing them away crying 'That's life!'. Implicit here is both sterility and, in the clashing sound, a hint perhaps, of the discord of Henry's marriage, exemplified also in his daughter's discords on the piano. The sound of stone striking stone heralds Henry's account of the sexual 'hammering', the long prelude to the engendering of Addie.

It is possible that the sea is trying to convey a more profound truth to Henry, that of his basic misconception about the life he is living, his deliberate avoidance (as in *Film*) of himself. By constantly escaping, as he does, into storytelling, Henry avoids definition as himself, denies his selfhood. This of course is the position of the creative artist, with which Beckett concerns himself in so many works; it is also the situation of the actor, losing his own identity in a multiplicity of roles. If *Embers* is interpreted in this way, the sea becomes the consciousness Henry seeks to avoid, as in *Not I*, where the 'buzzing' of the subconscious continually questions the story Mouth is telling, in order to try to bring it to her attention that the story is her own. When Henry says 'not a sound' he is thus successfully keeping his consciousness of reality at bay and taking refuge in fiction.

Henry, like Bolton in his major fiction, is living the embers of a life, with no future (as the negatives at the end of the play make clear) and only words to place between himself and despair. Either his fictions prevent him brooding upon an unwelcome reality, or that reality drives him to fiction. It appears that he has always told stories to pass the time. Ada draws attention to the fact that he never stops talking to himself and recommends a psychiatrist named Holloway, thus linking the fact of Henry's neurotic behaviour with the fictional doctor in his principal tale. An interesting ambiguity is introduced here: we have already remarked Henry's likeness to Bolton, so the possibility emerges that Bolton is a pseudonym, a mask or persona for Henry himself. Since, moreover, the Holloway in his story bears some resemblance to a doctor of that name, Henry's fiction now seems to contain elements of fact. He lives disguised in his stories, as with the third person narration in *Not I*. Like *Not I* also, the linking of words and excrement implies that what is said is not worth hearing. Ada remarks that Addie has heard Henry speaking 'in the lavatory' while Mouth in *Not I* rushes out occasionally to vent her flood of speech in the 'nearest lavatory'. It is one of Beckett's most despairing comments on the human situation.

The main problem with Henry's story is that 'I never finished it. . .I never finished anything, everything always went on for ever.' All Beckett's characters face a similar problem. The Unnamable's last words are 'I can't go on, I'll go on.' The latter appears to be uttering from a limbo beyond life and might reasonably expect to have reached the end, only to find that there is no end. Henry has a foreshadowing of such a situation in his opening speech:

> . . . that's what hell will be like, small chat to the babbling of Lethe about the good old days when we wished we were dead.

Ada's small talk that had tormented him in reality in the past now lives in his head. Henry is condemned endlessly to rehearse his experience, as are the characters in the later plays, or the aged Krapp, whose living is reduced to an ear bent towards his tape.

The level of unreality in *Embers* is extreme. Henry lives in a fiction, carries on internal conversations with imaginary voices, himself eavesdrops on his daughter and her teachers, tells himself a story that may be partly a truth he does not acknowledge and is accompanied throughout by a surreal sound purporting to be the sea. Although we remain uncertain about details such as Ada's whereabouts, or whether Henry's father drowned at sea or set up house in the Argentine, we have been able to establish something of Henry's current situation and state of mind. But the meaning of the Bolton and Holloway story remains ambiguous. That this fiction is significant is apparent from the amount of text devoted to it. We have already considered that Bolton might represent Henry and Holloway his doctor or psychiatrist. It is also sometimes suggested that Bolton and Holloway represent the two sides of Henry's nature. That the two men are mutually dependent and yet irreconcilable might thus hint at Henry's life of inaction, paralysed by opposing forces. Such an interpretation takes Bolton, imprisoned in his room, gazing from the window, to represent mind. He needs help from Holloway, who comes ready to minister to physical ills, with his black bag containing 'a shot'. But he cannot leave until Bolton releases him, and Bolton at first merely stares at him with 'the old blue eye.' Holloway does not respond to Bolton's plea when it finally comes, but, mesmerised by the stare, 'covers his face.' The situation remains unresolved: 'Old men, great trouble, no good.'

A rigid Cartesian parallel is unhelpful. It may equally be argued that Bolton's plea is for euthanasia, but that this, medical ethics must lead Holloway to reject, hence his lack of response to Bolton's begging. Bolton, holding aloft his lighted candle, may be seen as challenging Holloway to do a good deed (put him out of his misery) in a 'naughty world.'[12] But again this seems an over-simplification, for Bolton does not appear to take up Holloway's proffered shot, his 'Please!' seems to be directed towards something else. It seems in the end that the cure Bolton requires is beyond Holloway's competence to prescribe, a cure perhaps for the human situation in an absurd universe.

Embers is Beckett's most impenetrable play, John Pilling refers to its 'complex, almost molecular structure',[13] but clarity *per se* is not Beckett's object. As early as 1938, in an essay on the poet Denis Devlin, Beckett had remarked:

> The time is not perhaps altogether too green for the vile suggestion that art has nothing to do with clarity, does not dabble in the clear, and does not make clear.[14]

Writing to the American actress Jessica Tandy in 1973, regarding the pace at which she should play Mouth in *Not I*, Beckett showed that his view had remained consistent:

> I am not unduly concerned with intelligibility. I hope the piece may work on the nerves of the audience, not its intellect.[15]

The ambiguities in *Embers* 'work on the nerves of the audience' and are, perhaps, the play's main strength.

Pochade Radiophonique; Words and Music; Esquisse Radiophonique; Cascando

Beckett's remaining plays for radio will be considered as a group, since three of them (*Words and Music*, *Esquisse Radiophonique* and *Cascando*) were all written within days of each other, one in English and two in French, in late November and early December 1961. As discussed at the beginning of this study Beckett's published plays of the period 1956-76, starting with *All That Fall*, were all, with only minor exceptions, written in English as a first language. *Theatre II* and three short radio works (*Pochade Radiophonique*, *Esquisse Radiophonique*, and *Cascando*) were written first in French. Since this book is predominantly concerned with English plays I shall quote from the English translations of these French plays, except when discussing the drafts, where direct quotation will be made as required.

Words and Music, Esquisse Radiophonique and *Cascando* appear to be different approaches to a single theme, in the same manner that Beckett, shortly after the completion of *Play*, made notes for a further play on the triangular theme. These three radio plays are all concerned with the difficulties of artistic creation and the problems experienced by the writer. This is also the preoccupation in *Pochade Radiophonique*, for which the precise date of composition is unknown, but probably precedes the others. The French publication states: 'années 60?' and the English 'Circa 1960.'[16] This may not be reliable, however, since a similar description is given in *Ends and Odds* for *Esquisse Radiophonique*, although drafts date the latter precisely in November 1961.

Pochade Radiophonique

Pochade Radiophonique was not published until 1975.[17] Reading University has two typescripts prior to this publication.[18] The first of these is considerably older than the second and has manuscript alterations that are incorporated into the text of the second version. The play was first heard in Beckett's English translation on 13 April 1976,[19] under the title *Rough for Radio* and was subsequently published in *Ends and Odds*, this time entitled *Radio II*.

Despite the four characters in *Radio II*, the play appears to be an example of Beckett's natural mode of writing, a dialogue with the self, for which radio proved so appropriate a vehicle. *Radio II* is an internal monologue concerned with the authorial problem of finding words to satisfy the insistent urge to create. The difficulty of the creative process is seen in an extreme form in *Radio II*, with each character objectifying a part of that process. The Animator (or intellect) and writing hand (Stenographer) between them try to coerce the creative faculty or imagination (appropriately named 'Fox') into telling a story. But Fox, who has been kept bound and gagged until the others are ready for him, only lets loose a few words when attacked with a ruler by the sinister Dick, despite an embryo idea inside him ('I had my brother in my stomach.')

Dick is mute. His function is entirely physical, he never utters, only beats. Not one of the four characters is free. Animator is impelled in his investigation by a force he cannot resist, a force perhaps comparable with the stimulus behind the light in *Play*. The stenographer is similarly obliged to write down Fox's emergent phrases and check them back with Animator. All are trapped in and by the process of creation. They may dream of freedom (Animator's last line is 'Tomorrow, who knows, we may be free.') But freedom, if it ever comes, is likely to bring release only from one story to the next. Real freedom, as Victor Krap found in *Éléutheria*, is impossible. We do not know what lies behind the endless compulsion to create, any more than what lies behind the light in *Play*. It may be that the stimulus is involuntary, as irresistible as the life-force itself that sets the natural cycle in motion, and self-perpetuating merely because it has no option. The ambiguity is central to Beckett's repeated handling of the problem, in which his protagonists are driven to utter against their will and without knowing why.

Words and Music

The first reference to *Words and Music*, Beckett's next play for radio, is found in the 'Été 56' notebook at Reading University, where two brief notes are headed:

Words Music, Paris, Feb 16, 1961.[20]

The theme appears to have been well established in Beckett's mind at this time, since the notes refer to details, rather than the seeds of an idea, though the situation implied is not precisely that of the published text. The first note, for example, refers to a character not present in the later version:

Commands of Word (sic) faint, repeated clarion by Usher.

The 'Usher' might well be an early name for Croak, or first thoughts on what was to become the 'Opener' in the subsequent play, *Cascando*. The idea of an usher repeating commands seems also to have connections with a familiar Beckettian image, that of a court scene; but it is impossible to tell from the note whether the Usher was concerned in a trial, or heralding a performance.

The second note shows Beckett to have visualised an entire scene and to be considering his final effect:

End: diminishing sound of alternating words and music till close on a few syllables and a few notes.

Again this differs from the ensuing versions, where the only diminuendo is the gradual dying away of the sound of Croak's slippers. The published play ends with Music, cajoled by Words, giving a repetition of the 'well-head' passage.

A holograph and two typescripts of *Words and Music* are among the Samuel Beckett papers at Washington University, St. Louis. The holograph, which is entitled 'Word and Music', took precisely one week to write. It is headed 'Paris 20.11.61.' and dated at the close 'Ussy 27.11.61.' The name 'Croak' evolves on page 3 of the holograph. His first speech (on page 2) is headed 'Old Man's Whisper' and ensuing speeches are prefaced 'Whisper' until they are altered in favour of Croak. The first speech is then re-headed 'senile Croak'. Words and Music are referred to familiarly as Will and Louis, which may, as Clas Zilliacus suggests, have been an ironic nod in the direction of Shakespeare and Beethoven.[21] In the first typescript the two become the more neutral Joe and Bob.

In the holograph and first typescript the first theme proposed by Words is that of 'hope' not sloth, as it becomes in Typescript 2. Croak thus arrives on an appropriate irony in the holograph:

> By hope unvisited the soul — (*Pause.*) Listen! (*Distant sound of rapidly shuffling carpet slippers.*)

The sound of the slippers is subsequently increased, Expressionist fashion, to 'a deafening crescendo all sense of slippers gone, stops. Silence.' thus creating a Pinteresque sense of menace. By Typescript 2 (which is virtually identical with the Faber text) there is no longer an attempt to colour the listener's interpretation by establishing a moment of terror with the advent of Croak, and the 'crescendo' direction is omitted.

There is not enough information in the preliminary notes at Reading to suggest how like or unlike the final version of the play Beckett's first ideas were. The Washington drafts reveal only comparatively minor changes in the text, apart from linguistic polishing, which we shall look at in some detail when discussing Beckett's working method in Chapter 10.

Words and Music is often considered ambiguous by students coming to the play for the first time, but it seems to me one of the most easily accessible of Beckett's dramatic pieces. A. Alvarez points out that the play:

> illustrates vividly that split between the music the poet hears in his head and the leaden words at his command, and the slow, unwilling process of disciplining and refining these two elements until they finally chime together in a single work of art.[22]

A lyric may be defined as words sung to music and Beckett characterises both elements in this play that culminates in a lyric. The entire structure of *Words and Music* is reminiscent of musical composition, with themes tried out 'hesitantly' at first and refined through repetition until their final flowering. It is when Croak proposes the theme of age that Joe and Bob are at last heard to make efforts which, however faltering, are at least indicative of experience, rather than the gabble and sentiment previously emitted. These efforts gradually produce the first section of the lyric.

Joe's opening lines recall Adam's description of 'unregarded age in corners thrown' in *As You Like It*:

Words: Age is when...old age I mean...if that is what my Lord means...is when...if you're a man...were a man... huddled... nodding...the ingle...waiting –

Bob's ideas of an appropriate accompaniment gradually crystallise into an 'air' which he plays through alone, followed by a repeated invitation to Joe to join in, until at last, and very softly, Joe 'tries to sing' the entire lyric. The prosaic opening ('Shivering for the hag/To put the pan in the bed') is balanced by the romantic close:

The face in the ashes
That old starlight
On the earth again.

From the ashes of a love long lost or perhaps (as in *Play*) from the ashes of death, the face haunts Croak. Revisions in Typescript 1 emphasise his encounter with 'The face [ ] On the stairs', which is followed at once by his proposal of love as the theme for the day.

The prose description of the woman that comes after the first verse of the lyric is again carefully balanced between realism and romance. A romantic description, befitting Croak's emotion, is subsequently undercut by a parody of voluptuousness:

the great white rise and fall of the breasts, spreading as they mount and then subsiding to their natural -- aperture.

Bob, however, is inspired into a rash display of enthusiasm:

irrepressible burst of spreading and subsiding music.

The second part of the lyric culminates in Croak's departure, his exorcism temporarily completed, having faced the dreaded, longed-for agony of memory. Joe's sigh of satisfaction at the end of the play, after hearing a reprise of the 'wellhead' from Bob, contains also Croak's regret for lost youth and indeed the regrets of all Beckett's aged romantics for 'yesterday'.

It may be observed here that the music, although not composed by Beckett, is an integral part of this group of radio plays. Beckett envisaged the composition of *Words and Music* as the realisation of a 'long-cherished intention' — 'collaboration on an original work with his cousin, John Beckett'.[23] The result of this collaboration, *Words and Music,* was first broadcast by the BBC in November 1962 in Michael Bakewell's production. It is all too rarely heard. In order to make the play more accessible to the public a new version was produced by Katharine Worth in December 1973, for the University of London Audio-Visual Centre. The music, a new score, was composed, at Beckett's suggestion, by Humphrey Searle and the play was directed by David Clark.

The new music makes the play quite literally something else — a new work. This is the more interesting since Words, in both productions, was played by Patrick Magee — partnered each time by a different actor, which makes a comparison between his two performances particularly rewarding.[24] However a new score clearly goes far beyond the re-creation of a role by an actor, in transforming a play. This is especially evident in a play such as *Words and Music,* where music is an integral part of the text. Indeed so fundamental and potentially radical a change is it that collaboration between composer and author is desirable. In order that the music should be true to the spirit of the work as envisaged by the dramatist, he needs to be as fully involved as possible in the composition.

Esquisse Radiophonique

Words and Music was completed on 27 November 1961. On 29 November Beckett began *Esquisse Radiophonique* and finished it the following day, though it remained unpublished until 1973.[25] The French holograph is in the Mills Memorial Library at McMaster University, Hamilton, Ontario. Since the McMaster Library did not know about the publication of the play until it had taken place,[26] Beckett clearly retained a fair copy of the holograph, but was uncertain of the precise date of composition.

The published text is dated 'vers 1962-63?'. The play's first English publication in 1976 was entitled *Sketch for Radio Play;*[27] it was republished as *Radio I* in *Ends and Odds*.

The McMaster holograph is much crossed out and very difficult to decipher, but the published version appears to be a fair copy with small alterations, such as the substitution of 'Lui' and 'Elle' for 'homme' and 'femme' to describe the two human characters. It is a play for four characters: a man with two companions (as in *Words and Music*) though here called Music and Voice. The fourth character is an intrusive woman, who comes to hear Voice and Music. This is effected by turning separate knobs to the right, as in an old-fashioned radio. The two perform separately at first, at low volume; but they come together briefly and, when the woman has left, they perform together entirely.

As we have seen in Chapter 5 the man fears Voice and Music are about to leave him, since they have become very faint. He telephones his doctor urgently to inform him of the fact and expresses great surprise that, since Voice and Music cannot see or hear each other, they have managed to unite:

> *He:*. . .they're together. . .TOGETHER. . .yes. . .I don't know. . .like . . .(*hesitation*). . .one. . .the breathing. . .I don't know. . .(*vehement*). . . no!. . .never!. . .meet?. . .how could they meet?. . .

Unlike *Words and Music*, where the union is achieved with such difficulty, the coming together of Music and Voice appears to have been involuntary, with no assistance from the man. Indeed the union is expressly against his wishes, since it seems to have brought about the silencing of his two 'needs'. To his terror he realises that he can no longer summon his companions by turning the knobs, for they have an independent existence and have chosen to leave him. All he can do is await the doctor, who has already told him there is 'nothing to be done'.

The play as it stands is highly ambiguous. When read in conjunction with *Words and Music* and *Cascando*, however, it gains a new perspective. In *Words and Music* Croak forced his reluctant poetic imagination to coalesce in words. In *Radio I* 'he' can no longer summon either an imaginative idea or the words in which to clothe it, because both are failing. We hear them growing steadily fainter until finally there is silence. The lonely writer is left knowing he can hope for no assistance before noon the following day. Seen in this context, the end of the play is the writer's nightmare. The emphasis on 'tomorrow noon' and a 'breech' birth may even be seen to take on implications of a noon deadline, with no words, no ideas with which to perform the creative act, so that the work has to be dragged out, as in a breech birth. The writer is left with his 'needs' (the compulsion to create) but without the means to bring it about.

Cascando

Beckett abandoned *Esquisse Radiophonique* on 30 November 1961 and began *Cascando* the following day. The first page of the French holograph is dated 1 December 1961. A very full set of drafts for the play is to be found in the Harvard Theatre Collection, Harvard College Library and in the Samuel Beckett Papers at Washington University Libraries, St. Louis. Harvard has the earlier material and Washington the later. In a letter to Herbert Myrom accompanying the drafts sent to Harvard, Beckett described the material as follows:

> Herewith MSS. of *Cascando*. It tells its own shaky story. I Original MS. II Typescript of Voix I (Ouvreur). III Typescript of Voix 2 (élément soi.) IV Typescript of Voix 2 (élément histoire.) V Typescript of completed piece. VI Typescript of my English translation. VII Typescript of preceding revised.

He goes on to comment that:

> It is an unimportant work, but the best I have to offer. It does I suppose show in a way what passes for my mind and what passes for its work.[28]

There seems to be some confusion both in Beckett's description of the material and in Harvard's subsequent classification of it. Following the holograph which is written in two parts (Voix 1 and Voix 2)[29] Beckett made a typescript fair copy (Typescript I) again divided into two voices. He had little trouble with Voix I and, after making the fair copy, does not repeat this material until typing the 'completed piece'. Voix 2 was more difficult, however, and required three separate typescripts. The first is the fair copy already mentioned, while the second and third are headed separately in Beckett's hand: 'soi' and 'histoire'. When identifying the material for Harvard, Beckett misplaces half of the first typescript and instead of keeping Voix I and Voix 2 together, he labels Voix I Stage II and Voix 2 Stage IV. He then heads the second typescript (Stage III) 'élément soi' only, but he includes élément histoire here also, without identifying it. It is easier to appreciate the misplacement through internal textual evidence. A passage taken from the first speech of Voix 2 through its various stages of development elucidates:

Holograph
xxx...il regarde la vitre...de temps en temps...elle s'assombrit... ~~xxx xxx xxx ... xxx~~ **la terre** s'assombrit...
Beckett IV (ACTUALLY TYPESCRIPT I)
c'est long...il regarde la vitre...de temps en temps...elle s'assombrit...la terre s'assombrit...
Beckett III (ACTUALLY TYPESCRIPT 2, élément histoire)
c'est long...il ~~regarde la vitre~~ **leve la tête**...de temps en temps... **regarde la vitre** elle ~~s'assombrit~~ **brunit** ... la terre ~~s'assombrit~~ **brunit** ...
Beckett V (ACTUALLY TYPESCRIPT 3, entitled *Calando*)
c'est long...il leve la tête...de temps en temps...regarde la vitre...elle brunit...la terre brunit...

Such misplacement of material happens easily when collecting together several drafts of a work (we have observed a similar example in the early drafts of *Come and Go* at Reading University) but it shows that Beckett's ordering of the material needs careful checking before being accepted as the precise order of composition.

Beckett's description of the Harvard material is one of the most interesting features of the *Cascando* drafts. Not only are there two voices (the first of these subsequently named 'Ouvreur') but the second voice is divided into separate elements, that of the self (Soi) and that of the storyteller or narrator (Histoire). Investigation of the material reveals, moreover, a further subdivision, not mentioned in Beckett's description but evident in manuscript notes. Soi has a dual personality: Soi 1 and Soi 2. From Hamm to Mouth we are familiar with Beckett's protagonists telling themselves thinly disguised autobiographical stories to pass the time, but such precise identification of various elements of the protagonist is new. We have seen a division into separate elements such as Words and Music in the preceding plays for radio, but no preliminary material has come to light in which these elements are unequivocally stated to belong to the self, as they are in the *Cascando* drafts. Not only Voix 2 in its various guises, but Musique and Voix 1 are also part of the pattern of selfhood in *Cascando,* with Voix 1 supposedly in control of the rest, in that he releases them. By the end of the play, however, this function is open to question and Voix 2 and Musique seem to be acting independently, as happened with Music and Voice in the preceding play, *Radio I*.

Clas Zilliacus points out that when Musique and Voix occur together, it is only as Soi that Voix speaks. Histoire, the teller of tales (not only the self attempting to structure experience into stories, but perhaps the fantasiser also) always occurs alone.[30] Zilliacus also observes that Soi 2 appears to be the self's consciousness of guilt, characterised by the words 'coupable' 'innocent' and 'purgé'.[31] This Soi 2 material is the most noticeable omission from the later drafts of *Cascando*. Beckett refers to it in the margin of III as the 'motif coupable', but all overt mention of guilt is removed from subsequent drafts. 'Le coupable' is altered in III to 'le chercher', suggesting that Maunu, who is sought throughout the play, was originally conceived as the guilty one.

In the last of the Harvard typescripts in French the play is entitled *Calando* and Voix 1 and Voix 2 are brought together for the first time, instead of being written separately. Voix 1 is renamed 'Ouvreur', so that Voix 2 becomes the sole voice; but its various elements are no longer separated, nor are they in the subsequent Washington typescripts. The removal of the explicit elements of the self from the later drafts of the play is not, however, a typical example of developing ambiguity because the holograph is equally obscure. The division of Voix 2 into its three elements in the first typescript seems rather to have been so that Beckett himself could keep each separately in mind as he worked on developing the text.

Washington University has two typescripts of the French text that succeed the Harvard versions, but, beyond the emergence of the title *Cascando* in the first of these, there is little development. The second typescript contains what appear to be printer's markings and the text is identical with the 1966 Paris publication, except for a few small improvements in punctuation and presentation in the published version.

There are two typescripts of Beckett's English translation of the play at Harvard. The first has manuscript alterations, the second two spelling corrections only. The New York publication in 1963[32] is identical with the second Harvard typescript except for the penultimate speech of Voice, where the typescript reads 'I've had him' and the published version 'I've got him'. Three further typescripts of the translation are in Washington University Library. The first is a carbon copy of the final Harvard typescript, but with more extensive alterations. The second version omits most of the alterations from the first typescript, while adding new ones. The latter are incorporated into the last of the Washington typescripts, on which the London publication of the play in 1964 is based.[33]

Cascando is the last of Beckett's series of radio plays on the same theme and with a similar cast of characters. The fact that at one point Musique is weakening and has to be encouraged by Ouvreur links strongly with the failing sound in the preceding *Esquisse Radiophonique*. Ouvreur also recalls Animateur in *Pochade Radiophonique,* while Fox in the same play has much in common with the narrating voice (élément histoire) in *Cascando*. Fox's extreme reluctance to create is not, however, present in *Cascando* because Voix senses that at last he is on the track of the right story and is determined to pursue it to the end.

Voix, as Clas Zilliacus points out, is 'groping for the one story which would literally exhaust him, by exhaustively defining him.'[34] He seeks the story to end all stories. The desire to find such a story is expressed by Soi, and Histoire accordingly returns to an old story, that of Maunu, in the hope that it might prove to be the right one. Soi becomes increasingly certain that it *is* the right story and will culminate in a release from storytelling. A comparison may be made here with the later play *Not I*. The implication in *Cascando* is that if Soi could somehow tell his own story or 'say him',[35] the self would be able to unite, and, in so doing, achieve freedom. Similarly in *Not I* if Mouth could recognise or accept that she is telling her own story it is possible that she too would be allowed to stop repeating it. The more strenuously she denies her selfhood, the more powerless is the Auditor to help her.

It appears that Voix addresses himself as 'je' in *Cascando* when he is sure of his identity and as 'tu' when he is not. Since, however, the essential self is in its nature unnamable, those whom Voix addresses either by the pronouns 'je' or 'tu' or by name (Maunu) cannot be himself. The true self is nameless and no pronoun can pin it down. In this sense Mouth in *Not I* is right to deny her narration. The tale she is telling is only an approximation towards self-knowledge, the tale is truly *not* I because the real self eludes her. If real self-knowledge is impossible and consciousness remains a stranger to itself, O's predicament in *Film* is a permanent dilemma, insoluble by confrontation. Any attempt to reach the self brings knowledge of the label rather than the essence. The real self remains elusive and the label of identity cannot encompass it. In *The Unnamable* Beckett reveals such a self, agonisedly awaiting the freedom that would result from uniting with his true identity: 'it will be the silence [ ] I left myself behind in it, I'm waiting for me there'[36] and conscious that the many labels he has been given, the names by which he has been known, have never fully realised him.

Cascando remains full of ambiguities, whatever terms of reference are used for discussion. Whether, for example, it is interpreted as the self seeking its true identity, or the writer's search for the story of stories, the outcome remains in doubt. As observed in Chapter 5, however, the invasion of silence, cutting off the dialogue at the end of the play, does suggest a final culmination, however uncertain its nature.

It might be supposed that Beckett would not write one radio play in English, followed by two in French, on similar themes and without pausing between them, unless he were dissatisfied by each attempt and that he continued until, with *Cascando,* he approved of the result. *Words and Music* and *Cascando* were, however, written for collaboration with two different composers. John Beckett's score for *Words and Music* was, as we have seen, the fulfilment of a long-held intention, while Zilliacus quotes a letter from Marcel Mihalovici stating that 'L'idée de *Cascando* est de Beckett lui-même. Mais l'initiative d'écrire une oeuvre radiophonique avec mon ami était de moi.'[37] It would appear, therefore, that Beckett was merely carrying out two separate commitments, rather than making renewed attempts to write the same play.

Film

Film, written in 1963, is Beckett's only venture into cinema, although he has subsequently written five plays for the related medium of television. *Film* was written very quickly, moving from a first draft to a semi-finished text in the same notebook.[38] The notebook opens with 'notes for film' dated 5 April 1963. These are followed at once by a first draft, dated at its close 9 April 1963. A revised holograph draft, headed 'Outline sent to Grove'[39] follows, with the closing date 22 May 1963. Composition thus appears to have taken about six weeks from start to finish, suggesting that the idea was strongly present in Beckett's mind before he began to write. There are, however, important differences between the first draft and published text, both in the conception of the film and in the removal of detail, thus allowing a wider frame of reference for the final version. The main conceptual change is that Beckett first envisaged sound for his film. The preliminary notes contain the following suggestion and amendment:

Throughout Film ~~sounds~~ **NO** of things (feet, curtains etc.) but no speech

The first draft contains ideas for various sounds before Beckett changed his mind about them. O pants at the foot of the stairs and there is a 'crunch of broken glass' as he stamps on God's picture; however a note makes it clear that Beckett did not have a musical 'backing' of the kind typical in the silent cinema in mind for *Film*:

If music unavoidable, Schubert's Doppelgänger — with perhaps 'Ich bin nicht wild, komme nicht zu strafen'?

Once again 'Der Tod und das Mädchen' is Beckett's chosen musical signature, but he clearly decided after completing the first draft that sound was undesirable, and the second holograph is entirely silent, except for 'the "ssh!" from woman in part one'.

Precise identification of the subject of the film with the Bishop Berkeley dictum *esse est percipi* that forms an epigraph to the published text does not occur until the second draft. The preliminary notes to the first draft carry an introductory statement that might equally have prefaced *Cascando*, written some sixteen months earlier:

for one striving to see one striving not to be seen.

By the second page of notes, however, a hint of Berkeley appears:

'Percipi' Notes
Eye (E) One (O)
For Eye and one who would not be seen.[40]

The importance of *esse est percipi* is, however, somewhat undercut in the second draft, by some notes included subsequently in the published version:

Subject of film: search of non-being in flight from extraneous perception culminating in inescapability of self perception.
No truth value attaches to above. They are simply a structural and dramatic convenience.

A point on which a preliminary note is considerably more explicit than the later text, concerns the room. The note reads:

> His room or one he does not know? His mother's room.[41]

Having so decided Beckett is again at pains to point out the irrelevance of the information. In the first draft he describes the room thus:

> Small (10′×10′) miserable barely furnished room (boarded or tiled floor.) See sketch. It cannot be his (he would not keep pairs of eyes and a mirror.) It may be supposed that it is his mother's room, which he has not seen for a number of years and is to occupy momentarily, to look after the pets, until she comes out of hospital. This circumstance has no bearing on the film and is not otherwise indicated than by his photo on the wall.

This photograph is described on the facing page which bears a sketch of the room:

> ~~Recent large scowling photo of himself inscribed 'To my Mother, without rancour, Xmas 1929'~~.

Beckett decided immediately against personalising the room in this way and the entire note is crossed out. The only picture on the wall in the final text is that of God.

The dating of the film is confusing. Beckett's first thoughts in the preliminary notes were 'Period: ~~1913?~~ **1929**' and the published text states that the film takes place 'about 1929'. But the packet of photographs complicates the issue. The description of these photographs in the published text states that the man in the seventh photograph is precisely 30 years old, though 'looking over 40'. Since this photograph appears to be identical with the protagonist, it would mean that he was born in 1899 and graduated at 20 (photograph no. four) in 1919, already after the war. Yet photograph no. six (at age 25) shows him 'newly enlisted' (in 1924) and in no. seven he appears to have a war wound. Manuscript jottings in the notebook show that Beckett intended O to be about 50 when the film takes place. A marginal note in the first draft reads:

> O: aetat. 50
> 25 in 1914.

This would make him 50 in 1939 and born in 1899, which would also fit in with a first draft note that the mother's beflowered hat (in photograph no. two) is 'about 1890'. A further note on the same page is conclusive:

25 in 14
50 in 39

It is difficult to appreciate why Beckett did not keep to this dating and decided after all to set the film in 1929. If 0 were 50 in 1929, he would be 25 and 'newly enlisted' in 1904, just too late for the Boer War and a decade too early for 1914. It appears from the enlistment photograph that Beckett wished the sequence to include experience of the Great War. The first six photographs are all of smiling faces, but the seventh reveals a patch over the left eye and a 'grim expression'. It follows that, for the war photograph to be relevant, O has to be about 40 in 1929. It seems probable that Beckett would have preferred to be non-specific over such details, but was obliged to date the film for production purposes.

Beckett initially contemplated setting *Film* in the evening, but had to decide against this for a practical reason:

to remove possibility of his putting off light in room.

The main difficulty about the room is described in the first draft as the 'problem of dual perception' (E's perception of O, and O's of the room). Beckett expresses the problem on the first page of his preliminary notes:

In street **and stairs** all perception by E.
But in room?
H must perceive.
H perceiving perceived by E.
Express perhaps by simultaneous slightly incongruous images?

Beckett points out that since 'H. perceives only when he feels himself not seen, i.e. when E directly or nearly directly behind him', all E's images must be 'coupled with image of H seen from behind'. 'If insoluble', he concludes:

then assume identity of perceptions (E perceiving O's objects over O's shoulder) involving in foreground of all O's images[42] blurred nape and top of shoulder (and sacrificing principle that E's unique concert and perception is with and of O.)

Beckett was clearly dissatisfied with the above solution and contemplates in the first draft the 'possibility throughout of distinguishing two perceptions by a *quality* of image (filter oder was)?' The latter idea subsequently developed into the final one of a transition 'from greater to lesser and lesser to greater definition or luminosity'[43] for the separate perspectives. Whether or not this method is successful will be discussed in Chapter 11.

The Eye/I pun is, however, an effective one. E is, so to speak, O's blind eye. He has the function of making all with whom he comes into contact self aware. There is nothing intrinsically frightening in his image when at last it is presented to us at the end of the play. A sense of evil has been built up because of the looks of horror E arouses when perceived by others. In the first draft he appears to be neuter, a nameless menace:

> She feels E fixed on them and turns, raising her lorgnon, to look at it.

But when we finally see that E is O, the implication seems to be that he has no reality other than as an inner eye. The camera thus performs a function whereby each beholder sees himself. It holds a mirror up to nature and the observed sees himself reversed, as at the end of Miss La Trobe's historical pageant in Virginia Woolf's *Between the Acts*.[44] It is an uncomfortable experience and E's audience is no less outraged than Miss La Trobe's.

In *Film*, as soon as O, the conscious man, has closed his eyes, thus dropping his guard, the watchful subconscious takes over. The situation has Freudian implications. In the first draft, moreover, Beckett describes the final confrontation in Freudian terms, with E as alter ego:

> E = alter O (dénouement).

Having gained the upper hand, E, instead of vanishing when O starts awake, forces him to face himself in a real awakening. The film culminates in their confrontation in which, as Beckett points out in the first draft:

> O's face fully shown for first time, E shown for first time.

The fact that E stole upon O unawares recalls the narrator in *From An Abandoned Work*:

> there's no accounting for anything, with a mind like the one I always had, always on the alert against itself.[45]

The acceptance of selfhood would, it seems, as in *Not I*, involve the acknowledgement of a predicament beyond contemplation.

Two literary analogues are of great interest in connexion with *Film*, in their parallel treatment of the theme of the second self and as possible source material for Beckett. We have observed in the first draft Beckett's reference to 'Schubert's Doppelgänger' 'if music unavoidable' for the film. The doppelgänger theme has had many exponents, but none better known than Stevenson's *Dr. Jekyll and Mr. Hyde*. The following extracts reveal an extraordinary resemblance between the latter and Beckett's protagonist in *Film*.[46]

(a) ... he discharged the cab and ventured on foot, attired in his misfitting clothes, an object marked out for observation ...

(b) At all hours of the day and night I would be taken with the premonitory shudder; above all, if I slept, or even dozed for a moment in my chair, it was always as Hyde that I awakened.

(c) Hence the ape-like tricks that he would play me, [ ] destroying the portrait of my father;

(d) ...that insurgent horror was knit to him closer than a wife, closer than an eye; lay caged in his flesh, where he heard it mutter and felt it struggle to be born; and at every hour of weakness, and in the confidence of slumber, prevailed against him, and deposed him out of life.

It is of course mistaken to 'identify' O with Hyde and E with Jekyll. Beckett, it is true (in notes following the first draft) toys with the idea of making 'E tall' and 'O short (and) fat' which corresponds with the dual physique of Jekyll and Hyde. But *Film* is not concerned with representations of good and evil, only with the concept of the second self, of pursuer and pursued.

A further parallel that Beckett, a student of French literature, can hardly have missed, is Victor Hugo's poem 'La Conscience'.[47] 'Conscience' in French can mean either 'conscience' in the English sense, or 'consciousness' and the double meaning is important. The poem concerns a man haunted by an eye that stares at him unceasingly from the sky. He runs away from it, ever further, even to the grave, where, in the tomb, the eye awaits him. The man is Cain. He has been trying to escape consciousness of himself, the self that killed his brother, but his conscience will not let him rest. The eye/I is always present and, when he can run no further, must be faced in the tomb. Not only is a similar dichotomy the subject of *Film*, but *The Eye* was an early title for the film. Moreover Cain's attempts to hide (behind the fabric walls of a tent, for example) resemble O's compulsive drawing of the curtains and blotting out of eyes in an attempt to find security in the room. In both parallels the discrepancy between outer and inner man is apparent in the nagging unrest of the outer, hounded continually from within, so that he manifests signs of advanced paranoia. Such, too, is O's state of mind, and that of Joe, in the television play *Eh Joe,* Beckett's next venture into film.

Eh Joe

Eh Joe was written in 1965. The holograph is dated at start and close 13 April 1965 and 1 May 1965. It is followed by six undated typescripts (numbered 0-4 and 'final version'). The full set of drafts is in the Samuel Beckett Papers at Washington University, St. Louis.

The holograph reveals Beckett to have had a clear concept of the text he wanted from the outset, though changes made as the writing progresses show him once again avoiding the specific. The holograph, for example, makes it clear that the voice is telling her own story and describing her own suicide:

> Ever hear ~~what became of me?~~ **how I did it** . . . Just the announcement in the **Independent**?

Later in the holograph the denial of selfhood begins and (as in *Not I*) the announcement in the *Independent* describes 'her' not 'I'. By the first typescript all details of the death are given in the third person, though it is still apparent that the voice could not have known such details unless the experience were her own, and that Joe's conscience must have reconstructed the 'crime'. After the first suicide attempt ('lying down on sand with face in it warm night failure') a second attempt, that appears to have links with the boat at the end of *Cascando,* is described in the holograph:

> Boat out from Bullock cap xxx xxxx sitting in bow facing lights of land murmuring oh jo oh jo — there's love for you etc. till end whisper.

The protagonist is referred to as 'J' then 'Jack' on page 1 of the holograph, but becomes 'Joe' by page 3. The holograph (which was begun in blue ink and completed in black) was headed *Eh Joe* after completion, since the title is in black ink. In the first typescript (O) which is a fair copy of the holograph, the change of name has been forgotten and 'Jack' is typed into the text until page 3, where the holograph becomes Joe. The main innovation in Typescript 0 is that, whereas the holograph had been written phrasally, each phrase separated by three dots, a new line is now taken for each phrase, giving the play the appearance of a prose poem. The text is then divided in the margins into eleven numbered sections, between which the camera moves are to take place. In the ensuing typescript (1), sections 5 and 6 are merged and the resulting ten sections are numbered and reinstated as phrasal paragraphs throughout. Beckett was either dissatisfied with the 'poetic' formation, or had used it simply as a convenient method to establish where the camera moves should take place.

The phrasal technique adopted in *Eh Joe* was first used in *Radio I* (followed by *Cascando*) and appears later in *Not I*. It proved an efficient means of conveying the random nature of interior monologue; several phrases from *Eh Joe* return in *Not I* since Beckett's protagonists have a strong family relationship.

We have observed in Chapter five that the situation in *Eh Joe* is an extension of that in *Film*. The confrontation between O and the camera is the climax on which the latter ends. In *Eh Joe* the entire text is confrontation, since the opening 'business' in the room occurs before a word is spoken. As soon as Joe relaxes having ascertained that he is alone, the camera inches up, capturing him and the voice 'starts in' on him. The room has become 'the trap' (as Beckett describes it in notes following the second draft of *Film*) 'in which he has cornered O.' Echoes of *Film* are very obvious in the first draft of *Eh Joe*:

Noone can get at you **now** [ ] why don't you put out the light? [ ] **in case there's an eye you've forgotten.**

And the second draft is modified, in consequence:

~~in case there's an eye you've forgotten~~ **There might be a fly** ~~**looking at**~~ **watching you.**

Typescript 1 is the first draft to present a significant advance in the text of *Eh Joe*. It is succeeded by manuscript stage directions for the opening action in the room, as well as separate instructions for 'Voice', 'Face' and 'Camera' and several sketches of the set. These directions are then typed, revised in manuscript and finally added to the typescript as page one. A revision shows that Beckett originally thought of Joe in a chair, but realised a more telling image for a seducer would be alone on a bed. An afterthought in the notes for the face reveals Beckett already contemplating the mouth as a dramatic image. It reads 'mouth chiefly' and refers to the 'mounting tension of listening' being expressed mainly in the 'distorted' mouth. After being typed into Typescript 1 this direction is crossed out, but it shows the way in which Beckett's dramatic imagery is evolving, from the clay-baked faces in *Play* (1962/3) to a face in which expression is concentrated on the mouth in *Eh Joe* (1965) to the eventual mouth alone of *Not I* (1972). The importance of nagging repetition in disturbing Joe has already occurred to Beckett, who counts the number of repetitions of the title phrase 'Eh Joe' in the margins of Typescript 1.

Typescript 2 is headed 'text only', omitting the opening directions and some of the revisions made in Typescript 1. Typescript 3 restores the opening directions and contains on Page 3 a note written in French, showing Beckett either to have been thinking in French while revising the English text, or possibly to have been making a simultaneous French translation.[48] The penultimate section of the final speech in Typescript 3 is rewritten in manuscript, so as to emphasise phrases such as 'the hands' and 'the stones' through repetition. The word 'imagine' is also inserted several times; to imagine is precisely Joe's current predicament. These revisions are incorporated into Typescript 4 but are largely omitted from the final version. The exhortation 'imagine' remains, but the phrasal repetitions disappear — except for one final echo of 'the stones'.

The Faber text is closer to the unrevised Typescript 3 than to Typescript 5, the final draft. However Typescript 5 appears to have been used to rehearse Jack Macgowran, since certain phrases are underlined for emphasis and directions for an actor's movements are added in manuscript in the margins throughout. Moreover a blank page following the text contains what appear to be directorial jottings such as: 'Head down — up fraction on: How's yr. Lord'; 'brief smile for the green'; 'story faster'.

Typescripts 2-5 reveal Beckett's painstaking reworking of a text that had already virtually crystallised in Typescript 1, through four subsequent versions. These reworkings will be looked at in some detail in Chapter 10.

CHAPTER 9
'VAGUENING': STAGE AND *SANS*

Theatre I

Beckett's first attempt at a stage play in English came in December 1956, two months after he had finished *All That Fall* and the year in which he finally completed *Fin de partie*. Indeed the play was written while he was in the throes of preparing *Fin de partie* for its first performance and before he began the English translation, *Endgame*, in April 1957. The new play begins in a holograph notebook at Reading University and is entitled *The Gloaming*.[1] The play seems to have been abandoned after completion of the holograph; however in 1974 a later, French version of the play (entitled *Fragment de Théâtre*) was published in Paris.[2] Reading University also has a manuscript notebook and two typescripts of the French version.[3] Beckett is uncertain when these were written and queries: 'date?' on the cover of the manuscript and the play is thus dated only vaguely ('années 60'?) in the published text. Beckett then translated the French text into English. A further manuscript in English (entitled *Theatre Fragment I*) is dated 'Ussy 8.9.75' and is followed by two successive typescripts. These versions (which are all in Reading University Library) are a precise translation from the French.[4] The English version was first published by Grove Press (in *Ends and Odds*, 1976) under the title *Theatre I*.

There are only minor discrepancies between the French manuscript and its succeeding typescript drafts. The first typescript is a fair copy of the manuscript; the second typescript incorporates small manuscript revisions in the first one, and is identical with the published text.[5] The English translation and its two succeeding typescripts are also fair copies of each other. It is thus between *The Gloaming* and the manuscript in French that the main differences occur. Since all the French versions are almost identical and the English text is a precise translation of the French one, *The Gloaming* may be compared, for the reader's convenience, with the published text of *Theatre I*. Such a comparison also allows the reader to juxtapose *The Gloaming* (the original

English manuscript) with the play's final *translation* into English, a curious history indeed in the genesis of a text, and one that is unique in Beckett's dramatic writing.

Except for the ending of the play, the basic outline of *The Gloaming* corresponds with *Theatre I. The Gloaming* is, however, much wordier than *Theatre I,* indeed the latter contains several laconic exchanges between the two characters that strongly recall those between Vladimir and Estragon or Hamm and Clov. Perhaps the similarity of dialogue with *Godot* and *Fin de partie,* coupled with a less powerful dramatic situation in *Theatre I* resulted in Beckett's dissatisfaction with the final version, which (as also with *Theatre II*) he is reluctant to have performed. In the latest edition of the two plays he even retitles them: *Rough for Theatre I and II.*[6]

The scene in *The Gloaming* is 'a public place' and the two characters are named B (a blind beggar) and C (a cripple) instead of A and B as in *Theatre I,* and the text is considerably more detailed. A single line about the state of the trees in the published text, for example, (B: Hard to say. It's winter, you know.) originally read:

C: It is difficult to say. We are in winter, you know. They are black and bare — the evergreens included. One would have to cut into them, with a knife — I must remember to do that this afternoon. (*He takes out a memorandum and a pencil & writes.*) Check trees for sap. (*He puts them away.*) But is it worth it, one cannot inspect them all? But is it wise, for the peace of my mind? (*Pause.*) It is so long since I tried to make myself understood to anyone but myself that I . . .

At times, too, *The Gloaming* becomes heavy handed:

C: Let us keep these things for the long slow nights and days together, before the long silence when we only call for help. (*Pause.*) ~~The trouble~~ **The trouble** is when —
B: Then why tell me your trouble?
C: To enlist your sympathy. (*Pause.*) The trouble is when I want to turn and go home

In the final text this becomes succinctly:

B: Only one problem: the about-turn.

The quotation from Thomson's 'To Fortune' towards the end of *The Gloaming* ('Bid us sigh on from day to day/And wish and wish the soul away')[7] although so much in tune with Beckett's perception of human suffering, is omitted from the later versions.

There is a good deal of comic irony in *The Gloaming* that is cut from the later text:

C: You ~~went blind~~ **lost your sight** late in life.
B: I am not ~~old~~ **late in life.**
C: I mean you ~~were not born blind~~ **had it once.** (*Pause.*) Humility isn't your strong point, Billy, xx is it?

Or again when C enquires of B:

Why don't you walk round in a spiral? (*Pause.*) Have you no system? (*Pause.*)

There is at times a slapstick liveliness to the dialogue that is also cut, the tone of the final version becoming generally harsher. At one stage in *The Gloaming*, for example, B simply responds 'Coo!' (when C says he will point out the route for him) and C cheekily cries 'Tweet!' when B invites him to make a sound.

Interestingly, one ambiguity in *The Gloaming* is not present in the later text. The two men, it appears, may have been known to each other for some time, since C remarks to B towards the end of the play: 'Noone ~~can~~ **could** ever do anything for you, could they, Billy?' The final version ends, however, in an ambiguity entirely absent in *The Gloaming*. In Beckett's typical manner of creating a shock effect or sudden reversal at the end of a play, A wrests B's pole away from him in *Theatre I*, thus altering the balance of power. Since B is unable to move without the pole, the blind man at last appears to have taken the upper hand. The play ends here, with the resolution of the new situation left entirely ambiguous, whereas in *The Gloaming* the audience is shown what happens next:

B snatches the pole from his hand. Silence.
C: Yes. (*Pause.*) How shall we finish this now, Billy? (*Pause.*) By **your** having mercy on me? (*Pause.*) Then go our ways, saying, the last ~~thing~~ I did for anybody, anybody did for me, was xxx xxxxx mercy. (*Pause.*) No? (*Pause.*) It'd spoil it? (*Pause.*) It's going to be very cold, Billy, colder and colder. (*Pause.*) It's so long since I —
B throws the pole at C, who catches it. Silence. B listening in throughout above. C pushes himself backwards towards right wing halts at limit of stage watches B. Silence. C (sic)[8] *listening. He suddenly turns his head towards stool, having heard fiddle. He gropes towards stool, knocks into it.* ~~*Fiddle falls. He gropes to fiddle, picks it up, Fi*~~ **Fiddle falls. He gropes to fiddle, knocks over case and bowl.** *Complications of finding,* ~~*setting*~~ **setting** *up, knocking down, till finally all in place as at*

beginning and B sitting on stool holding fiddle. Silence, C watching, B listening.

C: Are you all right now, Billy? Have you everything you want? (*Pause.*) Will I go and have a look at the holly and come back and tell you? (*Pause.*) I ~~would~~ **wouldn't** come near you Billy, just enough for you to hear me and call out the word. (*Pause.*) ~~Is there nothing I can do for you, Billy?~~ **Will I go and get you a few sprouts?** (*Pause.*) Is there nothing I can do for you, Billy?
Pause

B: Bring me back to the hot summer ~~day~~ **evening** out in the bay with my father in the little rowboat, fishing for mackerel with a spinner. To the time when it was still time. 'Do you remember what they look like?' 'Yes, father, all blue and silver.'

Krapp's Last Tape

Krapp's Last Tape was written very quickly. It stemmed from Beckett, in December 1957, hearing Patrick Magee reading extracts from *Molloy* on the BBC Third Programme.[9] On 20 February 1958 Beckett drafted a text in the 'Été 56' notebook entitled simply *Magee Monologue.*[10] On 15 March 1958 he wrote to Jake Schwartz that he had for him 'four states, in typescript, with copious and dirty corrections, of a short stage monologue I have just written (in English) for Pat Magee. This was composed on the machine from a tangle of old notes, so I have not the MS. to offer you.'[11] By 5 April 1958 we learn from a further letter to Jake Schwartz that both the publication and first production of the play are going forward:

> I have written it for Pat Magee and George Devine and it will be played by the former at the Royal Court with Endgame. This will be next May or in the early autumn, I do not yet know which. [ ] It will be published in a coming number of Evergreen Review.

The writing was thus completed inside a month. The 'tangle of old notes' must, I think, refer to the 'Été 56' holograph versions, which appear to be in three stages. Stage 1 is a false start, in which the first tape heard records Krapp's thirtieth birthday. This version is broken off by a line drawn across the page below the text and a second attempt follows. Beckett did not, however, write out the opening of the monologue again, but began where he had decided revision was necessary, at the beginning of the taped voice. The second stage thus begins with Krapp having aged; it is now his thirty-seventh birthday. The remainder of the text is broadly similar to the final version. Beckett then revises the opening of the play (Stage 3) writing on the left hand blank pages of the notebook and thus facing the text he is revising; he breaks off at the words 'Thirty-seven today etc,' which is where Stage 2 begins. Stage 2 is then typed out (Typescript 1) and revised in manuscript. It is followed by three further typescripts which all contain the full text.

Krapp is called 'A' until a MS. addition to Typescript 2 in which the opening clowning with bananas also first appears; the clowning replaces some cumbersome stage business with the table in Stage 1. It seems likely that Beckett's main reason for abandoning Stage 1 was because it contained too much circumstantial detail. A recalls, for example, his nativity in North Great Georges St, making him a Dubliner born. The omission of a Dublin setting for a non-localized one is one of several instances of a movement away from the specific in the drafts of *Krapp's Last Tape*. It may be compared with the decision to remove pronunciation directions for an Irish accent from the drafts of *Not I*. Not unnaturally the voice Beckett hears when writing his monologues is an Irish one. But to set his plays in Ireland could prove limiting for actor and audience alike, providing problems of accent and perhaps distancing the plays into local curiosities, so that they lose the immediacy, the 'Everyman' effect that is one of their greatest strengths. A specific date variously tried out at the opening of Typescript 3 is also subsequently omitted:

~~April 1986.~~[12] **A late envening** (sic) **in ~~1985~~ the nineteen eighties.**

The corrected version remains in Typescript 4, but becomes 'in the future' in the final text.

Another point, clear in the holograph and subsequently obscured, concerns Krapp's vision. In Stage 2 he describes a sudden insight into his writing, a realisation that darkness is his true theme:

> . . . clear to me at last that the dark I have struggled to keep out of my work is in reality its true —

In ensuing drafts the passage becomes increasingly ambiguous until, in the final text, Krapp seems to be scoffing at a vision of life itself, rather than one of his artistic creativity. It is typical of Beckett's drafts to move from a narrow interpretation towards a wider one, as we have seen with *Play* and *Come and Go*. It is noticeable that in Stage 1 Krapp's sexual problems were of a very different order from the final text. Instead of his plans, in the published version, 'for a less . . . (*hesitates*) . . . engrossing sexual life', A says:

> what would help me more than anything, I think, is (*lowering his voice*) . . . sexual life. (*Pause.*) ~~With some partners~~. **a . . . a fuller . . . a more . . . more natural . . . a more . . . engrossing . . . absorbing** (*Enthusiastic*). Intercourse!

Such reflections lead the old man to stop the tape and pause for several swift drinks. He then reenters 'in a kind of shuffling dance', the first sign of the clowning that becomes so evident in later drafts. Stage 3, for example, gives stage directions for a clownish makeup:

> *Pallid face. Purple nose. Very near-sighted and hard of hearing.*

Beckett's description of the play as being 'composed on the machine' is somewhat misleading in view of the initial holograph versions, although certain vocabulary changes are made silently between typescripts. In these cases no manuscript alteration is made, but a typed change occurs in an ensuing version. Examples of this are the word 'widowhood' in Typescript 1 being replaced by 'viduity' in Typescript 2 and Krapp's age silently increasing from 37 (in Typescripts 1-3) to 39 in Typescript 4. All four typescripts are extensively corrected in manuscript, but the precise nature of these alterations need not trouble us here, since they are concerned not with radical change, but with the ways in which Beckett customarily refines his text, which is the subject of Chapter 10. The title first appears as a manuscript addition to Typescript 2: *Crapp's Last Tape*.

The speed with which the play was written and the lack of major alteration from first to last reveals that the idea and its method of execution were visualized clearly from the outset. Nonetheless some interesting jottings following the holograph text in the 'Été 56' notebook, show that Beckett wrote *Krapp* initially with very little idea of the mechanics of a tape recorder. The draft of a letter in the notebooks asks a friend to:

> beg, borrow, steal, cadge or even buy, and send me post haste, a prospectus [ ] of a tape-recorder.

Two diagrams of a tape recorder and some notes relating to them later in the notebook, show Beckett to have had access to a machine, though at what stage in the play's composition it is not clear. The tape recorder notes in the published version appear to have been written after the final drafting of the text, since a manuscript reminder of the necessity for some notes about the handling of the machine occurs at the end of Typescript 4.

A notebook Beckett prepared for his Schiller Theater production in 1969 draws attention to the light and darkness 'emblems' in the play,[13] and in the margin of the text that he used for the 1973 London production, a direct connexion is made with *Othello*, a play in which dark and light imagery is central. Where the word 'chrysolite' occurs on page 15, he writes:

> If heaven would make me such another world
> Of one entire and perfect chrysolite
> I'd not have sold her for it.
>
> *Othello V 2*[14]

Like Othello, too, Krapp has lost his love through his own folly.

In the interests of ambiguity Beckett has cut from recent productions Krapp's singing of the Baring-Gould hymn 'Now The Day is Over'; it is, as Knowlson observes, 'in Beckett's personal view, too clumsily explicit'.[15] Further alterations made by Beckett during production are discussed in Chapter 11.

Krapp's Last Tape shows the influence of Beckett's experience with radio in *All That Fall*, by introducing recorded sound into the stage action to develop his theme of the changing self. Krapp has the mechanical assistance of the tape recorder to bring into being his earlier selves, but he has changed so much that he cannot identify with them. At 39 he comments:

> Hard to believe I was ever that young whelp. The voice! Jesus! And the aspirations!

And the 69-year-old Krapp summarily dismisses the 39 year-old self:

> Just been listening to that stupid bastard I took myself for thirty years ago, hard to believe I was ever as bad as that. Thank God that's all done with anyway.

The two comments echo each other so precisely across thirty years that we are able to make the connexion he denies and see in the aged Krapp the younger men, their vices merely more pronounced, as, over the years, he has sunk into solitude. The old man has learned from experience, however, recognising that the time of real meaning in his past was a relationship with a woman, and not the intellectual vision that had so excited him at 39. It was a relationship he promptly denied; the episode is entered in his ledger as 'Farewell to love'. But, alone, at the end of life, the memory of perhaps his last meeting with the girl is the moment to which he clings.

Theatre II

The original manuscript for *Theatre II* was begun five months after the completion of *Krapp's Last Tape*. Dated 15.8.58 and written in French, it is contained in a notebook at Trinity College Dublin.[16] Beckett describes the 33 page manuscript as an 'Abandoned play'. There are in fact four separate attempts to develop the play in the manuscript notebook. The first of these consists of three pages, breaking off at the top of Page 4. It opens with a diagram for the set which is the same in every detail as the version finally published in 1976,[17] showing that Beckett's visual concept was clear from the outset. The initial dialogue is, however, very different:

Horloge Musique Mi do re soh. Soh re mi do. Mi re do soh. Soh re mi do. Fa.
Silence
B: Fa. Famiredo. Domirefa. Fa.
A: Déjà!
B: Fa. (*Un temps.*) Fa.
C commence à enjamber le rebord de la fenêtre.
B: Attendez!
(*C s'immobilise, une jambe dans le vide.*)

C's direct action, his arrested attempts to precipitate himself from the window, are the most distinctive feature of the first draft and are not present in later versions. B again interposes on Page 2:

C commence à prendre l'autre jambe par dessus le rebord
B: Attendez, Monsieur, un instant, je vous **en** prie, xxxx **pas de précipitation**, laissez nous finir, vous ne savez pas encore tout. (*C s'immobilise.*) [ ] Combien de misérables le seraient encore aujourd'hui s'ils avaient vu à quel point ils l'etaient!

Finally on Page 3 B's persuasions succeed in bringing C away from the brink: 'C ramène sa jambe, reprend sa pose au début.'

The relationship between A and B has echoes of Beckett's complementary couples in *Godot* and *Fin de partie*. Indeed a grotesque doodle on the back of the second page even visualises the idea of two in one since it shows, emerging from a single body, a huge head, from within which two smaller heads (one on top of the other) stare out. Most of the talking in the first draft is done by B, who criticizes his partner A for his apparent lack of interest in C's situation:

Nul vie humaine — le trésor irremplacable! repose entre nos mains et tu xx xxx xxxx **veux aller au** lit!

Just before the first attempt breaks off, B suggests that they should leave and give C a chance:

Allons-nous en. Laisser-lui une chance. Non le rien.

The second attempt, which begins on P4 immediately after the first one ends, has no directions for any movement from C — he simply stands before the window, as in the final version. The text is a condensed version of the first attempt, but with a larger share of the dialogue for A. It breaks off on P7 and the whole text is crossed through, except for the opening directions. Since the third attempt begins immediately with no such directions, it appears that Beckett wished those of the second version to stand. By the third attempt the dialogue is beginning to take a shape broadly similar to the published text; however on P9 this version also is abruptly ended. Overleaf directions for a fourth manuscript draft begin and this time the text is completed.

Although he abandoned the holograph Beckett clearly retained a fair copy, possibly a typescript on very faded paper held at Reading University Library.[18] This typescript is headed simply *Théâtre*; it is revised in manuscript and there are two pages of manuscript notes attached to it, in which Beckett reshapes some of the dialogue. Since there are numerous discrepancies between the holograph and this typescript there may be intervening drafts not as yet located, but it is also quite common for Beckett to make additional alterations straight onto the typewriter when making a fair copy of an earlier draft. By the typescript the names of A and B have stabilised to Bertrand (A) and Morvan (B) after considerable variation in the holograph (where, for example, in the first attempt, B had seemed intent on deliberate mystification by referring to A separately as 'Henri', 'Albert' and 'Armand'.)

Beckett also develops the vocabulary in the typescript. The mundane 'histoires de sexe' in the manuscript becomes 'histoires de fesses' (buttocks) and A's rather commonplace 'avenir noir' (black future) of the manuscript becomes the more suggestive 'avenir d'encre' (inky future.)

A second typescript at the Reading Library[19] tidies up Typescript 1 by making several small cuts straight onto the typewriter when copying the text, as well as incorporating actual corrections made in the earlier typescript. The French publication tallies largely with the second typescript, with one major difference. In the manuscript and both typescripts A timidly produces his handkerchief and extends it towards C's hand in the final stage directions, whereas in the published text he raises the handkerchief timidly towards C's face, thus strengthening the play's ending. The French edition is headed simply *Fragment de théâtre*, while the English translation becomes first *Theatre II* and finally *Rough for Theatre II*.[20] The translation is used for quotation in the ensuing discussion of the play.

The finished text of *Theatre II* is full of ambiguity. Precisely who A and B are and how they have the right to 'sum up' for C before letting him jump, is never clarified. It is as though they are there to pass judgement on C's life before he can leave it. Details such as which floor they are on are also deliberately confusing. B considers they are 'say twenty-five' metres above ground, allowing 'three to three and a half metres per floor'. This would mean they were on the seventh floor or even the eighth', but A comments: 'I could have sworn we were only on the sixth', thus contributing to the atmosphere of uncertainty.

A has the more imagination of the two. When B neatly tabulates the various areas of C's life, A enquires: 'May we not be mistaken?' For B everything is clear; the papers before him say it all:

> *B:* We have been to the best sources. All weighed and weighed again, checked and verified. Not a word here (*brandishing sheaf of papers*) that is not cast iron.

He flings the papers to the table, but they scatter on the floor and B's 'Shit!' in response comments also on the life the documents chronicle. A appears to have forgotten a good deal about C, again contributing to the atmosphere of uncertainty, though he stresses that a loss of memory is merciful: 'that's what saves us!' B is satisfied that there are no 'positive elements' in C's record, but A feels (in common with several characters in Beckett's later plays) that there must be 'something he said himself' that would be relevant. Thus B looks through the 'slim file' of 'confidences' and finds (among a typically Beckettian list of physical disorders) the note that C is 'morbidly sensitive to the opinion of others'. The discovery appears to provoke a power failure in B's lamp. Every time he tries to finish reading the passage relating to C's sensitivity, his lamp goes out in Expressionistic fashion, as though in direct response to C's wish for privacy.

The very presence of A and B and their judgemental attitude to his life assault C at his most vulnerable point. When B at last manages to read on, the lack of a main verb recalls Lucky's speech in *Godot*. The key sentence in C's 'confession', however, is never completed:

B: ah! I have it — '. . . I was unfortunately incapable . . .' Done it!

C's precise incapacity is never identified as the lamp again goes out, but B decides nonetheless that the investigation is over: 'There's the record, closed and final'. The language continues to ring with doubles entendres as A sums up:

A black future, an unpardonable past, so far as he can remember, inducements to linger on all equally preposterous and the best advice dead letter. Agreed?

A still feels, however, that 'To accumulate documents is not enough', whereas for B there is no problem in the paperwork: 'as far as I'm concerned the client is here and nowhere else.'

Just before the play ends a further ambiguous incident occurs, in the discovery of a caged bird that suddenly emits a 'brief burst of birdsong.' The determination of A and B to track down the bird and to pass judgement on it having done so, seems to have parallels with C's situation. Moreover, the two men are unable to help the bird, just as they have done nothing for C beyond offending his sensitivities. The brief burst of song after long silence might thus be seen as C's defiance of the two men, or indeed his jubilation at the completion of their investigation.

Standing at the open window C is as if poised at the door of his cage; his confrontation of 'the void' is reminiscent of Victor turning his back on humanity at the end of *Éleuthéria,* indeed C shares other traits with Victor as, for example, in his repeated absconding from home. C's back is turned on the audience throughout *Theatre II,* but the play ends in ambiguity, with the dramatic climax occurring after the last words have been spoken. A's sudden exclamation as he inspects C's face is followed by his proffering C a handkerchief. It is implied that C is weeping; whether at his 'record' or at his current situation is uncertain. Although apparently poised to leap, the vital action is not taken, perhaps the final evidence of C's incapacity. The restrained and ambiguous ending is more effective than C's clamberings on the windowsill, as Beckett must have realised since, after the first attempt in the manuscript, C remains motionless throughout the play.

Happy Days

The dating of *Happy Days* is puzzling. The first full holograph is dated 8 October 1960 at the opening and 14 January 1961 at its close. A holograph headed 'Rewrite' was begun two days later (16 January 1961) and the close of Act 1 is dated 31 January 1961. Act 2 was begun on 2 February 1961 and completed on '7.2.62' (the latter clearly an error for 1961). A final holograph was started on '29.3.62'. The first act of this was finished on 12 May '1961' and Act 2 was begun the following day, the full version being completed on 14 May. The last figure in both dates for Act 2 was hurriedly written and is not clear. The New York publication of the play in 1961 would seem to clinch the date of completion, were it not for an interview with Paul-Louis Mignon in June 1964, in which Beckett remarked that *Happy Days* had taken eighteen months to write, thus giving a new perspective to what had appeared dating errors:

> J'ai écrit *Godot*, vite, en un mois. *Oh les beaux jours* m'a demandé un an et demi![21]

On querying the matter with Beckett, his decision, in view of the play's prior publication, was the only one possible: 'Draft date 62 presumably a mistake.'[22]

The draft material for *Happy Days* is of great interest, as it shows Beckett interleaving holograph material with typescript. The typescript in each case is an attempt at a fair copy of the preceding holograph stage, and is improved on in turn by a new holograph version. There are nine stages in the play's draft development and the Roman numerals I-IX are used to distinguish these. The first draft was begun in the 'Été 56' notebook under the heading 'Female Solo'. But, after three pages, it was broken off. A second holograph (II) was begun on the same day (8 October 1960).[23] The play at this stage was in one act only. An undated typescript of the one act version (III) marks the next stage in the evolution of the play. It is followed by a further holograph version, in which the play appears in two acts for the first time (IV). After this come the first typescript of Act 2 (V) and then a typescript of the full play (VI). None of these typescripts is dated. The final holograph (VII, begun on 29 March) is followed by two further undated typescripts (VIII and IX).

So much preliminary material is available for this play that it seems appropriate to chronicle the main changes that occur from stage to stage. Gontarski observes that:

> In many ways, the early drafts of *Happy Days* are more 'realistic' than the printed version. The major structural and thematic alterations in the manuscripts demonstrate not an evolution toward fuller explanation of character and situation, but the opposite . . .[24]

We shall notice any movements towards imprecision as they occur in the drafts.

The 'Été 56' notebook not only contains the first holograph of *Happy Days*, but played a further part at various stages in the development of the text. After holograph I is broken off, six pages of jottings ensue, many of which find their way into the text later, for example:

> Not Mildred: Winnie
> Not Edward: Willie.

and:

> Cut out alarm clock. Invisible bell?

alterations which occur in Stages III and IV respectively. The title *Happy Days* is also found in these notes, in preference to an earlier jotting, which had suggested 'Title: "A low Comedy"'.

The most striking change between the first and second holograph is that a male figure (Tom) is also present onstage at the opening of Stage I, but is banished from view in Stage II. The first holograph, after describing the woman (W) reads:

> *Sitting on the lower ledge left, his back to the audience, a man, in striped pyjamas. He his* (sic) *sleeping, leaning so far forward that only his buttocks and foreshortened back are visible, his arms on his knees and his head on his arms. Bare flesh between trousers and coat of pyjamas.*

The above directions are repeated in the second holograph, with the additional information that Tom's pyjamas are of the 'same stripes as parasol',[25] but the entire passage is then crossed out and the following added:

To her right, behind mound and invisible from auditorium, **Tom**, *also sleeping.*

Beckett's second thoughts thus reject the rather obvious comedy of Tom's bottom, in favour of the woman's isolation.

As the second holograph progresses, Tom becomes 'Bee' (or B) and later 'Edward', but the woman remains 'W'. A passage of high comedy is introduced in this draft through B's newspaper:

B. 'Rocket strikes xxx Pomona.
Seven hundred thousand missing.'

(***Pause.*** *B turns page. W. resumes gesture xxx of hat towards head, suspends it as Bee reads.*) Rocket strikes —. One female lavatory attendant spared. (*Pause. B turns page. W resumes gesture of hat towards head, suspends it as Bee reads.*)

Rocket strikes —. ~~Six hundred and ninety fif~~ **eighty** ***3*** priests survive.

Further variations on the rocket theme appear in Stage III, but the idea has been omitted in Stage IV, Beckett choosing once again to avoid broad comedy.

Stage II closes with Edward defining a hog and returning to his newspaper, while W gazes happily before her. In Stage III the idea of W's smile fading at the end of the play is introduced. A manuscript alteration reads 'happy expression gone.' Other additions to Stage III establish the names Willie and Winnie. Winnie is first 'W' in Stage III, then 'M' (Mildred) and Willie 'Bee' and 'E' (Edward). Additions also provide early evidence of the network of quotation on which the play rests. M says:

I am lost, in the old sense of course (Quote: Lear 1.1.236?)

As well as providing the quotation reference Beckett has added in the margin:

lost me in your liking (Cordelia to Lear.)

Although this particular quotation disappears in Stage IV, it is the first indication of Beckett's intention to set the play in a literary context,[26] indeed against a backdrop of seventeenth to twentieth century poetry — from Shakespeare to Yeats — a device similar to that used by Virginia Woolf in *Between the Acts*.

Another example of emergent structure in Stage III is the fact that Beckett notes '30 minutes' at the bottom of a page two thirds of the way through the text. The idea of a two-act structure has now occurred to him and becomes the main innovation in the ensuing holograph (Stage IV). The reshaping of the play involved a good deal of cutting, but Act 2, at its first appearance in Stage IV, is much as the final version. Winnie's song at the end of the play is present (though unspecified) and her story of Mildred and the doll is there also. The doll, in its pearly necklet, seems to have some resemblance to Winnie herself and in the episode of undressing the doll there are sexual implications that seem to have a bearing on Winnie's situation, as if she had developed a fear of sex at this time, beyond which she had never progressed. Recollection of the mouse provokes screams in Winnie, thus making it clear that 'Mildred' is her childhood self. 'Mildred', as we have observed, was an early name for Winnie and the story is another example of a Beckett protagonist speaking autobiographically in the third person.

To link Winnie and Mildred still further, Beckett deliberately juxtaposes Winnie's recollection of the Shower/Cooker episode and the Mildred story. Below Winnie's account of the man's puzzlement over what she may be wearing 'underneath', Beckett notes 'continue Mildred', and picks up the story of Mildred and the mouse, thus counterpointing speculation as to Winnie's underwear by the tale of the undressed doll. A mouse, moreover, in Freudian terms, is a phallic symbol. Thus the terrified child might well have become the frigid wife. With this in mind, the mound may be seen as the tomb of Winnie's sexual nature, her distaste for physical contact leading Willie to retreat into his tunnel as the years of refusal pile up around his wife, until she has become unassailable. It is not suggested that this is the sole 'meaning' of the mound. Indeed a reference to 'tally-sticks' in Stage II seems to suggest that Winnie is making sexual demands on her husband, as does Maddy Rooney in *All That Fall*:

> There was a time, do you remember, when once a month was enough for me. (*Pause.*) Don't you remember? (*Pause.* ***Incredulous.***) Once a month! (*Pause.*) Then once a fortnight. (*Pause.*) The tally-sticks, don't you remember the tally-sticks Edward, they must be lying about somewhere still, every thirtieth xxx, then every fifteenth. (*Pause.*) Then weekly. I would wake up as usual, refreshed and without a care . . .

It is also Winnie who attacks her husband with a phallic-looking parasol, 'beak of handle emerging from sheath.' Reversing the picture again, however, Willie is the partner whose animal nature is emphasised in the play. A manuscript alteration in Stage III substitutes 'tail' for a reference to his bottom. There are also his 'hairy forearm', his tunnelling activities in the background, and his final arrival 'on all fours', while Beckett clearly intended his definition of a hog to be self-descriptive. Pornographic postcards are now Willie's only outlet, but who has refused whom in the marriage is ambiguous.

Sexual denial is, however, only one aspect of a mound that is capable of wide interpretation. It may be seen, for example, as the domestic trap, the mental rut, the accumulated trivia of daily living (surmounted by the handbag, emblem of such trivia) and the whole forming a rubbish heap that is also a grave and the heap of years of a dead marriage. That living is dying in Beckett's vocabulary is nowhere more clearly expressed than in the creeping atrophy of death in life in *Happy Days*.

Stage V, the first typescript of Act 2 follows. Manuscript alterations here begin to build up the literary background, 'shade', for example, becoming a Keatsian 'beechen green'. Willie and Winnie are revealed to have had at least one day of romance in the past. It took place in the setting common to Beckett protagonists:

> The sunshade you gave me ... that day ... the lake ... the ~~flags~~ **willows**.

It will be remembered that a discarded direction in Stage II linked Willie (then Tom) and the sunshade, by making Tom's pyjamas and the sunshade of identical stripes. This early detail provides a possible insight into the significance of the sunshade, as the emblem of Willie and Winnie's romance. It was their 'old style', a present from Willie in their romantic heyday, but is now seen to be wholly inadequate, no protection for Winnie against the sun's glare. It tires her arm to hold it up, but she is unable to put it down. Romance has not lasted for the couple, although the marriage yoke in which it resulted (the cause, perhaps, of the 'anthrax' on Willie's neck) cannot be broken.[27] All that remains is a merciless exposure to the reality of the situation. Finally, emphasising the death of love, the parasol goes up in smoke in Act I and Willie is not even aware of it. 'Do you know what has occurred, Willie?' Winnie enquires. But the parasol is there again on the mound intact in Act 2, as inescapable as the marriage itself.

Stage VI, the first typescript of both acts, is remarkable for a manuscript note beside the opening stage directions that reads simply 'vaguen'. The note is twice underlined and is explicit testimony to Beckett's policy of 'vaguening' the later drafts of his plays. His immediate concern in Stage VI is to modify the opening directions, which he does as follows:

Expanse of scorched grass rising front to low mound. The summit, 4' high and at exact centre of rise, is a flattened area about 3' square. The slopes leading up to it on either side are identical in contour. Effect of strict symmetry.

Expanse of scorched grass rising centre to low mound. From summit, a flattened area about 3' sq., the ground slopes gently down to front, left and right of stage. Behind mound abrupt drop to normal stage level.

In the margin of Act 1 a quotation from Gray's 'On a distant Prospect of Eton College' is identified ('And moody madness laughing wild/Amid severest woe.') Furthermore 'Wolfe' is noted in the margin of Act 2, beside the 'go forget me' passage,[28] showing Beckett to be steadily increasing the literary background to the play.

Stage VII, the final holograph, is headed 'Rewriting II'. The title *Happy Days* appears here for the first time. The text has now virtually crystallized, has much less alteration and is more legible. In the opening stage directions Winnie is further linked with the Mildred story by the addition of a 'pearl necklet' to her costume, as worn by the doll. Following the Shower/Cooker anecdote in Act 2, moreover, an unavailing cry for help is introduced into Winnie's text. She then returns to the Mildred story, which immediately culminates in a similar scream for help, thus strengthening the parallel between woman and child. The phrase 'what is that wonderful line?' is introduced in Stage VII to draw attention to the trellis of half-quotations on which the play is built. The quotation from *Romeo and Juliet* is written out on a blank left hand page:

Beauty's ensign yet
Is crimson in thy lips and in thy cheeks
And death's pale flag is not advanced there.

Stage VIII, the penultimate typescript, still has a good deal of alteration. The musical box tune, for example, is at last identified. 'When Irish Eyes are Smiling' had been suggested tentatively in

Stage V and rejected in Stage VI. Beckett now specifies:

the waltz duet 'I love you so' from *The Merry Widow*.

In Stage VIII also, the romantic water image develops into a precise echo of *Krapp's Last Tape*; 'the willows' (which had been changed from 'flags' in Stage V) now become 'the reeds'.

Stage IX has minimal textual alteration, but the substructure of quotations is identified in manuscript in the margins throughout, except for the opening line of Yeats's *At the Hawk's Well*, 'I call to the eye of the mind.' The latter is, however, included in a production notebook.[29] There are other possible literary echoes in the play, but Beckett does not identify these. The departure 'hand in hand' of the Shower/Cookers, for example, may recall the final lines of *Paradise Lost*:

They, hand in hand, with wandering steps and slow
Through Eden took their solitary way.

In Biblical terms Adam and Eve are the forebears of all Winnie's woe and a link with the poem is certainly appropriate for a play in which paradise is so conspicuously absent. Moreover Winnie sees the couple as representative of the human race ('last human kind to stray this way') and, as we have seen in Chapter 4, Act 2 of *Happy Days* opens with the first line of *Paradise Lost* Book III: 'Hail, holy light!' Winnie's literary background does not appear to help her predicament, nor would it make any difference were she able to recall the quotations fully. Her literary half-knowledge seems to be irrelevant to her situation, except in so far as it gives her pleasure, helping (like the habits and rituals with which she structures her day) to stave off the suffering of being.

'Habit', as Beckett points out in *Godot* 'is a great deadener'. The discussion of habit in Beckett's critique of Proust is also highly relevant to *Happy Days*. To omit or remove the protection of habit is to introduce 'suffering' which, says Beckett, 'opens a window on the real.'[30] It is such a confrontation with reality that Winnie experiences at the end of *Happy Days*. Throughout the play she has convinced herself that her greatest happiness would be for Willie to come round to her side of the mound; but, when he finally appears, she does, for a moment, see things as they are. First she chides him, in natural shock at his sudden appearance; next she plays out her fantasy that his arrival is a cause for rejoicing, and sings her song. Only then, when she is left facing the man as he is, does her smile fade. And before she can turn this too into fiction (through what Beckett describes in *Proust* as 'pernicious and incurable optimism')[31] the curtain falls.

The impact of Winnie's moment of truth at the end of the play is increased by the ambiguity surrounding the revolver that is lying on the mound. An early jotting in the 'Été 56' notebook reads:

She: Is it the revolver you are after, dear, or me.

This becomes in Stage VI:

Is it me you're after, Willie . . . Or is it something else?

The rephrasing of the question is an example of ambiguity developing in the play. 'Something else' contains the possibility of the revolver, but no more, and we are left with similar questions to those at the end of *All That Fall*. Willie enters 'dressed to kill' at the end of the play; but is he a ladykiller in the sartorial sense alone, or is it the gun beside his wife he is after; and if so, for whom is it intended? Is he at last about to silence the ceaseless chatter that had driven him into his tunnel and now forces him to attempt to scale the mound; or is it for himself that the gun is required? The ambiguities are beautifully balanced.

There seems to be a clue, however, in a marginal addition to Stage VIII. The revolver, despite its weight, always seems to come to the surface in Winnie's handbag and is thus ever present to her as an escape. But it is one she chooses to ignore: 'I'm tired of you.' Its constant surfacing, however, reminds her of a line from Browning: 'I say confusedly what comes uppermost';[32] Browning is also the name of a brand of revolver. Winnie goes on to refer to the gun as 'Brownie':

Ever uppermost, like Browning. (*Pause.*) **Brownie. (*Turning a little towards Willie.*) Remember Brownie, Willie? (*Pause.*) Remember how you used to keep on at me to take it away from you? Take it away, Winnie, take it away before I put myself out of my misery (*Pause. Back front, Derisive.*) *Your* misery!**

Winnie's scorn is as much for her husband's moaning as for his possible suicide; but this late addition to the text suggests the probable use to which the gun would be put, should Willie reach it.

The drafts of *Happy Days* thus help us to gain insights into the play that are largely obscured by ambiguities in the published version. Successive drafts also change the tone of the play considerably. The omission of the alarm clock in Stage IV, for example, in favour of an 'invisible bell' means that Winnie no longer controls 'the hour for waking' but is controlled by an unseen force similar to that generating the light in *Play* or the goad in *Acte sans paroles II*. The Stage IV 'Rewrite' also reduces the number of objects enumerated in Winnie's handbag, thus cutting down her pastimes and intensifying her isolation. In Stage II she had had a wider selection:

> ~~Down at the bottom in particular.~~ **The ~~xxxx~~ deeper layers in particular.** ~~God~~. **Heaven** knows what forgotten treasures, letters, ~~xxx~~ **favours,** ribbons, trinkets, petals, **dance cards with pencils,** theatre and concert programmes. (***Pause.*** *Break in voice.*) Prospectuses. (*Pause.* Do.[33]) Buttons.

Beckett clearly had it in mind in the early revisions in Stage II to emphasize Winnie's isolation by reducing the role of Willie, first banishing him from view and then cutting down his speeches. The result is a starkness both of image and situation at the opening of the play, in which no distraction or mitigation is permitted. As Gontarski points out, Beckett moves, in the drafts:

> not toward a naturalistic, precisely-defined physical world, but toward an abstract clarity, an image free of cluttering detail.[34]

The decision to make the play two acts instead of one also had the happy effect of intensifying Winnie's predicament. The largely comic tone of Act 1 gives place to the increasing horror of Act 2, and precisely because we have accepted the comedy of Winnie's situation in the first act, the implications of the second are the more chilling. The final result thus achieves the balance that Beckett had originally desired in *Fin de partie*:

> Act 1. Hilare. Act 2. Mortellement triste.[35]

Breath

Breath, as is well known, resulted from a request by Kenneth Tynan to Beckett for a short piece for the review *Oh! Calcutta* that Tynan was staging in New York. Among his unpublished MSS. Beckett found a text that he thought might be suitable and this was used by Tynan as the opening sequence of the American production of *Oh! Calcutta* on 17 June 1969. But Tynan decided to extend Beckett's stage directions to include nude figures:

Faint light onstage littered with miscellaneous rubbish, including naked people.[36]

Beckett promptly withdrew permission for the performance of his text and it did not appear in the subsequent London production of *Oh! Calcutta* in 1970.

I have been unable to trace the original manuscript of *Breath*, although two holograph versions and a typescript have come to light. Facing the text, in the first authorised publication of the work, is a photocopy of one holograph version; since there are no alterations, this appears to be a fair copy and the printed text is identical with it.[37] A typescript given to Francis Warner by Beckett in 1969 may predate the Calder text in that it is untitled, while the published holograph and text are headed *Breath*. The wording of Calder's text and the Warner typescript is identical and corresponds with the Faber text of 1971. Both are undated. Warner states that on asking Beckett whether he had any new work for performance in Oxford, Beckett gave him the typescript, remarking that he would be glad of a production of the work as it was intended to be performed, rather than the American travesty. Warner's production took place on 8 March 1970 at the Oxford Playhouse. When the production was revived at Hart House Theatre, Toronto, on 16 November 1970, Beckett gave Warner a holograph version for inclusion in the programme.This was written from memory and signed 'Samuel Beckett 1969'. The date is clearly the date of composition, since Beckett wrote this version in the summer of 1970.

There are several discrepancies between this holograph version and the Calder text. There is no reference to an opening and closing 'curtain', for example; instead Beckett writes 'Black' each time. Probably with Tynan's liberties with the text in mind, the first direction is made more ambiguous, describing 'miscellaneous *unidentifiable* rubbish'. The second direction reads 'faint cry' (rather than 'faint *brief* cry') and instructions for the second cry in direction 3 ('and immediately cry as before') are also omitted. Since this version was written from memory, however, it cannot be deemed a variant draft.

Lessness

The drafts of *Lessness* were written, according to Beckett, 'about 1969'; the draft material is undated. Since this work has already been discussed in Chapter 3 for the considerable insight it affords into Beckett's structural craftsmanship, it would seem inappropriate to exclude discussion of the draft material merely on the grounds that it is not a play. I have therefore decided to include a description of the drafts of *Lessness* at their chronological place in the exploration of draft material in this chapter.

The drafts, in the Beinecke Rare Book and Manuscript Library at Yale University, show Beckett at work translating *Lessness* from the French version, *Sans*. They are of particular interest for the explanatory material that Beckett sent with them. The extent of the Yale material is as follows: first there is what Beckett describes as a 'MS. reduction of French text to 6 statement groups for translation purposes'. There follow a heavily revised holograph of Beckett's first attempt at rendering these statement groups into English, and a typescript fair copy, also much altered. A holograph 'notation' of the sentence and paragraph order that resulted from the shuffling process ensues. This is identical with the holograph arrangement of *Sans* (headed 'Montage') that can be seen at Appendix II. After this come a holograph and corrected typescript of the first twelve paragraphs of *Lessness*. Finally there is a typescript of the whole text, also somewhat revised.

Beckett's explanatory material consists partly of the introduction to *Lessness* that appears on the dust jacket of the Calder text, together with what he describes in his analysis of the material sent to Yale as the 'key' to the work. The latter is a structural description, in which Beckett isolates the themes on which the work is based. It is here reproduced in full:

LESSNESS proceeds from PING.
It is composed of 6 statement groups each containing 10 sentences, i.e. 60 sentences in all.

These 60 are first given in a certain order and paragraph structure, then repeated in a different order and different paragraph structure.

The whole consists therefore of $2 \times 60 = 120$ sentences arranged and rearranged in $2 \times 12 = 24$ paragraphs.

Each statement group is formally differentiated and the 10 sentences composing it 'signed' by certain elements common to them all.

Group A — Collapse of refuge — Sign: 'True refuge'.

Group B — Outer world — Sign: 'earth . . . sky' juxtaposed or apart.

Group C — Body exposed — Sign: 'little body'.

Group D — Refuge forgotten — Sign: 'all gone from mind'.

Group E — Past and future denied — Sign: 'never' —
except in the one sentence 'figment dawn . . . . . etc.'.

Group F — Past and future affirmed — Sign: future tense'.[38]

Completing the key is a typescript of the finished translation, again in its statement groups, duly lettered and numbered, and a typescript of the sentence order and paragraph structure.

The composition of *Sans/Lessness* has already been discussed at some length. It is one of the most highly organised and, at the same time, the least formal of Beckett's works. To subject a careful structure to the hazard of the shuffling process is perhaps the most rigorous test of his work that a writer can devise, and that each new combination of sentences forms a satisfying whole indicates the quality of Beckett's achievement. The ambiguity of the final text is extreme. Beckett's Preface to the published text allows a reader some insight into its themes:

> *Lessness* has to do with the collapse of some such refuge as that last attempted in *Ping* and with the ensuing situation of the refugee.
>
> Ruin, exposure, wilderness, mindlessness, past and future denied and affirmed, are the categories, formally distinguishable, through which the writing winds, first in one disorder, then in another . . .

But such a Preface gives no indication of the precise structuring of *Lessness*. It gives the 'signature' to each family of sentences (and the reader will recognize these as they recur in the text) but the mathematical nature of the work is entirely obscured. The sentences cannot be recognized individually (as, for instance, A1 or F10) so that the piece cannot be read through from first to last and the development that we have observed in Chapter 3 appreciated.

It was not Beckett's purpose, however, for the work to be stripped to its roots in the manner in which we explored the text in Chapter 3. The rigorous structuring of each sentence has produced a text that will communicate landscape, mood and tone colour in no matter what order it is read. Each reordered text develops its own strength from a new juxtaposition of sentences, each sentence giving just enough information to add its particular colour to the pattern, but never enough to throw the work out of balance when shuffled. Nothing less than a perfect balance of language and statement has made this possible. The writing of *Lessness* reveals a development similar to that we have seen throughout the drafts of Beckett's plays. As the work evolves the original statement is obscured, until the final text has become a balancing of possibilities in the scales of ambiguity. As

Beckett remarked to Martin Esslin, when comparing his own method of working with that of James Joyce:

> The difference between Joyce and myself is that Joyce was a synthesiser. He tried to pack the whole world into a book, in as much detail as possible, and I am an analyser, I try to take as much of the detail away as possible.[39]

CHAPTER 10
WORKING METHOD

It is evident, as Gontarski comments, that knowing how an author works and 'what sorts of additions, excisions, or alterations he makes, is a valuable aid to literary criticism.'[1] Several conclusions about Beckett's working method may be drawn from a consideration of his draft material. Firstly, there is the question of planning a work. Where an initial plan is present among the drafts, Beckett's careful attention to detail is apparent. We have observed, for example, in Chapter 2, the outline for a play in which the potential text is timed before writing and we have noticed in Chapter 3 the extraordinary precision of planning of the sentence structure of *Lessness*, without which the text could not have emerged satisfactorily from the shuffling process. The early stages of *Come and Go* and *Not I* as seen in Chapter 7, again reveal meticulous structural planning to be part of Beckett's working method. Nonetheless he is also prepared to shape his plays according to the demands of the evolving text and sometimes to make radical changes, rather than stick rigidly to a preconceived plan. This is evident from the reshaping of both *Fin de partie* and *Happy Days*, where the act structure finally decided upon in each case reverses the original intention.

Careful self-analysis has been seen to be part of Beckett's approach when drafting a text. In the preliminary material for *Not I*, for example, we have observed him analysing the emerging text at various stages in its development. After writing the first fragment, *Kilcool*, he jotted aides-mémoire in the Trinity College notebook, to be borne in mind when attempting future drafts and went on to lay down eight themes on which the play should be based. Then, after writing the holograph of *Not I* some eight years later, Beckett made the 'analysis' of the text which can be seen at Appendix IV and decided that certain points required amplification. These, as we have observed, were subsequently drafted under the heading 'addenda'. Finally, after completing the play, Beckett produced the 'synopsis' which can be seen at Appendix V. The final text has thus emerged through an exhaustive process of repeated creation and analysis.

In our investigation of Beckett's manuscript material we have several times observed him thinking ahead while writing a draft; jotting, on a page facing an earlier section of text, notes that he subsequently incorporates into a later section. An early example of this process is the holograph of *All That Fall*, where, three pages before the end, Beckett notes the following:

Conversation with Jerry.
He runs off.
Mrs. K. calls to him. What kept the train late.
A child fell out of the carriage.
Pause.
Jerry runs off. **His** receding steps. Silence.
Storm of wind and rain.

These points all occur in the same order when the final page of text is drafted. A similar example occurs in *Words and Music*. The end of the play is once more being plotted, this time in the margin of the holograph; two pages before its close, the following note forecasts the shape the text will take:

End
Words: (*alarmed*). My Lord.
Departure of Croak.
Words recalls briefly themes. etc.

A last illustration, taken from the holograph of *Eh Joe*, is particularly interesting. Here a list of words facing the concluding passage of text is expanded into the final lines of the play:

Imagine
Stone
Joe Joe
stones
(more imagines) *lips* imagine
solitaire
eyes
~~girl~~ **June**
Breasts
Imagine
stones
fondling

Love for you
Eh Joe
Eh Joe

The encircled note is clearly crucial in the development of the final lines of *Eh Joe*. Since the word 'imagine' only appears three times in the entire preceding text it seems likely that Beckett realised that a concentration of the imperative in the final passage would effectively increase the pressure on Joe at the climax of the play. It is precisely his imaginative recreation of the girl's suicide and his resultant sense of guilt that has been haunting his imagination since her death. Beckett appears to have jotted down the list in response to the idea of increasing the imaginative pressure and then drafted the final passage on the opposite page. In response to the encircled note, he adds one more 'imagine' to the list of words (above) when drafting the text. It is evident from the manuscript that Beckett had some difficulty in arriving at the final lines and his changes of mind may be clearly seen as he develops the list of words and phrases:

~~Leave the rest to your imagination~~ **Now *imagine*** ... Before she went out ... Face in the hole ... ~~Joe Joe~~ ... **Lips on a *stone*** ... Thinking of you ... *Joe Joe* ... Moon gone ... From the shore ... From the ~~sea~~ **sea** ... Joe Joe ... To the *stones* ... Say it you now ... ~~say~~ **No one'll hear you** ... Say *Joe* ... It parts the *lips* ... *Imagine* the hands ... ~~small t~~ **The *solitaire*** ... Against a stone ... Imagine the *eyes* ... How they opened after ... ~~The xxxx xxx xxx xxx one~~ ... **Can you hear me, Joe?** ... ~~The girl for Him~~ **— one** ... ~~***Spirit of light***~~ ... **Month of *June*** ... **What year was that!**[2] ... Not even pregnant ... *Breasts* in the shingle ... And the *hands* ... **Before they go out** ... *Imagine* the hands ... What are they doing ... In the *stones* ... (*Image down, sound on*) What are they *fondling*? ... Until they grow quiet ... There's *love for you* ... ~~wouldn't~~ (*Image out, sound on.*) ~~**Istn't it Wasn't it**~~ **Isn't it, Joe?** ... Wasn't it, Joe? ... *Eh Joe*? ... Compared to us ... ~~Compared to you~~ ... **Compared to ~~God~~ Him**[3] ... *Eh Joe*?

End

The reduction and refining of Beckett's later writing takes place in every aspect of his work. From the spate of words of *The Unnamable* in prose, for example, to the first publication of *Lessness* on a single page of the *New Statesman*.[4] In drama the three acts of his first play, *Éleuthéria*, dwindle to the sigh of *Breath*, while the archetypal waiting situation in *Godot* is reduced to 121 words in *Come and Go*. With fewer words, the tendency to use a still bolder image has appeared in the plays. The dustbins of *Endgame*, for example, from which, at intervals, named human beings show themselves, give place to three nameless and immobile heads in urns in *Play* and finally to the disembodied mouth of *Not I*. As the text of the briefest plays is cut to a skeletal outline, detailed directions are required in order to convey meaning. Thus *Come and Go* has more directions than text and *Breath* consists entirely of directions.

An important part of Beckett's process of refining a text is the enrichment of language brought about by a rigorous cutting and shaping. A search for the allusive word may be noticed throughout the drafts and the choice of alliterative or assonantal words or phrases for euphonic purposes. In *Krapp's Last Tape*, for example, we can see how changing two words used in the holograph opens up wider possibilities in the text. In Typescript 2 'widowhood' becomes the archaic 'viduity' thus allowing Krapp some useful by-play with the dictionary. In Typescript 4 'moonstone' is changed to 'chrysolite', a word of great beauty which thus reflects and allows us to glimpse something of the beauty of the eyes Krapp remembers and also introduces links with the imagery of *Othello*, as discussed in Chapter 9.

The drafts of *Eh Joe* provide several further examples of the enrichment of language. In Typescript 1 'like ~~Waterford cut~~ **flint** glass' cleverly introduces the idea of stone that is picked up at the end of the play when the girl lies dying in the stones at the tide's edge. In the same draft 'no more old ~~chat~~ **lip** from her' puns on the incessant voice in Joe's head and the fact that it belongs to a cast-off mistress. In Typescript 2 'not another soul to ~~exterminate~~ **still'** both introduces ambiguity and greatly improves the aural effect. At times, however, Beckett realises his delight in assonance and alliteration should be curbed. Thus, in the final draft of 'Before *Come and Go*' at Reading University, he prunes Vi's description of being telephoned by Rose's husband, who 'was weeping over the wire' and Poppy's equally extravagant remark about Rose:

> Ghastly. I was aghast when I came in and saw her sitting there.

Beckett's word changes in the drafts frequently suggest the poet at work. It is interesting therefore to compare them with changes made when he is actually writing a poem. The development of the lyric from holograph to first typescript in *Words and Music* may be taken as an example here:

Holograph

Age is when ~~if you're~~ **to** a man
~~Crouching shivering over the dying~~ **Huddled over the ingle**
Waiting for the old hag
To put the ~~bottle~~ **jar** in the bed
And ~~come with~~ **bring** the toddy
She comes in the ashes
Who loved could not be won
Or won not loved
Comes in the ashes
Like in that old~~en~~ light
Her ~~eyes~~ **face** in the ashes
~~Like in t~~That old~~en~~ starlight
Lying on the earth again.

Typescript 1

Age is when to a man
Huddled over the ingle
~~Waiting~~ **Shivering** for the hag
To put the ~~jar~~ **pan** in the bed
And bring the toddy
She comes in the ashes
Who loved could not be won
Or won not loved
Or some~~thing else~~ other ~~thing~~ trouble
Comes in the ashes
Like in that old light
The face in the ashes
That old starlight
~~Lying o~~ **O**n the earth again.

'Huddled over the ingle' is both more economical, understressed (and consequently more telling) than 'crouching shivering over the dying'. 'Shivering', moreover, is used in the revision to add colour to the succeeding line. The idea of lost sexuality is present at the outset in 'comes in the ashes', but the verb is weakened by its earlier use in 'come with the toddy', which is therefore altered in the typescript to 'bring'. The removal of the archaism 'olden' from the penultimate line prevents the ensuing word 'starlight' from sounding over-sentimental, but in order to keep the rhythm, the word 'lying' with its implications of romantic delusion has then to be sacrificed from the last line. Verse two evolved easily in the holograph and there are only two main changes in it in the first typescript: 'dark' instead of 'still' and the omission of 'dear' from 'Through the dear scum'. The lyric has thus taken only two drafts to complete. There are no further changes in it in the second and final typescript.

The process of word polishing we have observed in the drafts of the plays is no different from that in the lyric. Having settled the basic form of the text, Beckett begins to shape the vocabulary until it is, as Zilliacus notices in the drafts of *All That Fall*, 'gradually enriched and enlivened.'[5] Beckett's linguistic alteration is of course considerably more than 'polishing'. The characteristic search for the evocative and resonant word to replace earlier more prosaic, non-dramatic vocabulary is his strength as both writer and dramatist. The process, generally one of rigorous selection combined with a limited accretion, may take many drafts to complete. In *Play*, for example, Woman 1's description of her rival evolves over five typescripts:

1

S 1 Horse face, spotty, calves like a ~~beefeater~~ **flunkey,** dugs you could —

This version remains in Typescripts 2 and 3. Typescript 4, however, not only adds a good deal of material, but splits the invective into two sections, with a speech from Woman 2 herself intervening:

4

W 1 ~~Horse face, spotty, calves like a flunkey, dugs you could —~~
Moon face, puffy, spots, 2 moles with hair, eyes passable, give her her due, mouth, blubber pout, jowls, no neck, dugs you could —
[*W 2*]
W 1 **Knobble knees, calves like a flunkey, varicose —**

5

W 1 ~~Moon~~**Pudding** face, puffy, spots, blubber mouth, jowls, no neck, dugs you could —
[*W 2*]
W 1 Calves like a flunkey —

To conclude this examination of Beckett at work I have attempted to reproduce a detailed record of four plays, as a practical illustration of his working method through successive drafts. To do this presents some intractable problems of both method and presentation: whether, for example, it is easier for the reader to assimilate information through a description of the material, or by looking at a chart. Clearly the method adopted must depend to some extent on the nature of the material for each play. Both have been attempted; in Appendix VII *Not I* is explored in chart form while the drafts of three further plays, *Play, That Time* and *Footfalls* are looked at chronologically.

CHAPTER 11
STAGECRAFT

It is a natural progression to look at Beckett's stagecraft in this chapter, since it is only in this way that the extra dimension to his dramatic writing can be appreciated. Having observed the painstaking creation of dramatic texts through numerous drafts, it is necessary to consider how they work onstage since, clearly, no play exists simply on the page, but needs to be brought to life in the theatre.

It is here that Beckett's dramatic imagination has been so exciting and uncompromising that it has had an incalculable influence on the contemporary theatre. As Peter Hall remarked after a performance of *Happy Days*, which was the National Theatre's opening production in 1976:

> Beckett has changed the way we do Shakespeare, the way we act, the way we write and the way we direct in the theatre.[1]

It was Kenneth Tynan who, on seeing *Waiting for Godot* some twenty years earlier, had realised that conventional concepts of dramatic possibility would no longer suffice. '*Waiting for Godot*', he said, 'forced me to re-examine the rules which have hitherto governed the drama; and, having done so, to pronounce them not elastic enough.'[2] Beckett has not only enlarged and extended 'the rules' by refusing to be bound by theatrical convention, but he even manages to 'make theatre out of the deliberate abnegation of the theatrical' as Gordon Macdougall, director of the Oxford Playhouse Theatre once suggested to me. Beckett's extraordinary restriction of the actor's movement and reduction of his vocal range to an unaccented monotone, is apparently anti-theatrical – contrary to every preconception about the nature of theatre. In performance, however, it is extraordinarily effective. Innovatory dramatic concepts of this kind have proved to be one of Beckett's greatest strengths as a dramatist. For audiences prepared to make the initial effort to overcome resistance to an unfamiliar theatrical technique, his plays have a direct subjective appeal.

Each part of Beckett's stagecraft is analysed in this chapter, in order to see how, why and indeed whether it works in the theatre. Since the art of theatre is the joining together of numerous parts to form a composite whole, it is obviously artificial to attempt to separate the parts from each other, isolating light from image, for example. At the same time it is essential to an understanding of the process of theatre to be able to see how each part operates and has its particular function in the formation of the whole. Most critics of Beckett's plays remark on his theatrical originality, but there is as yet no breakdown of his stagecraft into all its various components. In this chapter, therefore, the process of theatre as used by Beckett is discussed under headings such as *image and metaphor, space and setting, movement*, focussing, in each case, on the original nature of his dramatic concepts. Since each part of the process contributes to the same whole, it is inevitable that some repetition will occur in attempting to isolate each area for separate discussion. Moreover it is occasionally necessary for certain matters already raised in the previous investigations of pattern and drafts to reappear, with an altered focus. The focus here is the stage context. The plays are discussed *not* as texts, but dramatic artefacts — how they work in the theatre.

Beckett's theatrical choices are usually fundamentally simple. Having approached dramatic convention without preconception as to what may be attempted, he has experimented successfully in several branches of theatre: stage, radio, film and television, studying the potentialities of each medium. Indeed the apparent restrictions of each seem to stimulate him, resulting in the freshness of approach that is his dramatic signature. Since he creates each work for a particular genre, Beckett has until recently tended to resist directorial attempts to translate it from one medium to another. Of *All That Fall*, for example, he wrote:

It is no more theatre than *End-Game* is radio and to 'act' it is to kill it

adding:

If we can't keep our genres more or less distinct, or extricate them from the confusion that has them where they are, we might as well go home and lie down.[3]

Beckett's works for radio and for the camera are therefore discussed under separate headings.

IMAGE AND METAPHOR

Beckett demands more from the audience than they have been accustomed to give. Today's audiences are, however, becoming increasingly familiar with Beckett's dramatic terminology and increasingly prepared to think beyond the initial hurdle of the strangeness of the dramatic image, a woman stuck in a mound of earth, for example, heads emerging from urns, or a disembodied mouth. In 1955 audiences streamed from the theatre, outraged by the static nature of *Waiting for Godot*. Compared with the later plays, however, *Godot* now seems almost conventional. At least its characters converse, are relatively mobile and the play takes place in a stylised but recognisable setting; *Endgame* and *Krapp's Last Tape* are similar in style.

From *Happy Days* to *Footfalls*, however, Beckett's visual images become increasingly startling, in settings that have no pretensions to be representational, except in so far as they are dramatic metaphors, accurately reflecting a human predicament. Winnie's mound in *Happy Days* is a decisive instance of this and the extraordinary image communicates directly, as does the mouth speaking from space in *Not I*; moreover the gigantic figure of the auditor in *Not I* becomes a metaphor for pity and helplessness in the face of human suffering and error.

Comparing Beckett's plays with those of Sartre, John Fletcher describes the latter as 'competent dramatizations of political and philosophical discussions', whereas 'Beckett's are powerful and vital dramatic images in their own right.' Analysing the metaphor of *Fin de partie*, he points out that:

> (it) is the stage itself. Hamm, like a ham actor, plays to an imaginary audience. He delivers his 'story' in a theatrical manner, pausing every so often to comment on his own performance; likewise Nagg, in his tailor joke. Clov points his telescope at the audience and remarks ironically on their delirious enjoyment of the fun. We are in a world where all is illusion and all is play: we are in the theatre, but a theatre that Shakespeare would have understood — *theatrum mundi*, or all the world a stage.[4]

The stage as a metaphor for living is of course particularly appropriate to the cyclical view of existence revealed in Beckett's plays. Not only is a cyclic element already present in both text and action (in, for example, *Play* or *Not I*), but the nightly repetition of the play itself implies a similar inability to reach an end, in absolute terms, to that experienced by Beckett's protagonist narrators. Indeed the figure patiently paced out each night on her strip of stage by May in *Footfalls*:

> One two three four five six seven wheel
> one two three four five six seven wheel

may be seen as the visual equivalent of the mathematical symbol for infinity: ∞

Martin Esslin points to the immediate visual impact of Beckett's dramatic metaphors:

> Drama of the kind Beckett writes is poetry of concrete, three-dimensional stage images, complex metaphors communicable in a flash of visual intuitive understanding. [ ] In plays like *Not I, That Time* and *Footfalls* it is by no means essential that the audience in the theatre should be able to decode the complex story lines and intellectual puzzles they enshrine. On the contrary, what the audience should experience [ ] is precisely the *overall impact* of a single overwhelmingly powerful image . . .[5]

The boldness of Beckett's stage imagery develops markedly after *Krapp's Last Tape*. From a concentration on the head and face that began in *Happy Days*, was continued in *Play*, became conspicuous by default in *Film*, reappeared in *Eh Joe*, dwindled to a mouth in *Not I*, only to reemerge in *That Time*, Beckett turns to the opposite end of the body in *Footfalls* and uses not visible feet, but the sound that they make, as a metaphor for living and re-living. This calls to mind Giacometti's remark that he was sculpting not the human figure, but 'the shadow that is cast.'[6] Giacometti's work was certainly known to Beckett and he designed the tree for Beckett's Paris production of *Godot* in 1961. Rather like *Come and Go*, where the faces are shaded and light concentrates on the hands, *Footfalls* has 'least (light) on head'. Instead, the floor where May's feet pace unseen, hidden by her 'worn grey wrap' is emphasized, to prepare the way for her disappearance at the end of the play.

In *Footfalls* and *That Time* Beckett has dispensed with certain concrete metaphors from earlier plays, though still dealing with similar themes. In *Footfalls* the image of parents in dustbins so dominant in *Endgame* has disappeared, and instead the mother's voice emerges from the darkness in her daughter's mind.

Similarly the voices first heard on the tape recorder in *Krapp's Last Tape* are still present in *That Time*, but they now alternate in the skull of the old man whose sleeping face we see. The abandonment of the concrete image in the two later plays allows a more fluid, stream of consciousness approach to language. It is possible that Beckett's stage imagery has become more radical as his options steadily narrow, since a new image to express largely the same themes is required for each new play. On the other hand it can be argued that it has been possible for Beckett to adopt a less concrete approach as audiences become more familiar with his dramatic technique. His later images stem directly from *The Unnamable* and give visual embodiment to the predicament of a consciousness trapped and unable to cease.

SPACE AND SETTING

Part of the presentation of stage image is the manipulation of space, and here again Beckett shows himself to be a master craftsman. From the beginning his sets were economical: a divided set in *Éleuthéria*; a tree on a country road in *Godot*; a 'bare interior' that, with its high rear windows, is sometimes said to resemble a skull in *Endgame*; a table in *Krapp*, a mound in *Happy Days*. Thereafter, with the exception of the urns in *Play* and the bench in *Come and Go*, there is no stage furniture at all. Beckett's protagonists are either suspended in space (as in *Not I* and *That Time*) or pace a strip of stage (as in *Footfalls*). From 1976 onwards, as will be seen in the next chapter, there has been a return to a minimal use of stage furniture: a lamp and part of a pallet in *A Piece of Monologue*, a chair in *Rockaby*, a table, chairs and a book in *Ohio Impromptu*. *Catastrophe* has a realistic theatre interior, but with the stage bare, except for a chair and a plinth. In *What Where* the only 'furniture' is a megaphone, which turns out to be the protagonist! The chair in *Rockaby* also has elements of personification. Its 'inward curving arms' and W's reference to it as 'mother rocker' suggest the mother's embrace.

'All I want on the stage is a pair of blubbering lips' Beckett remarked to Desmond Ryan and his cousin John Beckett as early as 1958.[7] In achieving this object in 1972 with *Not I*, space became an important ingredient in Beckett's dramatic imagery and was used again in *That Time*. In both plays Beckett appropriates for his action what has always been considered unusable space outside the circus — mid-air itself. It is a challenge to convention similar to that represented by his prose in a literary context:

My little exploration is that whole zone of being that has always been set aside by artists as something unusable — as something by definition incompatible with art.[8]

Beckett creates in his audience an extraordinary awareness of offstage space. In *Godot*, for example, M. Godot remains unseen, but sends emissaries from his domain offstage; a boy is glimpsed from a window in *Fin de partie*. In the latter play too the audience is made aware of the blasted landscape and dead sea outside the windows, as of the bottle-filled offstage darkness in *Krapp's Last Tape*. Perhaps the most surprising example is Willie's unseen crawl in *Happy Days*, for which Beckett drew careful diagrams in a production notebook.[9]

In the mimes there are mysterious unseen forces, offstage tyrants who entice, command or prod Beckett's protagonists into action, catapulting the man back onstage in *Acte sans paroles I*, for instance, and then taunting him with descending and retreating 'comforts'. The merciless (if comic) goad in *Acte sans paroles II* is of the same species, as are the bells controlling Winnie's day in *Happy Days*. In the later plays the light in *Play* appears to be generated offstage, the voices in *That Time* sound from space above and to each side of the old man's head, while the women in *Come and Go* drift silently in and out of an enveloping darkness, like that into which May disappears at the end of *Footfalls*. Beckett in these ways makes maximum use of theatrical space, though he is often said to use only a very small portion of it.

MOVEMENT

The mimes were written in 1956, before the pattern of restricted movement set in *Fin de partie* became Beckett's dramatic 'signature'. To those familiar with the Beckett world the mimes often seem over-explicit. It should be remembered, however, that the object of mime is such clear visual communication with an audience that words are redundant. Beckett's comment on the mime Marcel Marceau points the difference between the languages of word and gesture: 'With Marceau', he remarked, 'I always feel the absence of words; the need for them.'[10] Marceau goes beyond straightforward communication through gesture to the kind of complexities for which words are more suitable. Beckett avoids such a trap in the *Actes sans paroles* which communicate directly — even with audiences who know nothing of his other work.

In the later plays, apart from the role of light in stage movement (to be discussed separately) and the ritualized movements in *Come and Go, Footfalls* and the later television plays, it is the minimal movement of static characters that holds audience attention. In *Happy Days*, for example, after the initial impact of the stage image is over, Beckett succeeds in holding attention by a series of small movements connected with the handbag and by a technique of arrested gesture, such as Winnie's delay in donning her hat. Winnie's slightest movements become extraordinarily important, since they are almost the only ones in the play. Moreover her running commentary on the movement in progress, whether her husband's or her own, focusses attention still further:

(*testing upper front teeth with thumb, indistinctly*) — good Lord! — (*pulling back corner of mouth, mouth open, do.*) — ah well — (*other corner, do.*) — no worse — (*abandons inspection, normal speech*) — no better, no worse — (*lays down mirror*) — no change — (*wipes fingers on grass*) — no pain —

In Act 2 only the infinitesimal movements of Winnie's face, of her eyes, nose and mouth are left, until the arrival of Willie, yet the concentration is such that attention does not flag. The same is true of *Not I*, where the luminous lips moving in darkness are sometimes described as a 'mesmeric' image. In *Eh Joe* where Joe's face dominates the camera, just before the woman's voice drops to a whisper at the end of the play, a manuscript note in the final typescript reads 'Eyes remember'. The direction does not appear in the published text and seems, therefore, to have been a rehearsal note; but it shows the immense concentration that Beckett was demanding from his actor, movement having dwindled to a flicker in the eyes. Jack Macgowran, for whom the play was written, called it 'the most gruelling 22 minutes I have ever had in my life', while acknowledging its suitability for television:

It's really photographing the mind. It's the nearest perfect play for television that you could come across, because the television camera photographs the mind better than anything else.[11]

STAGE DIRECTIONS

No playwright has more exacting stage directions than Beckett. To alter the directions may destroy the meaning of a play, as with a production of *Come and Go* I once saw, where, following a chatty confidence from Flo ('I can feel the rings') the curtain descended smartly, preventing any observation of the women's hands. Investigation of the form generally taken by Beckett's stage directions reveals, for example, that 'character' details are never given, though fairly detailed physical descriptions are sometimes present, as with Krapp, Winnie, Joe and May. The only interpretative hint as to character comes in the 'helpless compassion' note that follows the text of *Not I*. Notes on the text occur only in the later plays, from *Play* onwards. It is a natural result of the reduction of dialogue, of less requiring more. In *Come and Go*, for example, notes and stage directions form the bulk of the text and the latest plays for television, *Quad* and *Nacht und Träume*, consist entirely of directions for camera moves, with no words at all.

From *Play* onwards Beckett uses either silence (radio's tool for marking different phases in a text) or blackout (its stage equivalent) or a combination of the two to structure his plays into separate scenes. Thus *Play* is divided by blackouts, *Not I* and *That Time* by silence and *Footfalls* by both. Apart from such structural use, the most important function of Beckett's stage directions is to carry the climaxes of his plays. One of his most typical means of bringing about a climax is the use of surprise or shock endings, dramatic stings in the tail that are designed to throw the preceding text sharply into focus.

DRAMATIC CLIMAXES

The endings of Beckett's plays are generally a balancing of ambiguities. In *Godot* there is simply the contradiction between speech ('Yes, let's go') and direction ('They do not move'.) It is a situation of stalemate, already experienced at the end of the first act. *Endgame* also ends in impasse, Clov is dressed to leave but still present. Alec Reid remarks:

> The curtain falls with Clov standing on the threshold, but we must decide for ourselves whether he will cross it or not.[12]

It is in his first radio play that Beckett begins to develop the ambiguity of an ending to something approaching thriller proportions. The presentation of the ball to Mr. Rooney in *All That Fall* appears to link him with the child's death, of which the audience is told in the last lines of the play. As the listener speculates on this, directions for a twice-repeated:

Tempest of wind and rain

are given, and this becomes virtually an objective correlative for the growing suspicion aroused in the listener that Mr. Rooney may have murdered the child. A somewhat similar weight of suspicion occurs at the end of *Happy Days*, where, after smiling at Willie, Winnie's final direction reads:

Smile off. They look at each other. Long pause.

In this pause the audience recalls Willie's struggles to reach perhaps his wife, perhaps the gun. Since his back is to the auditorium we can gain no clue to his intention from his expression, but Peter Hall's 1975 National Theatre production, at which Beckett assisted, gave the play a distinctly menacing close.

The close of both *Cascando* and *That Time* is marked by a climactic silence. In *Eh Joe*, too, the actor Jack Macgowran felt the end of the play to be a silence achieved:

It's a little victory he has at the end in dismissing the voice; he finally crushes it.[13]

This is not necessarily the case, however, indeed rather the reverse. The woman's voice certainly drops to a whisper on the final page, but, in the penultimate stage direction, Joe's face fades also, and, in the last direction, the fading image and sibilant voice disappear together:

Voice and image out. End.

Again the outcome is ambiguous. In the context of the play Joe's escape from the voice is a possible interpretation, but in the wider context of Beckett's drama, escape from a situation of torture is rare.

Among the remaining works *Krapp's Last Tape* and *Embers* apparently end inconclusively, with Krapp and Henry still living in the past, as they were when the plays began. But the final direction in *Krapp's Last Tape*:

The tape runs on in silence.

may be seen as functional. Krapp's spool of life is almost wound, and the silent tape is both the time it has left to run and the silence into which he must pass. *Film* ends in a climax of self-confrontation, the precise reverse of *Not I* which closes on a final evasion of selfhood. In the disappearance of May at the end of *Footfalls* and the slow inclination of W's head at the end of *Rockaby* the dramatic situation is extended beyond the final words to register an ending for both characters. The latest stage plays, *Ohio Impromptu* and *Catastrophe* both culminate in heads being raised at the end in confrontation. Beckett is still using the same dramatic formula of presenting a final climax to the action and in several cases the climax introduces a shock effect that requires an audience to refocus its view of the play. The ambiguities on which the plays close are a major source of dramatic strength.

MAKEUP AND COSTUME

Beckett's makeup directions are extreme. In the earlier plays they range from the masklike 'very red' and 'very white' faces in *Endgame* to Krapp's 'White face. Purple nose. Disordered grey hair', the traditional makeup of the clown (an impression reinforced by an immense pair of narrow, pointed white boots). In the later plays hands rather than faces are emphasized by makeup in *Come and Go*; the faces in *Play* are 'so lost to age and aspect as to seem almost part of urns'; while the mouth, the only visible facial area in *Not I*, is customarily painted a luminous white, though there are as yet no makeup directions in the text.

Apart from Hamm's bloodstained handkerchief no costume colour is specified in *Godot* or *Endgame*. In subsequent plays, such as *Krapp's Last Tape* and *Footfalls*, Beckett specifies the colours he requires, either a contrast of black and white or the median colour, grey. The same colour scheme informs the world of the later prose, as for example in *Lessness*. In *Happy Days*, however, there is a chance for minor variation, in the club ribbon on Willie's boater and Winnie's bodice, striped parasol and 'small ornate brimless hat with crumpled feather.' The only precise colour suggestion in the stage directions for *Happy Days* is Winnie's hair: 'Blond for preference'.

Beckett's general practice in the later plays has been to make colour functionally relevant, either uniformly grey, or a contrast of dark and light. In *Come and Go*, moreover, the only play before *Quad* (1982) in which several shades are specified, the dulled floral colours have an organic function and are related directly to meaning.

TECHNICAL APPARATUS

It is by the introduction of pieces of technical apparatus as characters in their own right that Beckett achieves some of his most startling dramatic effects. The first of these, the tape recorder in *Krapp*, is conventional in so far as it is the machine's function to store voices and replay them as required. But the juxtaposition of Krapp's younger selves, so like and yet so different from the old man now listening to them, is an interesting dramatic innovation. Beckett instructed the actor Pierre Chabert in his 1975 Paris production of the play:

> to become as much as possible one body with the machine.[14]

The play is at once a commentary on Proust's vision of the changing self and the fusion of a dramatic technique hitherto thought proper only to radio, with a stage monologue. Having found the technique successful, Beckett adapted it for further use in *That Time*.

a) ***Light***

Inseparable from the stage image is the light that presents it, and, by the manipulation of light and darkness, gives it life. Beckett characteristically takes the use of light beyond the normal stage convention. Instead of merely animating the stage picture the technical apparatus, light itself, becomes a character in the action in certain plays and provides the necessary movement to prevent them becoming static. In *Play* light is often recognized in the programme as a fourth character, an inquisitor controlling the action. As Robert Wilcher points out, Beckett reverses:

> the usual theatrical convention that the lighting technician is subordinate to the actors. Instead of the light being there to serve the performer, the performer is in bondage to the light.[15]

Any actor who leaves the safety of the wings for the stage finds himself gripped by a spotlight, marked down while he delivers his lines. Beckett simply takes this dramatic fact further, imprisoning his actors in urns, so that any movement but that of the light is prohibited. Light's inquisitorial function of drawing speech from its victims is thus starkly revealed. The essential simplicity of harnessing a process already taking place in the theatre and drawing attention to it in itself, rather than using it as an accepted part of theatrical illusion is typical of Beckett's contribution to the contemporary stage.

Light has of course been used symbolically in the theatre by dramatists such as Maurice Maeterlinck[16] and designer-directors such as Edward Gordon Craig.[17] Beckett, however, goes further in *Play* not only personifying light, but using it to control the entire dramatic action. He does not ignore the fact that movement is necessary to animate the stage picture, but simply introduces a new kind of movement and paralyses conventional action.

In *Come and Go* and *Footfalls* although light is no longer a character as such, it is through light that the climax of both plays is reached, after completion of the text. In *Come and Go* the image of the hands in the spotlight questions the play's final lines. Both light and sound diminish steadily throughout *Footfalls* which, though a short play textually, seems thus to encompass aeons of time. The strong linear image produces an impression similar to that of a ripple gradually widening outwards until it is lost in an expanse of ocean. The protagonist in *Footfalls* seems to have departed into space at the end of the play, the light alone being left to register the absence of the body, its entry into another dimension. Similarly in *Rockaby*, where Beckett uses diminishing effects again, the climax of the play comes when W's head (held in a single spot) is slowly inclined.

Before writing *Footfalls* Beckett had experimented with diminishing light levels in *Play*, again making a climactic point by ending the play with light at 'normal strength'. *Play* is thus a catalytic play with regard to Beckett's use of light. Not only is light characterized in the play, but the possibility of eventual freedom from its scrutiny for the three characters, suggested by diminishing the light level is dispelled finally by raising it again, showing the illusory nature of any hope for freedom. The light level at the end of *Play* thus has something in common with the unrelieved 'blazing light' of *Happy Days* or the 'dazzling light' of *Act Without Words, I*. The tone of *Endgame*, however, is expressed by the opposite end of the lighting scale, the grey light of unrelieved gloom, while in *Godot* Beckett uses light to parody the naturalistic tradition by an exaggeratedly swift nightfall: 'The sun sets, the moon rises.' The parodic intention was particularly evident in Beckett's own production of the play at the Schiller Theater Berlin in 1975.

Beckett has thus used light with increasing subtlety throughout his dramatic career, to make functional points in the action and, in his most extreme concept, has given it a personality in its own right and a dramatic power within the framework of the play itself. The standard lamp that stands downstage centre 'faintly lit' in *A Piece of Monologue* is also dramatically powerful in that its failing thirty seconds before the end of the monologue provides the only action in the play. The 'skull-sized white globe' precisely on a level with Speaker's head, seems also to identify the lamp as a persona of Speaker.

b) *Camera*

Beckett's use of the camera is a further example of his personification of a technical apparatus. In *Film* the old man spends the entire film escaping the camera eye, only to be confronted by it at last. The camera has been used to personify his second self — it is his own inner eye that holds him in an ironic scrutiny. Beckett uses the camera as an externalization of the self once more in *Eh Joe*, the lens inching up on Joe while he listens to a voice in his head. The camera virtually becomes Joe's conscience, the means by which he is exposed, confronted by a self-knowledge he would rather evade.

The central dramatic idea here, as with Beckett's use of light, is both bold and simple. The camera exists as an apparatus capable of producing images of ourselves. Beckett simply explores this fact, using the camera to probe beyond the external image into the recesses of being. When Martin Held's Krapp (directed by Beckett at the Schiller Theater, Berlin in 1969) was recorded for television for Westdeutscher Rundfunk (Cologne) Beckett gave the television team a typescript entitled:

Suggestions for T.V. *Krapp.*[18]

In these suggestions Beckett calls for two cameras, A and B, and once again the apparatus is personified. A is described as 'mere eye', like the light in *Play*, but B is intelligent:

> This camera listens and its activity is affected by words spoken. It can thus be used, not only as 'savage eye', but as a means to distinguish in this recorded past those moments which matter little or nothing to Krapp from those which matter much or extremely.

In the later television plays ... *but the clouds* ... and *Nacht und Träume* Beckett uses the camera as both observer and observed. In both plays the protagonist sits to one side of the stage, observing a persona of himself performing certain actions. The camera in these plays becomes the mind's eye, externalising its images onstage.

SOUND

Beckett's first stage plays contain no extreme experiments with sound, though *Godot* is full of linguistic effects, such as Lucky's 'tirade', the comic routines of Vladimir and Estragon, and their occasional, haunting stichomythic exchanges. *Endgame* provides more of a foretaste of what is to come in Clov's few words from the heart spoken with 'fixed gaze, tonelessly towards auditorium'. But it is not until after his initial experience with radio that Beckett really begins to experiment with the possibilities of sound onstage. The radio plays should thus be considered first.

a) ***Radio Plays***

Surprisingly it was Donald McWhinnie, director of Beckett's first play for radio, *All That Fall*, who made the decision to use stylised rather than realistic sound effects in that play. Beckett was dubious about the decision but did not prevent McWhinnie from going ahead. The latter wrote to Beckett justifying his choice:

> Of course we have realistic recordings, but the difficulty is that it is almost impossible to obtain the right sort of timing and balance with realistic effects. By using good mimics I think we can get real style and shape into the thing. The other factor is that existing recordings are very familiar to our listeners and I do feel that without being extreme we need, in this particular case, to get away from standard realism.[19]

Martin Esslin notes that experiments undertaken to produce the sounds required for *All That Fall* led directly to the establishment of the B.B.C. Radiophonic Workshop, which, in turn, created the sound effects for *Embers*. It is likely that the success of *All That Fall* led Beckett to decide to continue his radio writing with non-realistic sound effects. At all events the sound of the sea in *Embers* is essentially non-realistic, as Henry explains at the outset:

> That sound you hear is the sea, (*Pause. Louder.*) I say that sound you hear is the sea, we are sitting on the strand. (*Pause.*) I mention it because the sound is so strange, so unlike the sound of the sea, that if you didn't see what it was you wouldn't know what it was.

However lacking in realism, the sound of the sea is a constant in *Embers*, audible 'whenever pause indicated' so that it is on the way to becoming a character in the action, a role subsequently achieved by Music, in the later plays for radio. As Zilliacus points out:

More than two hundred pauses are called for in the text of *Embers*. Thus the sea, which goads Henry on by surfacing in every one of them, achieves the dignity of a dramatis persona.[20]

Precisely because the medium is radio, the crucial enigma in *Embers* of whether Ada is present indeed, or simply in Henry's head is made possible. Beckett develops a similar ambiguity in *Cascando,* with regard to the identity of Woburn. Duckworth observes:

The play is, as Beckett explained it briefly to me 'about the character called Woburn who never appears'.[21]

In both plays Beckett uses as an integral part of his conception the fact that in an invisible medium neither presence nor absence can be taken for granted. Characters can come and go at will in radio, in the same way as they can pass in and out of a stream of consciousness in the novel. Thus to use this invisible medium in *Embers* for the invisible people in Henry's head is particularly appropriate. Radio is uniquely suited to Beckett's dramatic writing, since his plays are generally monologues, dramatic realisations of a stream of consciousness.

In *Radio II* Beckett takes the extraordinary step for a radio play of making one of the four characters, Dick, a mute. His presence is effectively registered, however, by his manipulation of a whip, with which he chastises Fox into speech. The virtuosity of Beckett's work for radio may thus be seen to cover the introduction of a mute into a spoken medium, the ambiguity as to whether voices heard are evocations or real presences, stylised sound effects, and, in the later plays, the characterization of music in its own right.

b) ***Musical Technique***

'All art', as Walter Pater pointed out, 'constantly aspires towards the condition of music.'[22] In his study of Proust Beckett draws attention to the musical element in his writing, commenting:

A book could be written on the significance of music in the work of Proust.[23]

The importance of music is continually evident in Beckett's own work, both as writer and director. In four plays a particular piece of music is used to develop a central theme: Schubert's *Death and the Maiden* Quartet is at the heart of *All That Fall,* while

Lehar's 'Merry Widow' waltz comments ironically on Winnie's situation in *Happy Days*. In *Ghost Trio* the woman F loves has become a melody (Beethoven's 'Ghost' trio) which haunts him like an *idée fixe*. In *Nacht und Träume* A's yearning for the benediction received from beloved hands in the past is expressed by Schubert's song of the same name, in which night with its dreams is begged to remain. The only words in this play are those of the song.

Beckett has also collaborated with several composers. John Beckett and Marcel Mihalovici have each written music for one of his radio plays and the latter describes Beckett as 'a remarkable musician' with 'an astonishing musical intuition, an intuition that I often used in my composition.'[24] More recently Beckett has written an original text entitled *Neither* for a one-act opera by Morton Feldman, first performed in Rome on 13 May 1977.[25] He has also specified that the four players in *Quad*, a play without words, should each be accompanied by a different percussive instrument (such as a drum, gong, triangle and woodblock). The instruments combine with the players' shuffling feet as the only sounds in the play.

A distinct progression in technique is evident from the use of Schubert's D Minor Quartet as a signature tune in Beckett's first radio play, *All That Fall*, to the use of music as a character in its own right in the subsequent plays for radio, *Words and Music*, *Radio I* and *Cascando*. In these plays Beckett uses music to give sound value to that which is beyond words. This, of course, is the function of music as an art form and Beckett characteristically attempts to harness the means of expression in its own right, rather than provide a libretto for which a score has to be set. In *Words and Music*, for instance, the coming together in the lyric of Joe and Bob is a fusion of equals, Joe creating the words and Bob the sounds that will evoke Croak's state of mind. Bob indeed strives to achieve not merely the complement of Joe's efforts to write a lyric, but its higher expression. His success is evident from Joe's repeated importunities at the end of the play for Bob to play the 'well head' music yet again.

It is for a musician to consider Beckett's interest in musical composition in relation to his technique with words. The actor Pierre Chabert draws the following analogy in an essay on *Krapp's Last Tape*:

> The writing and the composition of the text are perfectly musical insofar as they are organised around a network of repetitions, echoes,

alternances, oppositions and transpositions. This musical analogy can be analytically described on three levels: that of text alone considered like a score; that of the alternations between the two voices; that of the relationship between the recorded voice and the movement, thus bringing together all the factors which create the final 'score' and the staging of it.[26]

To attempt a close analogy between a particular musical form and a particular Beckett play tends to result in an arid series of possible identifications, with merely the virtuosity of the crossword puzzle. It may be observed, however, that Beckett uses musical terminology to describe his technique, referring for example to the repeat of *Play* as the *da capo*.[27] Similarly, when describing *Footfalls* to the actress Billie Whitelaw, Beckett called it 'a piece of chamber music'[28] and in the final rehearsals for the World Première of the play Beckett again said 'It's Chamber theatre and it must be perfect.'

c) ***Director/Conductor***

A Beckett play presents us with an experience that involves us in much the same way as we become involved when attending a symphony concert. The director's function is comparable with that of a conductor, as George Devine had the insight to appreciate in 1964:

> When working as a director on a Beckett play [ ] one has to think of the text as something like a musical score wherein the 'notes', the sights, the sounds, the pauses, have their own special inter-related rhythms, and out of their composition comes the dramatic impact.[29]

Today this has become the accepted view of a Beckett text. Peter Hall described the precise actions that Beckett indicated to Dame Peggy Ashcroft (when rehearsing Winnie with her for the 1975 National Theatre production of *Happy Days*) as becoming 'a kind of notation, like music' with Beckett as 'conductor'. The task of actor and director is, said Hall, 'to work *back*' from the notation, to reach 'the core of the text'. First 'the actor must get the actions right' (learn the notes) and only then can he begin to make the rôle his own.[30]

d) ***Pace***

Beckett frequently requires an unusually rapid pace for the delivery of his text. In *Cascando*, for example, although no directions as to pace are given in the published text, the holograph and first typescript of Voix 2 have a note 'débit rapide, haletant' (delivery rapid, panting.) Moreover manuscript notes in the margins of the first version of the full text (entitled *Calando*) time the speeches of Voix 2 throughout:

I 1 minute; II 30 sec; III 40 sec; IV 20 sec;
V 30 sec; VI 10 sec; VII 20 sec; VIII 20 sec;
IX 20 sec; X 20 sec; XI 20 sec; XII 10 sec;
XIII 15 sec; XIV 20 sec; XV 10 sec; XVI 10 sec;
XVII 10 sec; XVIII 10 sec.

The total of 5 minutes 55 seconds corresponds with a further manuscript note at the end of *Calando*:

Voix à elle) de 5 à 6 min.
Seul)
Musique
Ouvreur 5 —
Temps et silence 3 —

The total playing time for the text is thus envisaged as approximately 14 minutes, excluding musique. But, as Zilliacus points out, 'It would require an almost superhuman effort to obey these instructions' and 'Much of the text would necessarily be lost if delivered at the speed demanded.[31]

Directions for pace were omitted, at all events, from the final text of *Cascando*. In *Not I*, however, Beckett returned to the idea of a vocal delivery at top speed, although again there are no directions for pace in the text. In the 1973 Royal Court Theatre production, Beckett directed Billie Whitelaw at such speed that full intelligibility at first hearing was impossible. Rather did meaning accrue gradually through repetition as a torrent of sound emerged from an uncomprehending mouth, words streaming forth in tones and rhythms, like notes. Enoch Brater timed this production at 15 minutes, remarking that Beckett subsequently revised the manuscript, thus 'slowing the pace of the verbal onslaught' for Jessica Tandy's second attempt at the role, at the Lincoln Center, New York, in 1973.[32] Beckett, said Brater, 'specified 18 minutes' for the production, but pointed out to Miss Tandy that he was 'not unduly concerned with intelligibility', hoping the play would 'work on the nerves of the audience, not its intellect'.

e) *Voice*

Krapp's Last Tape, Beckett's first stage play after *All That Fall* at once reflects his work in the new medium of radio by fusing recording technique and visual image. It is with the voices in *Play*, however, that Beckett's real innovation in stage sound technique begins. The voices are to be 'toneless except where an expression is indicated'. When, moreover, the voices speak in chorus they are 'faint, largely unintelligible' and when isolated individually by the light, their strength of tone depends on the strength of the light beam, getting softer as the light diminishes. The monotonous computer-like tone emphasizes the routine of repetition to which the speaker is subjected.

Beckett thus deliberately restricts the vocal range of his actors, a pattern that becomes increasingly evident in subsequent plays. In *Come and Go*, for example, the voices are largely 'colourless' and 'as low as compatible with audibility', culminating in a stream of sound in *Not I*, where intelligibility is secondary to the vocal tone and pace. It is a similar development to that in Beckett's novels, where his writing culminates in the stream of words of *The Unnamable*. Mouth seems also to be foreshadowed (even to the buzzing that so troubles her throughout the play) in the following passage from *Molloy*:

> Yes, the words I heard, and heard distinctly, having quite a sensitive ear, were heard a first time, then a second, and often even a third, as pure sounds, free of all meaning. [ ] And the words I uttered myself, and which must nearly always have gone with an effort of intelligence, were often to me as the buzzing of an insect.[33]

Beckett in *Not I* is using the human voice as an instrument to convey mood more than meaning. Again the dramatic idea of using the spoken voice as an instrument is essentially a simple one. It is a commonplace in an actor's training that his voice *is* an instrument that requires great skill to tune to capacity. Beckett's deliberate denial of vocal range, requiring instead perhaps a monotone, perhaps breakneck speed, paradoxically takes the voice into a new dimension, where how it sounds rather than what it says makes the initial impact, the sense only gradually emerging through repetition. Using the voice in this way blurs the area between speech and song and highlights the similarities between poetic and musical technique. For the audience the experience of *Not I* is not unlike hearing a symphony for the first time, where the themes are not fully recognised as such until they are repeated. The main theme is introduced in the first movement and only gradually becomes familiar to the audience when it returns with variations in subsequent movements. By the end of the work, however, particular sequences of notes encapsulate the mood of the music and express for the audience what it is trying to say.

Beckett's handling of the voice in *Not I* seems also to have something in common with Artaud's ideas on language:

> To make metaphysics out of spoken language is to make language convey what it does not normally convey. That is to use it in a new, exceptional and unusual way, to give it its full, physical shock potential, to split it up and distribute it actively in space, to treat inflexions in a completely tangible manner and restore their shattering power and really to manifest something; [ ] and finally to consider language in the form of *Incantation*.[34]

When, moreover, Artaud describes his dramatic vision as 'very near to a tremendous scream, a human vocal source, a single, solitary human voice' uttering a cry,[35] Mouth in *Not I* seems to embody that vision. Beckett, however, describes himself as 'unaware of any influence from Artaud.'[36]

Beckett's latest experiments with the human voice include a 'dialogue' between a woman and her recorded voice in *Rockaby*; disembodied voices in *Ghost Trio* and *What Where* (the latter issuing from a megaphone) and a singing voice in *Nacht und Träume*, where the only words in the play are those of the song. Perhaps the most interesting experiment is W's voice in *. . . but the clouds. . .*, which has passed even beyond a whisper and merely mouths its words. An intently watching man picks up W's words, however, and murmurs them 'synchronous' with her moving lips. It is a logical extension from *Not I*. The lips still move, but the voice itself is no longer present; the technique recalls the vanishing of May at the end of *Footfalls*.

f) *Silence*

As discussed in Chapter 1 Beckett is preoccupied by the desirability of introducing silence into his work. In a manuscript notebook at Trinity College Dublin he even calculates ironically the number of pauses required 'to make (a) total silence of 24 hours'.[37] Ihab Hassan comments in a discussion of Beckett's use of language:

The syntax is often the syntax of nonsense, the grammar of absurdity. And silence, literal silence, invades the interchanges between human beings.[38]

Beckett manipulates stage silence as a counterweight to his use of sound. Predictably for a dramatist who has characterised music and light, he makes his silences take some of the burden of the action. The delicacy and economy of the ending of *Come and Go*, for example, is achieved by a dual aural/ visual effect. The echo of the final words in the succeeding silence is contradicted by the spotlit image of ringless hands. A similar contradiction occurs during the pauses in *Not I*, after Mouth has denied the stimulus urging her to self acceptance, and acknowledgement that 'she' is 'I'. The auditor's gestures of compassion decrease with each denial of selfhood, eloquently contradicting Mouth's reiterated lie in the silence which follows it. Thus 'the pauses' (as Zilliacus points out with regard to *Embers*) 'are not scattered dramatic effects, but integral parts of the total artistic statement.'[39]

In *That Time* the silence used throughout to mark the 'acts' or divisions in the play takes on a further meaning at the close. On realising that the three voices have ceased and silence has been achieved, the old man gives a toothless grin which is held until the image fades. Silence has 'invaded' the action here, as it does at the end of *Cascando* and the stage is speaking what Artaud calls 'its own concrete language'.[40] The 'specifically theatrical' in Artaud's terms is 'everything which cannot be expressed in words'.

Among the latest stage plays *Rockaby* (like *That Time*) is structured by silence. Throughout the play W bestirs herself to utter her one word 'more', after silence has fallen, until the recorded voice of her consciousness resumes its monologue. The play comes to a climax in a final silence, when W no longer demands and her consciousness ceases to utter. In *Catastrophe* a figure on a plinth centrestage remains mute throughout the play. When he finally raises his head a climactic silence, compounded of both helplessness and challenge is created, making a powerful dramatic statement.

In Beckett's most recent television plays silence again has a vital function. *Quad* is especially interesting in that here Beckett deliberately relinquishes speech. In *Quad 1* there are only percussive sounds and purposefully shuffling feet. In *Quad 2* the percussion has ceased, leaving the footsteps, now moving more slowly, as the sole remaining sounds, echoing eerily in an enclosing silence. In *Nacht und Träume*, Beckett's latest television play, Dreamer's most intense experience takes place in silence, as his mind's eye concentrates on an evocation of the past.

ACTING BECKETT

The French actor Pierre Chabert has observed that the Beckettian stage consists:

> of a rigorous mastery of theatrical space, where the word in its relationship to the gesture, the phrase to the movement, the language to the body, the writing to the direction, are all thought out and explored to their extreme limits.
>
> The result is a staging full of constraints, that must be read and performed like a musical score in terms of sound and vision, textually and spatially.[41]

Some of the 'constraints' are described by Brenda Bruce in a letter to James Knowlson recalling rehearsals of *Happy Days* in 1962:

> Beckett placing a metronome on the floor to keep me on the rhythm he wanted, which drove me into such a panic that I finally broke down.[42]

Similarly Billie Whitelaw described to Michael Davie how Beckett, when rehearsing *Not I* 'told me that in one place I had paused for two dots instead of three'.[43] Davie's description of Beckett rehearsing Rose Hill in *Footfalls* reveals the same technique:

> Beckett stood below the stage, his head about five feet away from the speaking woman. You felt an intense atmosphere of concentration. She kept her eyes fixed on Beckett as she rehearsed her lines; he kept his eyes fixed on hers. He had his head on one side; as she spoke, he moved his right hand an inch or two up and down, as if he were listening to, or conducting a piece of music, making very slight gestures.

The Beckett actor's movement is restricted, if not cut off altogether; he is denied the full range of his voice in the later plays and is sometimes deprived of his sight. In *Not I* except for his mouth he is entirely cut off from the audience by a blackout curtain. There are, as we have seen, no 'character' notes; 'Age undeterminable' is all the three women have to go on in *Come and Go*. There is thus nothing left to the Beckett actor but to master the notation of action allotted to him and then reach beyond his normal creation of an identity. He must first attempt to make himself a void, to create an inner space or channel, and then allow this to fill with Beckett's speech rhythms and repetitions until gradually an identification with the creative consciousness behind the lines takes place. The actor in fact 'tunes in' to Beckett rather than creating his own character. At best his imaginative identification is so strong that a fusion of actor and author takes place, which in turn creates the extraordinary impact Beckett's plays often have on audiences.

It is perhaps to some extent a consciousness of the freedom from 'character' in the conventional sense that leads so many actors, despite the constraints outlined above, to remark on the 'freedom' they experience when performing Beckett's plays. Moreover the energy demanded for the delivery of monologues such as Winnie's or Mouth's has a cathartic effect on the actor. Beckett's hope, as Ruby Cohn points out, is that severely imposed limits will demand more of the actor, thus extending, rather than inhibiting, his emotional range.[44]

BECKETT AS DIRECTOR

a) *Production Notebooks*

The preparation of minutely detailed production notebooks before rehearsals begin characterises Beckett as a director, as we have observed in the notebook for his production of *Happy Days* in Berlin in 1971.[45] Further examination of this notebook reveals that it is Beckett's practice to divide a text into numbered sections, noting its particular characteristics in detail. In *Happy Days*, for example, he makes lists of movement, gesture, facial expression, laughter. Repetitions are carefully counted, variations on a theme noted and occasionally a small sketch of an object or diagram of a movement is made. Beckett's concern is clearly both to structure the play into workable sections for rehearsal purposes and to bring out the patterning in the text, its balance and contrast. The extraordinary detail of his notes for the stage properties to be used in *Happy Days* is particularly revealing. Beckett's intention is for the objects listed to be both manifestly inefficient and in a state of dilapidation paralleling that of the protagonist. The toothbrush, for example, has 'hardly any hairs left', the lipstick is 'visibly *zu ende*', the pearl necklace 'more thread than pearls' and the parasol:

faded red and yellow striped, mangy fringe, diminutive canopy, disproportionately long telescopable stick.[46]

The disproportion between the component parts of the various properties reflects the disproportion in the text, in Winnie and Willie's marriage, for example, or their unequal contributions to the dialogue. The revolver with its 'short butt and long muzzle' is a further example. Beckett even notes tiny details, such as that the mirror should be 'small, square (because of round mag. glass) long handle'. He has visualised the scene with such concentration that the smallest contrast between square mirror and round magnifying glass becomes relevant.

Beside the list of properties Beckett sketches the 'old fashioned steel' spectacles he requires for Winnie and the kind of parasol he envisages, noting, at the top of the list:

Generally speaking:
Conspicuousness.
Inadequacy or exiguity of primary element (brush, glass), as compared with secondary (handle etc.)
Narrowness and elongation
Agedness, endingness.

b) *Beckett in Rehearsal*

Peter Hall, commenting on Beckett's detailed vision of a play before the first rehearsal, remarked:

It became clear in rehearsal that Beckett had a complete visual picture of the play in his head and that is how he rehearsed.

He did not, said Hall, discuss 'how Winnie feels but what she does' and even 'which hand she does it with'. Beckett had told Dame Peggy Ashcroft 'On that line you pick up that, on the other this', thus giving her a complete choreography of small actions.[47]

From such rehearsal experiences an oral tradition of Beckett directing his plays is gradually accumulating and this is particularly interesting in cases where precise directions are not present in the text, as with the pace of *Not I*. The extension of meaning in *Krapp's Last Tape* resulting from the introduction of the 'hain' or awareness of death into the later productions of the play is another example. Beckett described the hain to me as follows:

Freund Hain (or Hein = Heinrich)
= Death (easeful) the Scytheman[48]

He also pointed out that Matthias Claudius, the Eighteenth Century German poet, author of 'Der Tod und das Mädchen' 'dedicates to Freund Hain his collected works'. No instructions for the hain are present in the English text, though Beckett has used it in all productions in which he has been concerned since Martin Held's Schiller Theater Krapp in 1969. In his preparatory work for the 1977 San Quentin Drama Workshop production, with Rick Cluchey, Beckett makes a note on the action of the hain:

Having finished reading from ledger he stands and stoops over recorder to adjust reels. This action interrupted by sense of presence behind him in shadows. He turns slowly (left), still stooped, long look, comes back slowly front, completes action, sits, assumes listening position, switches on, etc. Same interruption exactly towards end of play as he adjusts reels for lake passage.[49]

The rehearsal situation also sometimes leads Beckett to make a remark to his actors or give an explanation that presents new insights into the text. Ruby Cohn, for example, notes that Beckett likened Willie to an old turtle, very much of the earth. His subsequent comment that:

Winnie's fate is all the more pathetic because this weightless being is devoured by the earth

is thus directly relevant to Beckett's view of the marriage.[50] In the 1975 Schiller Theater production of *Godot* Beckett again linked his characters to earth and sky, as Walter D. Asmus noted in his rehearsal diary:

'Estragon' (Beckett explained) 'is on the ground, he belongs to the stone. Vladimir is light, he is oriented towards the sky. He belongs to the tree.'[51]

Beckett pointed out later that the two 'are, in fact, inseparable'. Asmus also describes Beckett at the first rehearsal plunging into Lucky's monologue, dividing it up for rehearsal purposes and outlining its main themes:

'We are going to divide it into three parts and the second part is going to be divided again into two sections. The first part is about the indifference of heaven, about divine apathy. This part ends with "but not so fast ..." The second part starts off with "considering what is more", and is about man, who is shrinking — about man who is dwindling. Not only the dwindling is important here, but the shrinking too. These two points represent the two under-sections of the second part. The theme of the third part is 'the earth abode of stones' and starts with "considering what is more, much more grave".' Beckett is very concerned to be exact in his explanations and repeat certain ideas, underlining them with short gestures while we are looking for them and marking them.

Material such as the Asmus diary enables us to see not only Beckett the director, skilfully establishing rehearsal procedure with his cast, but the playwright intent on sharing his vision with his actors.

c) ***Production Changes***

At a panel discussion in Toronto in 1971, Jack Macgowran was asked by A. N. Jeffares:

'Do you have experience of, for instance, Beckett's plays being altered at all, or have they come, as it were, perfect onto the stage?'

Macgowran replied:

'No they haven't come perfect onto the stage all the time ... Beckett himself made many alterations the more he became acquainted with the theatre.'[52]

The ability to compromise when circumstances warrant within the particular production is characteristic of Beckett as director. Despite the apparent stringency of his stage directions, he himself adopts a fluid approach to his text when problems arise, though, as has been shown with *Come and Go*, it is generally unwise for other directors to do the same. In a notebook prepared for the 1975 National Theatre production of *Happy Days*, for example, Beckett suggests cutting the sunshade exploding into flame 'if change not feasible technically' and also notes: 'perhaps cut breaking and discarding of mirror'.[53]

In the original text of *Footfalls* (as can be seen in Appendix VII) seven steps are taken to cover the lighted strip of stage. But when the play entered rehearsal and it was found that nine steps made a more satisfying stage image, Beckett at once increased the number of steps taken in the first production to nine and also altered subsequent texts accordingly. Later texts of *Footfalls* also replace the south door of the church by the north. When asked about this Beckett explained:

> That is a correction. South Door is too warm, North Door is colder. You feel cold. The whole time, in the way you hold your body too. Everything is frost and night.[54]

Again, while rehearsing *Play* in Paris in 1964, Beckett decided that the play would be 'dramatically more effective' if a diminution of light and voice occurred in the repeat.[55] Notes for alternative ways of performing the repeat were therefore included in the next Faber edition of the text (1968). Certain alterations in the 1969 Schiller Theater production of *Krapp's Last Tape* are also 'incorporated into the text published in *Das letzte Band Regiebuch der Berliner Inszenierung*', as James Knowlson observes.[56] The English text of *Krapp* was not altered, however, nor are the revised directions for the repeat of *Play* preferred alternatives. Indeed Beckett's opinion when consulted about the repeat in 1976 was : 'Exact repeat preferred.'[57]

It may be inferred from this that Beckett is reluctant to tamper with the text he has finally arrived at after the lengthy process of its evolution through numerous drafts has been completed. The case of *Not I* lends weight to such a view. When rehearsing *Not I* for the London première in January 1973, Beckett from the outset encountered problems in lighting the auditor and was finally forced to prune his gestures. The actor Brian Miller explains:

> There are four gestures indicated in the script for the Auditor but I don't do them now because they couldn't be seen, so Beckett worked out a final bowing of the head into hands on the final — 'She . . . She'.[58]

In a subsequent production in Paris Beckett cut the auditor altogether, leaving only Madeleine Renaud as Mouth. Nonetheless both auditor and gestures remain in the text. The French translation of the play was made after Beckett's experience of the lighting problems in London, but the notes for Auditeur in *Pas moi* do not reflect these difficulties in any way and are identical with the English text.

It would seem, therefore, that although variations (even radical changes) may take place in a particular production, the original text generally remains the authoritative version and is rarely altered. Alterations regularly take place in Beckett's productions, either for practical reasons or reasons of artistic judgement, but they generally remain *ad hoc*. Beckett may incorporate such changes into his next production, but very few achieve the permanence of textual alteration.[59]

The role of accident during rehearsal has also produced some interesting results. Alan Schneider has described how 'eyes' began to proliferate in the studio once the film crew became alive to the possibilities of pairs of holes, such as the folder in which O's photographs were kept.[60] Similarly what Beckett referred to as 'originally an accident — heaven sent'[61] was the faint glimmer of light coming from Krapp's tape recorder at the end of the play when the rest of the stage was in darkness. The implications of a glimmer of light at this point so impressed Beckett that, as Knowlson points out, he included the 'voyant blanc du magnétophone dans l'obscurité' among the play's light emblems.[62]

d) *Production Problems*

There are sometimes real difficulties in realising Beckett's dramatic concepts and transferring them from page to stage. Several of these difficulties concern lighting: for audiences accustomed to regarding the limit of light's stage capacity as achieving subtle effects of shading and providing an appropriate setting for the actors, suddenly to find it making points in its own right may be disorientating. Once the new technique has been registered, however, it is, paradoxically, easier for an audience to accept a full characterization of light, as in *Play*, than to appreciate the final effect in *Come and Go*. Since light in *Come and Go* has revealed the stage picture in the conventional manner throughout, an audience does not suspect that the last few seconds' focus are adding a new dimension to the play, are in fact, refocussing it. In *Footfalls*, although the directions call for dim lighting: 'strongest at floor level, less on body, least on head' Beckett nonetheless told me he found in rehearsal that it was necessary to have a narrow spotlight to reveal May's face, when she stands at each end of the lightstrip.

The lighting problem in *Not I* arises because audience attention is mesmerized from the outset by the luminous, moving mouth and finds it difficult in the pauses to switch its attention across the stage. The two images were separately inspired; Mouth by a Caravaggio painting of the head of St. John the Baptist in St. John's Pro-Cathedral, Malta[63] and the auditor by a djellaba-clad woman silently listening for the arrival of her child, whom Beckett had seen in North Africa.[64] The auditor's helplessness in the face of Mouth's refusal to accept selfhood is, however, an integral part of the dramatic vision. This aspect of the play is lost if the listening figure is cut although, as Beckett realised, the play is still intelligible to audiences with Mouth alone.

Problems also arose in translating *Film* from the page, and the result is perhaps slighter and less powerful than its realisation in the imagination when reading the scenario. The problem is partly one of audience reaction. It has always been a convention of cinema photography that the camera is all-seeing, capable both of recording a scene and of being the protagonist's eyes. Independent recording of the room in *Film* will thus be taken as a matter of course by the audience rather than as the perceptions of O's alter ego. Moreover when shots of the room are handled both in greater definition and more blurred, in an attempt to achieve the dual perception of E (the pursuer) and O (the old man) it is quite possible that an audience will fail to register these nuances and may even regard them as deficiencies of the camera. Suspicion that someone may be following O grows during the film, partly suggested by the looks of horror that the camera reveals on the faces of passers by, as it tracks O down the street. But the sense of pursuit tends to be lost on O's arrival in the room, in his concentration on blotting out the eyes he encounters there. Inside the room, therefore, there is no clear reason why an audience should take the dual perception as other than a matter of course, until O is finally stalked in his sleep. Beckett, in other words, is demanding a high degree of sophistication from his audiences, requiring them to treat the normal in cinema terms as abnormal, and also to develop a paranoiac fear of the camera as pursuer. Martin Dodsworth suggests that Schneider should have resisted Beckett's wish for a dual perspective:

> An audience unprejudiced by a reading of the scenario is [ ] not likely to understand the difference between O shots and E shots until E confronts O, if then. Simply to have more of these different-quality shots is not to make them more acceptable or comprehensible for the audience.[65]

It may be necessary to register these failures in the communication of Beckett's dramatic concepts in order to obtain a balanced view of his technique, but they are infinitesimal in comparison with the revitalizing effect of his dramatic imagination in the theatre over the past three decades. *Come and Go* and *Not I* are, moreover, undeniably stimulating dramatic experiences, even if the desired effect is not fully communicated to an audience unfamiliar with the text. And for those who are prepared to abandon their preconceptions as to what theatre should be and open their minds to Beckett's dramatic vocabulary, the plays remain alive long after the final curtain, as Watt found with 'all the incidents of note proposed to (him) during his stay in Mr. Knott's house'. Contrary to Watt's experience, however, rather than losing meaning during the process of recapitulation, the plays go on expanding in the mind:

> . . . in the sense that it was not ended, when it was past, but continued to unfold, in Watt's head, from beginning to end, over and over again, the complex connexions of its lights and shadows, the passing from silence to sound and from sound to silence, the stillness before the movement and the stillness after, the quickenings and retardings, the approaches and the separations, all the shifting detail of its march and ordinance, according to the irrevocable caprice of its taking place.[66]

CHAPTER 12

CONCLUSIONS 1956-76

Studying Beckett's plays of the period 1956-76 from the perspectives of genesis and development, structure and performance has enabled us to gain a rounded view not only of each individual play, but of a considerable body of dramatic works. From this twenty year span of plays it is now possible to drawn certain conclusions as to Beckett's creative process. In discussing in the early chapters the precision of planning in Beckett's writing, we have observed the recurrence of a particular pattern in the plays, a cyclic movement, reflecting Beckett's constant theme of the human life cycle, in a precise fusion of content with form. The virtuosity of his dramatic writing has been seen to lie not in variation of theme, but in the many different ways in which the same theme is treated; the continual refining both of language and image until all that remains is the essence of an idea, a skeleton, which the audience is forced to flesh for itself.

The reduction in scale of Beckett's dramatic oeuvre is especially evident when comparing his later plays with the first plays in French (though here also a reduction is apparent, from the three acts of *Éleuthéria* to the long one act of *Fin de partie*). We have observed, however, that implicit in the brevity of the later plays is the concept of an infinite repetition, exemplified in the repeat of *Play*, or (in its most extreme form) in *Breath*. The shrinkage of the text may be seen as a natural development from the *trilogy*, a way of demonstrating more concisely Beckett's view of the cyclic nature of existence. Moreover the use of visual symbols as dramatic metaphors in the plays, Winnie's mound, for example, or the urns in *Play*, has made the plays more accessible than many of the novels, to a public increasingly prepared to accept the Beckett universe on its own terms, rather than demanding that those terms should be different.

Beckett shows people at their extremity, with no choices left to make, unable, even, to choose to stop; '. . . you must go on, I can't go on, I'll go on' are the Unnamable's last words, while the decision to leave the stage at the end of *Godot* merely results in immobility. Man is shown to be in an absurd situation in which there is 'nothing to be done' but continue to play out the comedy in the hope of an eventual conclusion. The fact that significant change is impossible in Beckett's terms is reflected in the cyclic structure of the plays. His protagonists cannot break out of their limited cycle of experience and apparently even in death are found repeating it to themselves, unable to understand why they are speaking or to find meaning in the experience recounted. By a merciful self-delusion, however, such experience is often distanced, as in *Not I*, into third person narration. The self can only be faced at one remove, and, when recognition presses uncomfortably close, is deliberately denied. Thus, where drama traditionally presents protagonist and antagonist in action, Beckett's characters are in self-conflict. When the plays that follow *All That Fall* begin, the 'action' in traditional terms has already taken place. From *Krapp's Last Tape* onwards all that is left in most of the plays is recapitulation, a struggle with voices in the head, and a masochism that both demands and dreads the assaults of memory, 'all the dead voices' that will not be silent.

Unlike Brecht, who believed that to present a problem on the stage presented also an implied solution, in the desirability of social change, Beckett has no solutions to offer. Nor does he believe that it is the task of the artist to provide any. Writing in 1938 of the poet Denis Devlin, he comments on the limitations of an art in which 'solution (is) clapped on problem like a snuffer on a candle'.[1] Instead he confronts his audience with the problem, the image of human suffering. This, he says, is 'how it is'.

The rigorous patterning in which Beckett's nightmare vision is enclosed is itself an ironic comment on the shapelessness of most human experience. Attempts to structure living can be only partial, because the unpredictable can never be excluded. Art, on the other hand, in the nature of the word, means a shaping and selection of material, exclusion of the unpredictable. The problem for the contemporary artist, as Beckett remarked to Tom Driver, is to 'admit the chaos'[2] to allow the unpredictable and unformulable into the text.Throwing open his highly organized structure, *Sans*, to the hazard of a chance arrangement may be seen precisely as an attempt to 'admit the chaos' by making unpredictability functional in a work of art.

The second area of investigation, Beckett's manuscripts, reveals how the ultimate shape of the plays evolves over numerous drafts; it is a study of the creative process in action. The process of drafting each play, moreover, may be seen as a microcosm of the development of Beckett's oeuvre as a whole, a refining and scaling down of the text. A meticulous craftsmanship of both structure and language has been evident throughout the drafts. A tendency for the text to develop, as the drafts progress, from the concrete and comparatively straightforward to the indefinite and more complex has also been observed. Such development is part of the refining process and increasing ambiguity becomes as much the signature of a study of Beckett's drafts as a circular motif is characteristic of his structure.

The plays gain in power from a balancing of possibilities. To try to pin down a Beckett play like a moth on a naturalist's board is to impoverish the text and hamper its resonance. As Duckworth pointed out when editing *Godot*:

> It is impossible to summarize Beckett's novels and plays without divesting them of almost all significance.[3]

It is thus important to keep the evolutionary aspect in mind when studying Beckett's draft material and not to diminish the final text by too literal interpretation. Nonetheless a knowledge of the process by which the final version was arrived at and the ideas from which it grew can greatly enrich both our understanding of the plays and of Beckett's craftsmanship as a writer.

In the study of Beckett's stagecraft his theatrical innovation may be seen to some extent as a natural consequence of his growth as a writer and the search for new ways to express familiar themes. But, as we have seen, Beckett has considered the particular qualities of each medium in which he has worked with an eye uncluttered by convention. The result has been the introduction of dramatic effects which make use of the distinctive nature of each medium: effects such as the personification of light, music and the camera, or the unorthodox use of stage movement in the frantically working lips in *Not I*. Beckett in these ways has extended contemporary concepts of dramatic possibility and that he is still approaching the theatre with originality and freshness is apparent in the commentaries on the latest plays, which close this study. Beckett's plays have been, in Katharine Worth's words, 'one of the great freeing influences on modern theatre' and, as she concludes:

> It would be hard to overestimate Beckett's importance as the opener of the door to this disturbing freedom.[4]

EPILOGUE
THE LATEST PLAYS

Beckett's interest in visual communication developed greatly in the mid seventies, leading (more than a decade after the completion of *Film* and *Eh Joe*) to renewed experiment in the medium of television, with the writing of four new plays for television between 1975-82 (transmitted 1977-83). The third of these, *Quad*, is perhaps Beckett's most radical dramatic experiment. Martin Esslin commented in his introduction to the first BBC transmission of *Quad* on 16 December 1982, that in recent years Beckett:

> has become more and more fascinated with the television medium and in particular with the fact that television allows him to project the images in his mind directly, with the minimum use of language and the utmost economy and precision.

In *Quad* indeed Beckett dispenses with language altogether. The possibilities of close-up shots in television mean that he is able to experiment with imagery of greater subtlety than is possible in the theatre. The camera's ability to isolate an image is particularly suited to the concentration and intensity of Beckett's dramatic style. It can, for example, focus audience attention on one small detail. It is also possible for the camera to create an illusion of movement, by zooming in on close-up shots or by dissolving from one shot to another. This is of great benefit to Beckett, whose increasing tendency is towards static theatre. Finally, of course, the camera can both freeze and perpetuate the image. The moment of creation is not only preserved but is capable of exact repetition.

Even *Not I*, one of Beckett's most successful plays in the theatre, is capable of televisual experiment — not, as it was originally conceived, a mouth pulsating in darkness, but with the mouth filling the entire television screen, giving the play a different kind of impact. Beckett is reputed to have refused to have anything to do with the making of the BBC television *Not I* (which was shown on 17.4.77. as part of the 'Lively Arts' programme *Shades*) but to have been delighted with the result, the new image of Mouth.

Five new stage plays have appeared since 1979. Of these, *Rockaby* can be seen as a direct successor to *Footfalls*, while *A Piece of Monologue* is much closer to the world of Beckett's prose fiction than any previous play. *Catastrophe* marks a new departure for Beckett into political statement and *What Where* also seems to have political overtones, as well as affinities with *Quad II*. Beckett is still actively engaged in redefining the frontiers of dramatic art and seeing new possibilities for theatre.

The epilogue consists of explorations of the latest plays,[1] with regard to matters of structure, theme and interpretation and dramatic technique. As Beckett's dramatic work since 1976 has moved ever further into the region of abstraction and experiment (in *Quad*, for example, and *What Where*) it may increase the accessibility of some of the latest plays for the reader to analyse their action. This is especially true of the television plays. Whereas to read a play allows the imagination to play on the text,in the television plays there may be no text (as in the third scene of *Ghost Trio*, for example, and in *Quad*) and it is sometimes quite difficult to 'read' the action simply in terms of camera shots and to appreciate the dramatic effects Beckett was aiming for. Even the latest stage plays may need to be brought to the mind's eye. *What Where*, for example, needs close attention in order to follow the progression of the action, since the play relies heavily on repetition and the four characters are virtually identical.

The commentary on each play can stand on its own as well as forming part of the exploration of the latest plays. The commentaries will look at each of the latest plays in the light of knowledge of Beckett's previous work, gained through the detailed study in earlier chapters of patterning, manuscript and stagecraft. Should a theme or technique be shared with an earlier work, this will be discussed in the course of each commentary, as will Beckett's continuing dramatic innovation in the latest plays. Although each commentary is separate, the television and stage plays have each been grouped together in chronological order. In this way it is possible to see how the plays habitually develop from and stimulate each other. The four television plays are discussed first, since *Ghost Trio* was written the same year as *Footfalls* — and it is with *Ghost Trio* that Beckett's latest experiments in visual communication may be said to begin.

I: TELEVISION 1977-84

GHOST TRIO

Ghost Trio[1] was written in English in 1975 and first produced for BBC television on 17.4.77. (with ... *but the clouds* ... and *Not I*) in a 'Lively Arts' programme that Beckett himself entitled *Shades*. The action of *Ghost Trio* is combined with passages from the *Largo* of Beethoven's fifth piano trio, known as 'The Ghost'. The extreme precision of planning that is Beckett's normal practice in constructing a work is very well suited to the demands of television, where a play is built up frame by frame. The set diagram for *Ghost Trio* is exact to a millimetre; each scene is structured into numbered camera moves and there is a trio of scenes: I. Pre-action II. Action III. Re-action. This scene division is a highly typical Beckett sequence, with repetition built into the play's structure.

As with Beckett's previous play for television, *Eh Joe*, the protagonist is a male figure who does not speak and the text is spoken by a female voice. In *Eh Joe* Joe listened to a voice in his head; in *Ghost Trio* the voice (V) is more impersonal. She is a narrator, describing the scene for the viewer, yet she also has intimate knowledge of the protagonist (F), knowing what he will do before he does it. When the play opens with a general shot of the set, V sounds like a recorded message from a guide:

> Good evening. Mine is a faint voice. Kindly tune accordingly. (*Pause*.) Good evening. Mine is a faint voice. Kindly tune accordingly.

She begins by describing the various aspects of the room and then invites the audience to 'look closer' almost as though she were the voice of the camera. The camera then focusses in close-up on various rectangles around the room, some horizontal and some vertical, so that the play here becomes a statement of shapes, rather in the manner of Cubist art. It is as though Beckett had been contemplating a room through a camera lens, noticing how it framed its shots and had then incorporated the frame itself into his play, using it to isolate a piece of wall or floor. The window measures 0.70×1.50 metres and the camera creates rectangles of wall and floor of precisely the same measurements, thus echoing and balancing the image. Yet when the camera moves on the the rectangles are no longer seen as such, but have merged back into the totality of floor and wall, thus contributing to the impression of ghostliness that might be expected from a play of this title. V also comments 'dust' as the camera rests on each of these images, stating dismissively: 'Having seen that specimen of floor you have seen it all.' There is a further balance of image between the vertical door and horizontal pallet, which might be described as grave-shaped images, since both measure 0.70×2 metres. The rectangular pillow at the head of the pallet gives depth to that image and some relief for the eye.

The play's lighting seems indeed to be supernatural:

> The light: faint, omnipresent. No visible source. As if all luminous. Faintly luminous. No shadow. (*Pause.*) No shadow. Colour: none. All grey. Shades of grey.

This recalls May's description of herself as 'a pale shade of grey' in *Footfalls*, also written in 1975. There is too the idea of isolating a piece of floor in *Footfalls* and an emphasis on the rectangle in the strip of light.

V's last words in Scene One: 'Sole sign of life a seated figure' bring the camera to focus on F as a climax to the scene. Each time the door has been seen in earlier shots, there has been a sound of faint music. F sits on a stool beside the door, bowed over a small rectangular object in his lap. As the camera approaches him the music becomes slightly louder and the object is gradually identified as a small cassette recorder. The music again increases in pitch as the camera closes in on the hands clutching the cassette and the bowed head hiding the face. The camera inching up on the protagonist in this way recalls both *Film* and *Eh Joe*. Here, however, it does not maintain its position, but retreats gradually, causing the music to become fainter, until the general view of the room (as in the opening shot) is reached and having thus come full circle, the 'Pre-action' ends.

In Scene One V has been an objective recorder, acting as intermediary between scene and audience. In Scene Two ('Action') she at once demonstrates that she is also the omniscient narrator, with inner knowledge of F: 'He will now think he hears her' she says and F immediately performs the relevant actions by 'raising his head sharply' and listening in a 'tense pose'. In a sense, therefore, V initiates the action. F remains on the alert throughout Scene Two, in agonised expectation of a woman's arrival. Beckett's original title for *Ghost Trio* was *Tryst*. The tension of waiting is more extreme than that created in earlier plays, such as *Waiting for Godot* or *Come and Go*, because it is reinforced by the urgency of the music and because F has no companions to help him support the situation. In *Eh Joe* Joe has been trying to throttle the woman in his head; here, as in *Krapp's Last Tape* and *Words and Music,* F's whole being is concentrated on the memory of 'her' and he is very moving in his isolation and repeatedly baffled hope. He may indeed have succeeded in summoning her ghost, since it is a woman's voice that is in the room with him, though he does not appear to be conscious of this. It is of course possible that V's 'recorded voice' is trapped, like the music, in F's cassette. On the other hand, although she herself remains unseen, V can see F even when the camera cannot, as when his face in the mirror surprises her, but the camera (and thus the audience) cannot see it.

Nearly all the camera shots in Scene Two are taken from A, the most distant point of the set. The 'Action' consists of F looking out of the door (which has no knob and 'closes slowly of itself') and then out of the window, which closes in the same manner. F turns next to the pallet and to the mirror at its head, but from position A the camera fails to register his face. F returns to his stool and 'settles into opening pose, bowed over cassette', whereupon the five climactic shots from Scene One (in which the camera inches up to and then away from F) are repeated. There is a development from Scene One, however, in that a further sequence of action ensues, with F once more going to the door, looking out, and finally returning to stool and cassette. As the climax to Scene Two music is heard without the camera closing in on F. The practice in Scene One had been for music to become audible as the camera approached F. Here it occurs and increases while the camera remains unmoving at the most distant point from F, until V calls a halt, emphasising her control of events. When the music stops V's last word 'Repeat' closes the scene.

V's instruction leads directly into Scene Three: 'Re-action'. She does not speak at all in this scene; but there is no need for further words, the camera now speaks for itself. It begins by observing F and then closes in on him (as in Scenes 1 and 2). The pattern of repeated action is already well established, but there are some advances in Scene Three. F repeats the actions of going to the door and window as in Scene Two, for example, but this time both have developed a 'crescendo' and 'decrescendo' creak. Moreover an empty corridor can now be seen from the door, a 'long narrow grey rectangle' (exactly paralleling the window in width) its 'far end in darkness' and from the window there is now a view of night and falling rain. The two sequences of action are precisely balanced. A preoccupation with rectangles also returns in Scene Three. The corridor is rectangular and the cassette on the stool is a 'small grey rectangle on larger rectangle'. The camera also dwells on the pillow on the pallet and shows the mirror (which is the same dimensions as the cassette) 'against larger rectangle of wall'.

F's face is at last seen in the mirror. The sight seems to disconcert him, so that he bows his head and returns to his now familiar pose on the stool, where once again he listens intently. This time approaching steps are heard by the audience and two 'faint' knocks at the door. F opens it to find a small boy in shining wet oilskins, who twice 'faintly' shakes his head, then turns and goes. The camera observes 'his slow recession till he vanishes in darkness at end of corridor'. Interestingly, in Beckett's production of the play for German television, the boy does not wear oilskins, nor does he turn to go, but backs slowly away down the corridor. Again echoing the previous scene the camera returns to its observation point (A) before closing in on F, who is so bowed over the cassette that it cannot be distinguished. In the silence following the end of the *Largo* movement F raises his head, so that his face is clearly seen by the camera. It is the first time he has confronted the camera head on; earlier the camera had caught simply his reflection in the mirror. This climactic confrontation may be compared with the end of *Film*, where O meets the camera eye at last and finds it is his own. With this in mind the camera can be seen to have a double function in *Ghost Trio*, partly acting as objective recorder and partly bringing the self to face reality and come to terms with itself.

The music seems to be an externalisation of F's yearning for 'her'. His thoughts persistently return to the *Largo* and the intensity of his feeling is expressed by the music's increases in volume. In a sense 'she' *is* the music. It expresses her presence in F's consciousness in much the same way as Croak urged both Words and Music to express his memory of 'the face on the stairs'. In *Ghost Trio* it is the central movement of Beethoven's Fifth Piano Trio that expresses 'her' for F, the movement which, because of its haunting quality, resulted in the work as a whole becoming known as 'The Ghost'. It is in the silence following this movement that the play ends.

Structurally emphasis on the figure three is omnipresent, as might be anticipated from the play's title. There are three scenes and three main camera positions, moreover the number of shots increases by three in each scene: there are 35 shots in Scene One, 38 in Scene Two and 41 in Scene Three. There are also three main elements in the action: F (the image) combined with music and voice. Perhaps the final trio is that of F, the boy, and the ghost of 'her' in the music, so that she is both present and not present in true ghostly fashion (as with the recorded voice).

The boy's shake of the head is ambiguous. He may be saying she is not coming or that it is not yet time for F to follow him and thus, perhaps rejoin her. It is almost as though the boy were F's youth, coming to tell him he has not yet reached the end of his course and backing away into the past. His faint headshake leaves F in the same dilemma as Vladimir and Estragon in *En attendant Godot*; it is necessary to keep on waiting in case Godot comes tomorrow. The boy's arrival at this juncture naturally links the play with the boy messenger at the end of each act of *Godot*. In Beckett's Schiller Theater production of *Godot* in 1976 moreover, the messenger also left the stage backwards. As in Godot too, there is an implicit sense of potential recurrence at the end of *Ghost Trio*. The repetition that has already occurred from scene to scene may be envisaged as recurring in further scenes. The audience is seeing, even experiencing with F, part of an ongoing process of waiting.

Technically the precision required to synchronize each bar of the music with F's movements and with camera action is exacting for sound recordist actor and cameraman alike, so that the play becomes an extraordinary fusion of the visual aural and dramatic arts.

. . . BUT THE CLOUDS . . .

. . . but the clouds . . . was written in English in the late autumn of 1976 and was first transmitted by the BBC on 17.4.77 in a programme entitled *Shades*, on which Beckett himself had worked closely with the director, Donald McWhinnie. From a concentration on music and visual art in *Ghost Trio*, Beckett turns to a poem as a stimulus for memory in *. . . but the clouds . . .* . The poem is W. B. Yeats's 'The Tower', thus confirming once more Beckett's appreciation of Yeats's work. In the last verse of the poem the poet gradually schools himself to the acceptance of his own inevitable physical decline and to the 'worse evil' that life brings, the death of friends or of those brilliant with life and promise. In the end, thinks the poet, the emotion aroused by such matters will become distanced, until it seems no more than a cloud in the gathering dusk:

Now shall I make my soul,
Compelling it to study
In a learned school
Till the wreck of body,
Slow decay of blood,
Testy delirium
Or dull decrepitude,
Or what worse evil come –
The death of friends, or death
Of every brilliant eye
That made a catch in the breath –
Seem but the clouds of the sky
When the horizon fades;
Or a bird's sleepy cry
Among the deepening shades.

There are three separate images in ... *but the clouds* ...; the first, M, is both strange and difficult to realise satisfactorily with the camera:

Near shot from behind of man sitting on invisible stool bowed over invisible table. Light grey robe and skullcap. Dark ground. Same shot throughout.

The BBC production took a side view, with M's right elbow as the central camera focus, his arms folded across his chest, the left hand holding the right arm. An emphasis on crossed arms had also emerged during rehearsal of *Footfalls* in 1976, where May developed a posture in which she seemed to be hugging herself, thus expressing her isolation.

The second image in ... *but the clouds* ..., a woman's face, also in close-up and 'reduced as far as possible to eyes and mouth', materialises at intervals. It is an image that recalls the end of *Eh Joe*, on the way towards the reduction to mouth alone of *Not I*. The final image is the most striking dramatically and is also where the action is focussed. It consists of a circle of light (about five metres in diameter) 'surrounded by deep shadow'. A male figure, M1, a persona of M, continually enters and leaves the circle, changing his costume from hat and greatcoat to robe and skullcap, depending on whether he is coming in or going out. The robe and skullcap worn by both M and M1 seem to be intended as a visual link (for the audience) between the two men; however, the BBC film relied on forging the link by dissolving from M to M1 during M's speech, since M's exact costume could not be identified from the image of his folded arms, and his head was also hard to distinguish. The 'doppelgänger' theme is fully explicit in the text. The directions read:

M1: M in set. Hat and greatcoat dark, robe and skullcap light.

Beckett first experimented with personnified aspects of the self in the radio plays. Croak, for example, in *Words and Music,* is seen alongside his creative impulse, externalised into the personae of Music and Words. In . . . *but the clouds* . . . , however, Beckett is concerned not with fragments of the self, but the whole person. The protagonist, M, sees himself whole, (as at the end of *Film*) held in the light circle of the imagination.

There are four areas specified in the circle. Division into the roads (West) the sanctum, (North) and the closet, (East) may recall the Greek classical theatre convention of entry stage right or left meaning that the actor was coming from the city or the country. The fourth position is the central point of the circle, which receives maximum light. M1 stands here, (in direct contrast with Beckett's next play for television, *Quad,* in which the centre of the lighted area is zealously avoided throughout.) The camera position is far South of the circle, overlooking it. From a diagram in the text it looks as though the camera eye is imprisoning the light circle.

A pattern in M1's comings and goings in the circle is soon established. He comes in from the roads in hat and greatcoat and stands centre stage before entering the closet to change. Emerging in 'robe and skull' he stands centre stage before vanishing into his sanctum. He then performs these actions in reverse order, coming from the sanctum, changing in the closet and going off to the roads. There are thus two distinct sequences of action (a) arrival and (b) departure, which take place as follows: A A B A B. Since M is dressed in M1's costume for entering the sanctum, M, speaking from the shadows, might be presumed to be in the sanctum, 'crouched, where none could see me, in the dark'; he is stated to be 'bowed over invisible table'. He might, on the other hand, be viewing the circle from another sanctum, through the camera eye which also sees from the shadows.

The action of . . . *but the clouds* . . . consists of M reliving past experience with such intensity that he can see himself performing his daily routine. As he recapitulates his actions, M1 carries them out in the light circle, precisely as stated by M. When, for example, M says: 'I came in', M1 enters the circle. The circle is, as it were, the canvas of M's memory, and functions like a camera lens, framing the past. When M1 stands in the centre of the circle, he may be said to be awaiting M's instructions at the point of strongest light, or greatest creativity. M, in the chair, sees himself in the circle and corrects the image: 'No,' he says, if his recollection is inaccurate, and M1 disappears. M repeats himself until he is satisfied with his recollection and M1 has enacted the scene correctly. At this juncture M says: 'Right', like a director signifying approval. Again, after M1 has performed the third series of movements, M, as though at rehearsal, says: 'Let us now run through it again.'

The purpose of M's recapitulation is to recapture his memory 'of her'. His routine was to return from the roads, settle in the sanctum and:

> beg, of her, to appear, to me. Such had long been my use and wont. No sound, a begging of the mind, to her, to appear, to me. Deep down into the dead of night, until I wearied, and ceased.

Occasionally she appears, almost like a muse. M. the author-narrator, shuts himself in the cold North shadow of the writer's sanctum, begging the creative impulse to come to him. Had 'she' never come he could have 'busied (himself) with something else' or done nothing, but he is caught in the writer's trap, the expectation of inspiration. It is equally possible, on the other hand, that W is a lost love (as in many other Beckett plays) and the poem that she mouths to M a statement about herself, as though she were one of those with whose death M has yet to come to terms:

> Those unseeing eyes I so begged when alive to look at me

appears to suggest her death and the BBC film took this view by focussing in closeup on W's face during these lines. The ambiguities of the play allow for several possibilities, however, and W can be seen as a dead love or a muse or indeed both.

M's evocation of W is at its most intense when he asks her first to look at, then speak to him and she frames some words from the poem. M joins with her, so that the phrase '. . . but the clouds . . .' sounds like a refrain and thus becomes intelligible to the audience. Beckett brilliantly juxtaposes these murmured words with some high comedy over the numerous occasions she had failed to appear to him:

when I begged in vain, deep down into the dead of night, until I wearied, and ceased, and busied myself with something else, more ... rewarding, such as ... such as ... cube roots, for example, or with nothing, busied myself with nothing, that MINE

At the same time the passage is harsh enough ('that MINE') for Beckett to maintain the overall intensity; he is therefore able to build to the climax of the play, in which M speaks more of the verse, while the camera eye gives him another glimpse of W's face, before the final fade out.

The play requires careful synchronisation of the threefold image and the narrating voice. Beckett here takes his experiments with the human voice in the theatre beyond even the extremities of the sigh in *Breath* and the vocal pace of *Not I*. In ... *but the clouds* ... W has no voice, it is beyond even a whisper, yet its presence is felt, as she mouths the words of the poem. The audience try at first to lip read, then V's 'murmur synchronous with lips' enables them to hear. W's soundless voice and M1's complete silence, coupled with the fact that M himself does not speak, but his voice, sometimes as a murmur, comes from V (in Beckett's typical manner of recorded reverie) make the play most interesting vocally. Another experiment that Beckett makes in ... *but the clouds* ... is to have no camera moves at all, but simply to dissolve from fixed shot to fixed shot. There is enough movement in the dissolves and in M1's passage in and out of the circle to satisfy the eye.

A strong sense of the passage of time is created by M1's coming and going; indeed the daily routine of human life is shown to be governed in the circle, as in the world, by the sun. M1 leaves the circle from the East, 'at break of day', 'to walk the roads' and returns from the West, having 'brought night home'. Such language is extraordinarily evocative, as also with M1's 'robe and skull'. The shrouded ghostliness implied here is echoed in M1's silent appearance from and disappearance into the surrounding shadows and also in W's materialisation and vanishing and her soundless voice. Creatively this is a rich play, in which Beckett fuses several disparate elements and experimental techniques.

QUAD

Quad was conceived and written for television in 1981. It was filmed in Germany for Südefunks, Stuttgart and first transmitted in 1982 by Süddeutscher Rundfunk, under the title *Quadrat 1 and* 2. In association with Arena productions it was shown on BBC television on 16 December 1982 and was published by Faber in 1984. The original manuscript of *Quadrat* is at Reading University.[2] The film was directed by Beckett himself, assisted by Bruno Voges. The cast listed in the film credits gives 2M 2F and 4 percussion. In fact, since the figures all wear long robes with cowled heads, it is impossible to distinguish sex and the Faber text simply calls for four 'players', numbered 1–4.

The choice of costume recalls the directions for the auditor in *Not I*: 'sex undeterminable, enveloped from head to foot in loose black djellaba with hood.' In *Quad* the directions read: 'Gowns reaching to ground, cowls hiding faces.' The only difference is that in *Quad* the robes are coloured: 1 is in white, 2 in yellow, 3 in blue and 4 in red. Beckett wishes the four players to be 'As alike in build as possible' and considers 'Adolescents a possibility. Sex indifferent.'

The scene is a square of stage dimly lit from above and 'fading out into dark'. There are also four differently coloured lights 'clustered together'. Each player has his own light, the same colour as his costume; it is 'turned on when he enters, kept on while he paces, turned off when he exits.' The result is a constantly changing motion of light and colour as the characters come and go. Interestingly *Come and Go* is Beckett's only other play to make a feature of colour (other than black, white or grey) and again the characters enter and leave the stage in a precisely mapped sequence of movement, which is also to be found in *Quad*.

A similar effect to the fluctuation of light and colour is achieved aurally by the use of percussion. There are four percussive sounds; Beckett suggests a drum for 1, a gong for 2, a triangle for 3 and a woodblock for 4, though the sounds used in the television film appear to differ somewhat from this suggestion. As with the light, each sound comes and goes with the entry and exit of its particular character. The percussion is 'pianissimo throughout' and in order to relieve the ear further it is also intermittent, thus allowing the footsteps alone to be heard at intervals. Footsteps shuffling in sudden silence prove most effective dramatically. The players' backs are bent and they look towards the ground as they cover the square with extreme rapidity. Like the other effects in *Quad* the footsteps of the players have a particular sound, so that (as in *Footfalls*) the audience becomes strongly aware of them. The percussion sits at the back of the stage, barely visible, on a raised podium – a somewhat similar arrangement to that of the Japanese theatre. There is no speech.

The action of *Quad*, presented in the text like a mathematical formula, clearly recalls the unpublished 'J M Mime' at Trinity College Dublin[3]. In the mime, however, there were only two characters, a son and his father or mother and the action consisted of starting from the centre of the square and returning to the same spot 'by greatest number of paths'. In *Quad*, the four players all sedulously avoid the centre. Each side of the square takes six paces to cover. The course of movements prescribed for each player takes him right round the outside edge of the square, interspersing these straight lines by crossing at intervals, diagonally back and forth from each corner of the square, but always skirting the centre. By the time his course of movements is completed, a small central square has been paced by each player around the empty central space, thus forming a precise geometrical figure.[4]

There are four series of movements in the piece. Each series takes six stages to complete, building up from one player to four and then reducing to one again. In each series the four players, each entering from a particular corner, go through their prescribed courses of movement four times — except for the last player to arrive, who has completed only three of his courses when the series ends, thus leaving him alone onstage to begin the second series. The pattern is perhaps most easily followed if expressed in the colours of each player, thus:

	SERIES 1				SERIES 2			
Stage 1	white				yellow			
Stage 2	white	blue			yellow	white		
Stage 3	white	blue	red		yellow	white	red	
Stage 4	white	blue	red	yellow	yellow	white	red	blue
Stage 5		blue	red	yellow		white	red	blue
Stage 6			red	yellow			red	blue

	SERIES 3				SERIES 4			
Stage 1	blue				red			
Stage 2	blue	yellow			red	blue		
Stage 3	blue	yellow	white		red	blue	yellow	
Stage 4	blue	yellow	white	red	red	blue	yellow	white
Stage 5		yellow	white	red		blue	yellow	white
Stage 6			white	red			yellow	white

The four series of six stages each thus produce a total of twenty four stages. As in *Lessness* Beckett seems preoccupied with a number suggesting the measurement of time. The piece ends where it began, having come full circle and gone through every combination, so that the light finally fades when white is left alone on stage once more, ready to begin the whole process anew, in a typical Beckett *da capo*. The direction reads: 'Without interruption begin repeat and fade out on 1 pacing alone.' Time has no interruption.

There is thus a constant ebb and flow of colour, movement and sound, rising to a crescendo with all four players present and a gradually reducing diminuendo as they leave the stage one by one. This continual fluctuation and change, combined with the repetition of pattern, seems to mirror the natural cycle of creation. The figures have no discernible purpose, apart from negotiating their courses and avoiding both the centre and each other, and could thus be seen as embodying the life force — coming and going because they have no option. Seen by the camera from above they hurry about the square, staking out their territory and negotiating complicated manoeuvres, not unlike a group of ants.

Their avoidance of the centre is clearly a metaphor capable of wide interpretation, as with Winnie's mound in *Happy Days*. The small empty square in the middle of the figure round which the players pace, surrounded by the much larger square of light, could suggest the flight from self, the 'I' Beckett's characters so carefully avoid, in such works as *Film* and *Not I*. The deliberate avoidance of contact with each other, though present in the same square of light, is also a familiar theme in Beckett, whose characters frequently choose isolation, as with Krapp, for example, or Listener in *That Time*. Beckett acknowledges a problem in moving round the centre space 'without rupture of rhythm when three or four players cross paths at this point'. He goes on to consider how best to 'exploit' this 'if ruptures accepted', offering as a solution the idea of the centre being 'supposed a danger zone. Hence deviation. Manoeuvre established at outset by first solo at first diagonal.'

The four swiftly moving figures executing their courses, crossing and recrossing the square, is an extraordinarily complex manoeuvre and it is not surprising that Beckett should state in the notes: 'Some ballet training desirable.' Rehearsal must indeed have been much like a dance routine, perhaps even somewhat akin to army drill. There is a comic element to this persistent, self-absorbed scurrying about the square, even perhaps the sense of a board game in the fact that the four are described as 'players' and are seen moving across the square in a prescribed fashion. In these terms the piece could be seen to link with *Play*, where the possibility that the light is playing a game with the three heads is ever present. In *Quad* it remains a possibility that the figures move without volition, merely because they must. There is even a more sinister possibility behind the title of the piece. That there is a pun in 'quad' and 'quod' (slang for gaol) can hardly have escaped Beckett. Since, moreover, one of his Paris apartments overlooked the Santé prison, he must have been conscious of the rhythm of life as lived in a prison over a long period. With this in mind the players following their prescribed course of movements around a sqaure could be seen as 'doing time' in the most literal sense of the term, and exercising within the precise limits of the prison yard.

The tempo of *Quad* is stated to be rapid. Beckett anticipated one pace per second, which, 'allowing for time lost at angles and centre' would give a playing time of approximately twenty-five minutes. He found, however, that this was an overestimate and that it could be performed in fifteen minutes. A variation on the play, *Quad II*, appears in the German television film as a coda to *Quad I*. This came about fortuitously. When Beckett had approved the completed version in colour after the filming in Stuttgart, the director happened to remark that the play also looked good on the black and white monitor. Beckett was intrigued and suggested a black and white recording of one circuit only, slower and with no percussion, simply the sound of shuffling feet. This was duly done and the black and white version became *Quad II*. It is dramatically effective for the two versions to succeed each other, as tried out in the Stuttgart film. *Quad II* seems a natural succession or second act to *Quad I*, in Beckett's now accepted and habitual style (in *Footfalls*, for example) where slowing and fading effects of light and motion are used to represent distance and the passage of time. When Beckett saw the black and white version, he said: 'Good. That's 100,000 years later.'[5]

Not since *Lessness* has Beckett produced a work to so extreme a formula. His delight in pattern is here taken to the limits of mathematical precision, at last dispensing with words altogether, which, since *Breath* in 1969, has seemed a logical possibility. *Quad* is not a mime, it is more akin to dance. Martin Esslin, in some remarks made before the screening of *Quad* on BBC television, termed it appropriately 'a poem without words.'

NACHT UND TRÄUME

Nacht und Träume was written in 1982 for Süddeutscher Rundfunk.[6] It marks Beckett's continuing interest in the possibilities the camera holds for his work. Both the image and the basic technique of materialising the protagonist's longings have something in common with his earlier play for television ... *but the clouds* .... There are also, as will be seen, certain elements in the image that first occurred in the stage plays *A Piece of Monologue* and *Ohio Impromptu*.

An integral part of what Beckett describes as the 'elements' of *Nacht und Träume* is the exquisite Schubert song (Opus 43 No 2) that gives the play its title. The words, by Matthias von Collin, describe the way in which human dreams well up at night, like moonlight through space, and how man hears them with longing, so that he cries out at daybreak for the dreams to return. The dual protagonist in *Nacht und Träume* is the Dreamer (called A) and his 'dreamt self' (B). The last seven bars of the song are used, where the dreamer cries out for the return of his dream. A sits at a table in the left foreground of the camera image. His right profile is seen — head bowed, grey hair, and hands resting on the table, reminiscent of *Ohio Impromptu*. Unlike the stage play, however, the camera is able to focus particularly on the 'head, hands and section of table on which they rest' so that these alone are clearly visible. This image improves on the close-up technique of a man seen from behind: 'sitting on invisible stool bowed over invisible table' in ... *but the clouds* ... , which is a difficult image to realise satisfactorily.

Nacht und Träume opens to reveal A in: 'a dark empty room lit only by evening light from a window set high in back wall.' Such a scene could suggest a room in a prison or a monk's cell perhaps, but a specific location is not important and would restrict the play's resonance. As a male voice hums the end of the song, the evening light fades. It is likely that the voice would be recorded (although this is not stated in the text) because the figure of A is presented as a listener and viewer, a dreamer rather than an active participant in the action. The last three bars of the song are then sung, whereupon A bows his head onto his hands and the light on him fades. He remains just visible during the ensuing dream, in which light comes up on B, his double. It appears that B materialises, since he is: 'on an invisible podium about 4 feet above floor level,' to the right of centre stage. He is seated at a table, in precisely the same attitude as the dreaming A, but 'exhibiting the other outline' as M instructs M1 to do in ... *but the clouds* ... . B presents his opposite profile to the audience: 'faintly lit by kinder light than A's,' the light of the imagination. Beckett had already used identical doubles or 'doppelgängers' in two earlier works for the camera, *Film* and *. . . but the clouds . . .* , as well as in the stage play *Ohio Impromptu*.

The central action of *Nacht und Träume* is the materialisation in space of a pair of hands, which minister to B's needs. This recalls 'The hands. Seen from above' in *Ill Seen Ill Said*, as well as the hands that appeared to Speaker in *A Piece of Monologue*, once he had managed to penetrate 'Beyond that black beyond'. This time, however, the hands are also seen by the audience. Only B can see the face belonging to the hands, however, and he gazes up at it. The climax of the dream has the right hand (R) clasped between both B's hands, on the table, with B's bowed head resting on them. The left hand (L) 'rests gently on B's head'. The dream fades here and light comes up on A, who raises his head 'to its opening position.'

A precise repetition of the earlier scene follows, from the song being hummed and light going down on A, to the materialisation of B, as before. This time, however, the camera shots on B get progressively closer, 'losing A' from the picture. Dream has taken over from reality. The dream is filmed 'in close-up and slower motion' until B's head is once more resting on the clasped hands on the table. At this point, before L can come to rest on B's head, the camera slowly withdraws: 'to opening viewpoint, recovering A', and the dream fades, leaving A alone for the final fade out.

The immediate recapitulation shows A to be trapped in fantasy. The process of reverie or recapitulation of a remembered event is a continuum, familiar in Beckett's drama. The scene will continue to enact itself in A's imagination, perhaps in slower motion each time, until it has managed to fade from the mind, (as with the increasing dimness of light and slowness of pacing in *Footfalls*, until May finally disappears). Slow motion is also used in Beckett's preceding play for television, where *Quad II* marks a deliberate reduction in tempo from *Quad I*.

The technical requirements of this short play are again very demanding, as has come to be expected with Beckett's dramatic works. The successful materialisation of the dream requires great skill in its realisation. B's table should appear in space, and the materialisation of the hands has to be achieved with no shadow of the form to which they belong. The difficulty of avoiding a human outline, once light is focussed on any part of the body, was apparent in the Royal Court Theatre production of *Not I* in January 1973, where, despite a very narrow light beam focussed on the Mouth, Billie Whitelaw's head was faintly visible. Television, however, has the advantage of the ability to achieve complicated camera effects piecemeal, by careful editing. In Beckett's production for German television a central door, not mentioned in the text, was shown in the shots of A, disappearing in the shots of B, as though A had entered the world of B through the door of memory.

II: THEATRE 1979-84

A PIECE OF MONOLOGUE

A Piece of Monologue, a prose fragment, was revised for publication in the *Kenyon Review* in 1979, following a request in 1978 from Martin Esslin for a work to include in the review.[1] The actor David Warrilow, who had performed *The Lost Ones* for the Mabou Mines Company asked Beckett for a work he could perform on the subject of death. Beckett answered this request also with *A Piece of Monologue* and Warrilow performed it in New York in the Autumn of 1979 and at Stanford University, California, in the Spring of 1983.

A Piece of Monologue is precisely what it says, a piece of prose capable of dramatic performance. It is less a play than an image with words. There is no action as such and thus no stage directions, simply the words and the image. The words are so suggestive that effective radio performance would be possible. The image is entirely static, except for light from a lamp, which begins to fail thirty seconds before the end of the play, leaving, after it has gone out, 'faint diffuse light' on set and Speaker. Speaker stands downstage, 'well off centre' to the left of the audience. Two metres to his left, at precisely the same level and height as himself, is a standard lamp with a 'skull-sized white globe, faintly lit.' The white foot of a pallet bed is just visible to the extreme right of the audience, again at the same level as Speaker and lamp.

A Piece of Monologue, like so many of Beckett's works for the theatre, is concerned with recapitulation. Speaker seems largely divorced from the narrating self, whose memories we hear, and only vaguely conscious that he is speaking:

> Stands staring beyond half hearing what he's saying. He? The words falling from his mouth. Making do with his mouth.

As in *Not I* words stream from his mouth and the narration is in the third person; but whereas Mouth repeatedly denied her selfhood, in *A Piece of Monologue* the narration is implicitly understood to be Speaker's own story, because his costume, as well as the scene onstage, are both identical with those in the narrative. Speaker indeed describes both his costume and the set in theatrical terms, as though he were a stage designer, or setting up camera shots:

> Gown and socks white to take faint light. Once white. Hair white to take faint light. Foot of pallet just visible edge of frame. Once white to take faint light.

There are several examples of this staging process in the text, as if Speaker has so distanced the scene and objectified it in the mind's eye, so separated it from himself, that it has become a set for television, seen through a camera lens:

> White foot of pallet edge of frame stage left

Always his description tallies with the stage picture the audience see before them.

The theme of birth and death so familiar in Beckett plays from Pozzo's outburst in *Godot* to the miniature life cycle of *Breath* is set explicitly in the opening line of *A Piece of Monologue*:

> Birth was the death of him.

The sentence is repeated almost immediately and the harsh and uncompromising tone of the first words is reinforced by two following lines:

> Ghastly grinning ever since. Up at the lid to come.

It is a wholly negative perception of life: 'From funeral to funeral. To now.' Speaker is entirely precise about 'now'. There have been, he says: 'Thirty thousand nights' from birth to 'This night' (making him in fact just over 82) a grotesque comic detail typical of Beckett and one not immediately apparent, unless to an audience of mathematicians.

The word 'Birth' in *A Piece of Monologue* acts as a trigger to memory, as in *Not I*: ('out . . . into this world . . .'). In *Not I* Mouth circles round a particular group of memories of the past, in which she remains trapped. In *A Piece of Monologue* Speaker describes a series of actions that are performed nightly. Since he is identified by the audience with the figure he describes, these actions still seem to be continuing, although he makes no move during the play. He is, however, no less trapped than Mouth. The play is structured round two tracks of memory that entangle him. One concerns birth and the lighting of a lamp, the other death and a funeral. The memory of birth seems to link that event with the room in which Speaker is now standing:

> Born dead of night. Sun long sunk behind the larches. New needles turning green. In the room dark gaining. Till faint light from standard lamp. Wick turned low, And now. This night. Up at nightfall. Every nightfall. Faint light in room.

Speaker keeps going over his nightly routine: (rising, going to the window, then lighting the lamp and going to the wall) refining it to an almost telegraphic form:

> So nightly. Up. Socks. Nightgown. Window. Lamp. Backs away to edge of light and stands facing blank wall.

Then, as he sinks deeper into memory and penetrates 'the deeper coil',[2] a window seems to open on the past and he seems to be looking right back to an earlier night, when other hands lit the lamp. The hands materialise for him:

> There in the end slowly a faint hand. Holding aloft a lighted spill. In light of spill faintly the hand and milk white globe. Then second hand. In light of spill. Takes off globe and disappears.

The lamp seems to be the same as the one he himself lights nightly, but the room is different. Instead of the white pallet there is a 'glimmer of brass bedrail'. The room appears to be as he had known it in childhood, the remembered hands lighting the lamp and turning the wick low.

The second memory haunting Speaker ('dark slowly parts again') is of:

> Grey light. Rain pelting. Umbrellas round a grave. Seen from above. Streaming black canopies. Black ditch beneath. Rain bubbling in the black mud.

It is another picture seen as through a camera lens:

> Coffin out of frame. Whose? Fade. Gone.

The two memory tracks revolve 'again and again' though at times a welcome respite occurs:

Dark whole again. Blest dark.

As is usual with Beckett protagonists, Speaker's isolation is extreme. He has even stripped the photographs from his wall (as in *Film*) photographs: 'of . . . he all but said of loved ones.' This wry remark recurs in the play, always in the same form. He has tried to banish 'loved ones' from his memory, to destroy them, as he had destroyed the photographs:

Ripped from the wall and torn to shreds.

But his words keep betraying him: 'he all but said loved one' and he finally admits the funeral that haunts him is that of a woman:

Coffin on its way. Loved one . . . he all but said loved one on his way. Her way.

He is left with nothing but memories:

Facing the blank wall. Dying on.

The wall is described as facing East, the position of the altar in a church. Filled with family photographs it has been a kind of shrine for him. Now its blankness emphasises his isolation, only discoloured patches remain to show where the photographs had been. Even the sounds of life seem to have deserted him:

Room once full of sounds. Faint sounds. Whence unknown. Fewer and fainter as time wore on.

Rain still falls at times, however, (described, like mercy in *The Merchant of Venice* as: 'dropping gentle on the place beneath. Even now.')

Speaker's recapitulation sometimes gives additional information, at others verges on shorthand; it is almost continuous:

Again and again. Again and again gone.

As he goes on staring into the past ('Eyes glued to pane. As if looking his last') he manages to see 'beyond through rift in dark to other dark. Further dark.' It is there that the ghosts are:

Beyond that black beyond. Ghost light. Ghost nights. Ghost rooms. Ghost graves. Ghost . . . he all but said ghost loved ones. Waiting on the rip word.

Waiting for the word to be uttered that will bring them back, setting the flight of memories in motion again, like pulling the rip cord of a parachute to initiate the downward spiral. 'Birth' has been the rip word in the course of the play. He has tried to think of other things, more practical matters, but in the end accepts that there is only one subject of importance:

There are no other matters. Never were other matters. Never two matters. Never but the one matter. The dead and gone. The dying and going. From the word go. The word begone.

This was his subject in the first line and he has come full circle. It is also Beckett's subject, throughout his oeuvre.

The globe fades in the room at the end of the play. Speaker draws attention to it, thus making a final tie between himself and the narrative. The dying light is the more effective for there having been no other stage action throughout the monologue. Although the globe fades, however, 'the other' does not. Speaker remains 'barely visible in diffuse light', but still there. He has commented on this other light in the course of the play, wondering where it comes from, since there is none from the window. Now he stresses its continued presence in the room, and the figure of Speaker is seen by the audience still to be there within it. This seems to make the close of the play a continuum rather than an ending. It is as if the globe represents the nightly energy that allows Speaker to recapitulate the past. When it goes out Speaker remains, containing the past within himself, to be energised once more when the lamp comes on again. The birth of the light will act as a 'rip word' to start speech flowing again. It is like May in *Footfalls* slipping out at nightfall to pace her strip of floor and recapitulate her cycle of memories, waiting, at the end of the play, for the energy to complete the last lap before she is lost to sight. Speaker's lamp, like the light on May's strip, is 'faint' at the opening of *A Piece of Monologue*; were it to come on again, the chances are it would diminish further, but the 'skull-sized' globe would still manage to energise Speaker once more. As Beckett says in *For To End Yet Again*: 'Thus then the skull makes to glimmer again in lieu of going out.'[3]

ROCKABY

Rockaby was written in English and first performed at the State University of New York at Buffalo in 1981.[4] The play is a natural successor or companion to *Footfalls*. Beckett had Billie Whitelaw in mind to perform both plays; both are concerned with the mother-daughter relationship, and in both Beckett makes use of gradually diminishing light and sound.

As in *That Time* the protagonist, W, is largely a listener. The text appears to consist of her own recorded voice (V) to which she listens, while being slowly rocked in a rocking chair. She does not control the rock, and, at certain points in the play, the chair stops. In the ensuing lengthy pause W bestirs herself to say: 'more', whereupon, after a further pause, rock and voice begin again 'together'. It is as though tape and chair combined represent W's involuntary memory, and the only control she is capable of exerting over it is to encourage its continuance when it has temporarily halted.

The basic structure of *Rockaby* closely resembles *Not I*: the text of both plays is broken by silences. In *Not I* one phrase only results in silence, in *Rockaby* three different phrases mark the scene endings. In both plays the text consists largely of repetition from scene to scene. The text of *Not I* is expressed phrasally, in stream of consciousness form, each phrase separated by three dots. *Rockaby*, on the other hand, which is considerably shorter, seems more to resemble a poem on the page, since there is generally only one phrase to a line. The technique of phrasal repetition is the same as *Not I*, but pared right down.

There are four scenes in *Rockaby*. The play opens on a silence, until W says softly: 'more', thus suggesting that the audience is eavesdropping on a process that has been going on for some time. Three more silences occur during the play and there is another at its close, so that the text takes place between a framework of five pauses, making four scenes in all. In the first scene V, narrating in the third person, tells how 'she' had searched 'all eyes/all sides' for 'another creature like herself', 'another living soul', an endeavour that had proved fruitless, until one day she made up her mind it was 'time she stopped'. The last phrase sounds like a knell through the play, occurring three times in Scene 1, twice in Scenes 2 and 3 and once in Scene 4; it is also the closing phrase in Scenes 1 and 3. Each time it is repeated, like a refrain, in which W joins:

V: time she stopped
V and W: *time she stopped*

In the last scene, however, W remains silent and the phrase occurs with a variation:

V: time she stopped
let down the blind and stopped

Scene 2 repeats the themes of Scene 1 and adds impetus to the text by relating how, having finally abandoned 'going to and fro' outside, she:

Went back in and sat
at her window
let up the blind and sat
quiet at her window
only window
facing other windows
other only windows

The new information is built up fragmentarily, phrase by phrase, each extending the repeated language in each line by one extra detail. It is, in microcosm, the same technique as that by which the play is structured. Each scene repeats the themes of earlier scenes and, in a development almost musical in form, adds one new theme or movement to the pattern.

Scene 2 ends on the phrase 'one other living soul.' 'She' is still in search of someone to share her solitude. By Scene 3, however, her ambition has dwindled to seeking simply:

for a blind up
one blind up
no more
never mind a face
behind the pane
famished eyes
like hers
to see
be seen

In the final movement (Scene 4) even this is abandoned and she realises there is nothing further to be done, but go:

down the steep stair
let down the blind and down

right down
into the old rocker
mother rocker

The play thus forms a steady reduction from scene to scene, so that it follows, in miniature, the passage of a life (presumably the listener's); a gradual narrowing of horizon and hope until a final acceptance — even a welcoming — of the inevitable is reached; at first she goes about in the world, seeking a companion; then she withdraws, still seeking, to her window. In Scene 3 she hopes only for a sign of life ('one blind up', 'never mind a face') and at last accepts that her place is where she began, in the chair whose arms, say the stage directions 'suggest embrace', the 'mother rocker' in which her mother died. As the rocking finally ceases and W's head 'comes to rest', it seems that the daughter has also decided to follow her mother to the grave. In a sense she has even become her mother, as with May in *Footfalls*. This is evident from V's description of the mother as:

dead one night
in the rocker
in her best black
head fallen

W, says the costume directions, is wearing a 'black, lacy, high-necked evening gown' and an 'incongruous flimsy head-dress set askew' and at the end of the play her head gently falls. The head-dress 'askew' seems to tally with V's statement that the mother had: 'gone off her head/but harmless.'

Again like *Footfalls*, *Rockaby* seems partly the mother's story and partly the daughter's. W is, at the same time, both mother and daughter and yet fully neither. Jung's notion of the child who was never properly born seems once more relevant here.[5] Mother-dominated (as is May in *Footfalls*) W seems never to have found herself entirely, never to have become her own person. Her lack of a true sense of identity brings with it a lack of confidence and of the capacity to find companionship; hence her extreme isolation and final return to the arms where she began. Her attempt to escape her home and go into the world has failed. However the ambiguities in the language also allow for quite another interpretation. W's going:

down the steep stair
time she went right down

was her own other
own other living soul

may be compared with entering 'the deeper coil' of the mind that so alarmed Murphy. W could be seen here as penetrating the subconscious and accepting and uniting with the person she finds there, and thus becoming at last 'her own other' or complete self. In these terms even the chair may be seen as W finally embracing herself, while held in the 'inward curving arms'.

It is interesting to compare this embrace of the chair with the attitude adopted by Billie Whitelaw while rehearsing *Footfalls* with Beckett. Her arms were used to hug herself, expressing both May's isolation and her rejection of other companionship. Unlike May W has sought company and failed to find it. Her final embrace of herself may be seen as a more positive action than May's. Instead of seeking for some meaning in her experience, as does May, W is able finally to shrug life off: 'fuck life' as Billie Whitelaw said so memorably in her performance of *Rockaby* at the National Theatre in 1982. It was spoken in a light tone of acceptance and dismissal of experience and marked a distinct extension from May's persevering recapitulation in *Footfalls*, or Mouth, whose unswerving denial of selfhood in *Not I* leaves her perpetually haunted by the past. On the other hand the bitterness in the final lines of *Rockaby* can never be extinguished entirely, however gently they are spoken. Inevitably they have a forcible impact on an audience, more so than the dead rat in the reeds (or death of romantic love) in *That Time*, with which they may be compared, because they are more immediately explicit:

saying to the rocker
rock her off
stop her eyes
fuck life
stop her eyes
rock her off
rock her off

W hides nothing from herself. Life has brought her nothing but a final acceptance of the fact that nothing should have been expected from it. Understandably she wishes such negative experience to cease and a distinct ending appears to take place. Beckett says W's head has finally 'come to rest' and her eyes are 'closed for good', language charged with death. There is also a sense of completion, of having come full circle, at the end of the play, as with the smile at the end of *That Time*.

As in *That Time* also, Beckett uses eyes to achieve a particular dramatic effect. In *Rockaby* they are used to reinforce the sense of dwindling that develops in the play from scene to scene. Beckett states they should be 'now closed, now open in unblinking gaze', with the proportions 'about equal' in the first scene, but becoming increasingly closed in Scenes 2 and 3, closing finally half way through the last scene. Light is also part of the fading process in *Rockaby*, as it had been in *Footfalls*. When the play opens, a subdued spot falls first 'on face alone' and this remains 'constant throughout', only fading out in the final moments of the play. When light first comes up on the chair it is also subdued, leaving the rest of the stage in darkness, but the end of each scene is marked by a 'faint fade of light' on the chair, until it goes out altogether just before the end of the play, leaving only the spot on the face. W remains visible to the audience throughout, however, because light catches the highly polished chair and jet sequins on her dress, as she rocks gently 'in and out of light'.

Each scene is further structured by the closing phrase echoing, in precise synchronisation with the chair coming to rest and the fading light. Even W's voice contributes to the dwindling effect, by becoming increasingly softer when she breaks the silence after each scene by calling 'more'. Moreover when she joins in the refrain 'time she stopped' her voice also becomes progressively softer from Scenes 1 to 3 and has died out by Scene 4. The recorded voice (V) also weakens at the end of the play, so that her final words 'rock her off' echo in a whisper. Beckett had first used echo in *Footfalls*, with the diminishing echo of the chime between scenes giving an effect of distancing, combined with recurrence. In *Rockaby* the effect is enhanced by the echoing voice between scenes steadily reducing to a whisper. Beckett has in fact used every possible means of achieving diminishing effects in *Rockaby* and the play requires considerable technical skill to synchronize them precisely.

OHIO IMPROMPTU

Ohio Impromptu was written in English for performance at the Beckett Symposium at Ohio State University, Columbus, in May 1981.[6] After experimenting with a dual persona (M and M1) in his television play ... *but the clouds* ... and, earlier, with O and

E in *Film*, Beckett introduces a visual double or doppelgänger into *Ohio Impromptu*. For the first time he portrays both the listening and speaking figures familiar in earlier stage plays and confirms that they are one and the same. In *That Time* and *Rockaby*, for example, separation occurred between a listening figure and recorded voices (assumed to be voices in the head, externalised on tape for the benefit of an audience). A duality between listener and speaker was thus established and Beckett develops this in *Ohio Impromptu* into the image of two old men, Listener (L) and Reader (R), 'as alike in appearance as possible'. Both men are identically dressed in long black coats and both have long white hair. They are seated at a table centre stage, which is the only lighted area. Both sit with bowed heads propped on their right hands, both have their left hands on the table. In the centre of the table is one hat only, black and wide-brimmed, which could thus belong to either man. Neither face is fully seen. R is seated at the right of the table (as seen from the audience) with his head bent over the book. He thus presents only his profile to most of the audience and that consists largely of the specified long white hair. L's face is also largely shielded by hair falling around his bowed head, although he sits facing the audience, towards the right end of the long side of the table.

The action consists of R reading from the book in front of him. At times L interrupts him by knocking on the table with his left hand. There are always two knocks, following a set pattern. The first is a signal that R should repeat the penultimate words heard. When R has done this a pause occurs, during which a second knock from L signals that R may continue reading. There are six such occasions where L interrupts the narrative. The first occurs at the opening of the play and the last at the end. On the final occasion, however, when L signals R to continue reading, R closes the book and, in the silence that follows, the two men simultaneously 'lower their right hands to table, raise their heads and look at each other. Unblinking. Expressionless.' The confrontation of self and self (as at the end of *Film*) and, at the same time, both registering that the story is finally told, makes a most effective dramatic climax.

The story R reads describes the end of a life, the book is 'open at last pages'. It tells of a man having left the home 'where they had been so long together' after the death of his 'dear ' companion. The repeated use of the word 'dear' contrasts noticeably with *A Piece of Monologue*, where Speaker could not bring himself to use endearments: 'he all but said loved one.' The man in R's story had hoped 'some measure of relief might flow' from the unfamiliarity of his new surroundings, but the move had been a mistake. The dear one had warned him in dreams of the danger of leaving the home they had known, where 'my shade will comfort you'. From his new room the isle of swans is visible, and:

> Day after day he could be seen slowly pacing the islet. Hour after hour. In his long black coat no matter what the weather and old world Latin Quarter hat.

The man in the story is thus specifically identified, as to costume, with the two men seated at the table. In his solitary state he notices couples — how even the 'two arms' of the stream joyously rejoin each other at the tip of the island and flow 'united on'. Echoing Lady Macbeth (Act V Scene I) he realises he cannot return to the old haunts: 'What he had done alone could not be undone.' He develops nightmares 'In this extremity' (again like Lady Macbeth) which had not troubled him since childhood. Here, in the middle of the sombre narration, a shaft of grotesque humour typical of Beckett emerges. R starts to turn back the pages, to recapitulate 'the fearful symptoms described at length page forty paragraph four', until 'checked by L's left hand.' Beckett looks coldly at old age as well as compassionately, but the grim nature of his vision is at times relieved by laughter.

The end of the narrative tells how one night, when wakeful as usual:

> a man appeared to him and said, I have been sent by — and here he named the dear name — to comfort you.

The man read to him until dawn 'Then disappeared without a word'. This happened quite often thereafter until, 'with never a word exchanged they grew to be as one.' *Rockaby*, Beckett's previous play, will be recalled here, where almost W's final action was to become 'her own other.' The audience is naturally confirmed, by this time, in its identification of the narrative with the Reader and Listener on stage. The narrative goes on to relate that one night the visitor had remained after closing the book, eventually stating that the dear one had told him there was 'No need to go to him again, even were it in your power.' At this news the two men had 'sat on until turned to stone', both:

> Buried in who knows what profounds of mind
> Of mindlessness.

In consequence they failed to register the arrival of day, or perhaps it never came: 'From the street no sound of reawakening.' The narrative is not clear on this point; what is clear, however, is that it has now come to an end. These last pages have been the swansong.

The play opened with the line: 'Little is left to tell.' It is now rounded off by: 'Nothing is left to tell.' R closes the book, his action clearly paralleling its closure in the narrative. L, as usual, requests more of the story, but R does not — cannot comply: 'The sad tale (has been) a last time told.' In the ensuing silence, as L and R both register their new situation and simultaneously raise their heads to regard each other for the first time, Beckett manages to bring yet another play to a dramatic climax after the text has ended. As the two men appear now to be incontrovertibly identified with the two men in the story R has read, R must now leave, it is not in his 'power' to stay. Since L's story has been told, however, and the two men have grown 'to be as one' the likelihood is that this is the end for L also. In this realisation the two men look at each other, but no decisive action is taken; as at the end of *Endgame* Clov is prepared to go, but has not left when the curtain falls.

The narrative may of course be supposed to be entirely fictional. This is made especially apparent when R relates various reasons why the two men in the story may not have registered the new dawn. On the other hand, since much of what is being read is almost simultaneously enacted for the audience by the two men onstage, it appears that the narration is an up to the minute account of their final situation. Art becomes life as the two men stare at each other at the end of the play, and life art.

Technically this play does not have the complicated effects of *Rockaby* that preceded it, although the precise synchronisation of appearance, attitude and movement of L and R is very demanding for the actors. The use of knocking to represent speech (the first knock meaning 'repeat' and the second: 'continue') is a new idea and the resulting repetition of passages gives the play stylistically (as with *Rockaby*) somewhat the effect of a poem.

CATASTROPHE

This play marks a departure from Beckett's other work for the theatre, since it makes a political statement — albeit on humanitarian grounds. It was written in French in 1982 for performance at the Avignon Festival on 21 July 1982. The evening was organised by AIDA (L'Association internationale de défense des artistes victimes de la répression dans le monde) on behalf of Vaclav Havel, the Czech playwright, imprisoned for his political beliefs. In the most extreme torture for one living by his pen, all writing materials were denied to Havel. Beckett and Arthur Miller both wrote plays dedicated to Havel for the occasion. The first publication of Beckett's English translation of *Catastrophe* was in the *New Yorker*, in January 1983.[7]

The play is set in a theatre. There are four characters: the director (D) his female assistant (A) Luke, the lighting technician (L) heard offstage but not seen and the protagonist (P) who stands unspeaking centre stage throughout 'on a black block 18' high.' The action consists of the assistant's manipulation of the figure on the block, in order to achieve an image that satisfies the director. D is extremely authoritarian, his instructions domineering and frequently irritable, and the assistant's suggestions are timid in consequence. D gives his orders from the comfort of an armchair; he is, at the same time, a parody of directorial dictatorship and an image of the authoritarian state. He is even dressed in the standard wear of leaders of the Eastern bloc, in a fur coat and matching fur toque. The assistant continually takes notes of the director's wishes, thus emphasising the writing materials Havel lacks. In her white 'coverall' she operates on the silent figure on the block in an almost clinical fashion, emphasised by the language: 'How's the skull?' enquires D. A hospital is of course an effective method of demonstrating state control, but in Havel's case the theatre is a particularly apt choice of metaphor, reflecting the dramatist's plight.

The protagonist in *Catastrophe* appears entirely divorced from his surroundings — a cross between a statue and a puppet. He is dressed as though bereaved:

Black wide-brimmed hat. Black dressing gown to ankles. Barefoot. Head bowed. Hands in pockets.

The assistant, who might be said to be carrying out state orders, has arranged his figure so as to present a carefully selected view to the audience or public at large. Getting the image right is a political necessity no less than a requirement of theatre as an art form:

D: . . . Why the plinth?
A: To let the stalls see the feet.
(*Pause.*)

D: Why the hat?
A: To help hide the face.
(*Pause.*)
D: Why the gown?
A: To have him all black.

The director is anxious both to develop the image and also that no inconvenient details should be apparent. The hands, for example, (which A says are 'crippled') must not draw attention to their inactivity by being hidden in the pockets, nor, when exposed, should the fists be clenched. A notes D's wishes: 'Hands limp.' He orders the figure to be stripped, revealing:

P in old grey pyjamas, head bowed, fists clenched.

A comments that he is shivering, but D is unimpressed: 'Not all that.' He orders the hat to be removed and both head and hands to be whitened, thus presenting a stronger image. A unclenches the hands and timidly suggests joining them, so that the figure stands on the plinth as if in prayer. When she again comments on P's shivering, D's triumphant sadism is apparent: 'Bless his heart.' However her suggestion that there might be 'a little . . . gag?', thus emphasising the figure's predicament, meets with an explosion of anger:

D: For God's sake! This craze for explicitation!
Every i dotted to death! Little gag! For God's sake!
A: Sure he won't utter?
D: Not a squeak.

D reflects Beckett's own dislike of 'explicitation' here, a wish to leave at least something to the audience's imagination. The mute figure, hands raised as if in supplication, makes its own comment — though not, of course, the one D has in mind. Where he would wish the figure to appear to be expressing contrition for past misdemeanours, the actual effect is to enlist audience sympathy on humanitarian grounds.

At this point D leaves the stage, in order to 'see how it looks from the house', thus allowing comic relief as A 'subsides' into his armchair, only to 'spring to her feet no sooner seated' and wipe the chair vigorously, so that no trace of the tyrant can contaminate her, perhaps. Since D now calls his orders from off-stage, there is a growing sense of being overlooked and of manipulation by unseen power, a subject that had interested

Beckett in earlier works, such as *Act Without Words I*. The head now has to be further bowed and more of the body exposed: 'Bare the neck', A is told. The legs are also progressively stripped to above the knee and 'all flesh' is to be whitened.

The image is now ready for lighting and the electrician is instructed to black out the stage, leaving A in shadow and light on P alone. D asks for light to isolate the head. Scorning A's suggestion that P should 'raise his head . . . an instant . . . show his face', D is quite satisfied with the image as it stands: 'There's our catastrophe. In the bag.' He merely wishes to see it once more before leaving for his political meeting ('Step on it. I have a caucus.') At the command: 'Now. . . let 'em have it' the gradual isolation of P's head by the light (as in *Play*) is again achieved. D's satisfaction is conveyed expressionistically. In the final words of the play he imagines the applause to come: 'He'll have them on their feet. I can hear it from here' and, after a pause, a 'Distant storm of applause' is heard.

P then performs the one act of his own volition in the play, he raises his head and 'fixes the audience', which is aghast. 'The applause falters, dies' and there is a long pause before the light fades. Beckett has once again achieved a dramatic climax by light and image alone. P's silent gaze is more eloquent than language and the final comment is Havel's. D's carefully prepared political statement has been silently challenged — the performance has gone beyond the director's control. For him, it is a catastrophe.

WHAT WHERE

What Where was first performed at the Harold Clurman Theatre, New York, on 15 June 1983. The names of its characters (Bam Bom Bim and Bem) recall Pim Bom and Bem in *How It Is*: 'one syllable m at the end all that matters.'[8] They appear to be a quadruple identity, reminiscent of *Quad II*, with four players 'as alike as possible', all with the 'same long grey hair' and long grey gowns. The idea of a multiple identity had also been present in *How It Is*:

> there are millions of us and there are three I place myself at my point of view Bem is Bom Bom Bem let us say Bom it's preferable Bom then me and Pim me in the middle.[9]

A fifth character in *What Where* (V) is the voice of Bam, present 'in the shape of a small megaphone at head level.' This divorce between the actor and his voice, already familiar in Beckett in plays such as *That Time* and *Rockaby*, is here given visible and comic form, yet with sinister implications as the play progresses.

From his commanding position downstage left of the four players (as seen from the audience) V may be seen as directing proceedings in the playing area (P) a rectangular area 3×2 metres upstage right of V, like a stage within a stage; a megaphone is standard equipment for certain directors, as for example on a film set. V 'surrounded by shadow' downstage (the auditor's position in *Not I*) overlooks the playing area and his voice from the dark is precisely what an actor expects of a director during lighting rehearsals. V indeed controls the action by the operation of light on the playing area, stating that he is switching on or off. It is almost as though we are hearing the voice of the light operator in *Play* at last. The playing area (which, like V, is 'dimly lit' and shadow encircled) is divided into W(est) N(orth) and E(ast), as was the light circle in . . . *but the clouds* . . . . South is not mentioned in either play, recalling Beckett's remark when rehearsing *Footfalls* that South is 'too warm'.[10] As in . . . *but the clouds* . . . also, the action of *What Where* is controlled by a demanding voice. In both plays there are false starts and V (M's voice in . . . *but the clouds* . . . and Bam's in *What Where*) demands repetition, until accuracy is achieved.

V refers to the four players and himself as 'the last five', an interesting calculation, since Bam and he (if not more of the identical players) are one and the same. Bam is present when V first switches on the playing area, standing (W) 'head haught' with Bom (at N) 'head bowed'. V does not like what he sees and switches off at once. When he 'starts again' Bam is alone and V approves: 'Good./I am alone.' Bom re-enters still with bowed head and Bim follows, 'head haught', like Bam. After a pause Bim goes out again, followed by Bom and reappears, after a further pause, with his head also bowed. It is as though in their brief time together Bom had been able to communicate his despair to Bim. A pattern is thus established in which precisely the same actions are performed by the remaining players; it is not unlike the exposition of a Fugue in Four Parts. Bem, the last to enter, inherits Bim's bowed head and finally passes it on to Bam. When this happens, V closes the action: 'Good./I switch off.'

The next sequence of action begins at once, as in *Quad*: 'I start again.' This time, however, V says: 'Now with words.', as though the first version were a mime and movement rehearsal and the actors are now ready for the dialogue. Precisely the same series of actions is repeated by the four players, in the same order, but with the addition of dialogue, so that a rhythm of repeated language is also established. In the first dialogue Bam establishes from Bom that 'he didn't say anything', despite having been given 'the works.' V regards this as a false start. As with the first silent version, however, when Bam substitutes: 'He didn't say it' for 'he didn't say anything' V approves, so that the dialogue continues past the point where it was previously stopped, until Bam refuses to believe Bom:

Bam: It's a lie. (*Pause.*) He said it to you. (*Pause.*) Confess he said it to you. (*Pause.*) You'll be given the works until you confess.

Bim enters here and Bam asks him to take Bom away and make him confess:

Bim: What must he confess?
Bam: That he said it to him.
Bim: Is that all?
Bam: Yes.

Bam's response to Bim does not satisfy V, however, and he makes him repeat it:

Bim: Is that all?
Bam: And what.
V: Good.

Presumably V is trying to get at what (if anything) was said, thus establishing the 'What' of the play's title.

A repetition of Bam's interrogation of Bom takes place, this time with Bim. The only difference is that after a false start, V manages to make Bam substitute the word 'Where' for 'it' or 'what'.

Bam: You gave him the works?
Bim: Yes.
Bam: And he didn't say it?
Bim: No.
V: Not good.
I start again.
Bam: Well?
Bim: Nothing.
Bam: He didn't say where?
V: Good.

Bim: Where?
V: Ah!
Bam: Where.
Bim: No.

Thus the second word in the title is also established. The pattern is then repeated, as in the silent version. Bam does not believe that Bim was not told 'where' and he is given 'the works' by Bem, who, in his turn, is not believed by Bam. The interrogation has been becoming progressively shorter and has dwindled to only two questions by the time that Bem enters with bowed head:

Bam: Well?
Bem: Nothing.
Bam: He didn't say where?
Bem: No.

Bam himself has to leave the stage in order to give Bem 'the works' and his own head is bowed when he returns: 'In the end I appear/Reappear' states V calmly. He does not comment on Bam's bowed head, but registers with pleasure that he is alone once more. The action completed, he switches off:

V: Good.
I am alone
In the present as were I still.
It is winter.
Without journey.
Time passes.
That is all.
Make sense who may.
I switch off.

Light goes first from the playing area and, after a pause, from V. Throughout the play V has commented in similar lines when alone, on the season and the passage of time. In the first (silent) sequence, it was spring, after the interrogation of Bom it is summer; autumn follows Bim's interrogation and winter, Bem's. The repeated phrases echo each other like a refrain in verse.

Repeated patterns of language and action characterise the play. V initiates the action both by manipulating the light on the playing area and by pushing Bam (i.e. himself) into pursuing the enquiry. There is a strong sense of menace in the interrogation and apparent torture of Bom Bim and Bem. Bam is never given 'the works', the play ends just as his turn has come, but there is no one left to interrogate him. There may be connections here with the political theme of Beckett's preceding play, *Catastrophe*. *What Where* also seems to have something in common with the plan for a play at Trinity College Dublin (discussed earlier in connection with *Play*)[11] in which a man is seated downstage with his head up, while two women, who sit upstage facing him, have their heads bowed; at the end of the play the man's head also is bowed. A diagram for the projected play suggests a fourth character also, thus increasing possible links between the fragment and *What Where*.

The interrogation takes place in order to ascertain whether 'it' had been said and 'what' and 'where' it was. Despite Bam's apparent certainty to the contrary, the possibility (even likelihood) remains that Bom Bim and Bem were telling the truth, that nothing had been said, that indeed there was nothing to say. Bam's bowed head at the end of the play might thus represent his final acknowledgement of this. His insistence that there must be some secret to be told or knowledge to be gained links the play with earlier works. In *Play* and *Not I*, for example, the characters suspect or hope that if they could only find the right words, they would no longer be forced to go on speaking. But they have no idea what words they might be. Bom Bim and Bem are both torturers and tortured, but they seem equally puzzled about the supposed secret, and, since they are quite sure nothing has been said, might not even recognise it if they heard it, as Mouth says in *Not I*: '. . . something she didn't know herself . . . wouldn't know if she heard . . . then forgiven . . .'. The fact that Bam refuses to believe the others, to accept that there is 'nothing' to be told, could link with May's obsessive attempt to register her steps in *Footfalls*, or find meaning in her existence.

In 1985 Beckett cut *What Where* radically for a Stuttgart (Süddeutscher Rundfunk) television production, entitled *Waswo*. Interestingly, in view of his earlier reluctance to adapt works for other genres, he greatly prefers the cut version. Tightening the play for television (Beckett's comment was that he ''couldn't have made it much tighter without splitting!'')[12] involved dispensing with movement, and the series of entrances and exits is cut in favour of light isolating the men's faces. Feeling that the play worked much better like this, Beckett recommended a similar form of presentation for a 1986 stage production in Paris, which also improved on the original version.

The fact that he prefers the television version of *What Where* and was prepared to cut the play for the camera marks Beckett's increasing interest in images on a screen. Indeed when asked in September 1986 whether he felt he had now come through the theatre into television, he replied: "I would think so. There are so many possibilities in television."[13]

APPENDIX I

MANUSCRIPT CHART

All That Fall to *Footfalls*

1956—1976

University collections are abbreviated to one word; full details in acknowledgements.

Title	Year of Writing	First Language	Holograph and Collection	Typescript and Collection
All That Fall	1956	English	1 RUL 1 Texas	1 Texas 1 Washington
The Gloaming/ Theatre I	1956	English (French)	2 RUL 1 RUL	2 RUL 2 RUL
Krapp's Last Tape	1958	English	3 RUL	4 Texas
Theatre II	1958	French	1 TCD	2 RUL
Embers	c.1958	English		1 TCD 1 Texas
Happy Days	1960-61	English	1 RUL 3 Ohio	5 Ohio
Pochade Radiophonique/ Radio II	c.1960	French (English)	 1 RUL	2 RUL 1 RUL
Words and Music	1961	English	1 RUL 1 Washington	2 Washington
Esquisse Radiophonique/ Radio I	1961	French	1 Ontario	
Cascando	1961	French (English)	1 Harvard	4 Harvard 2 Washington 2 Harvard 3 Washington
"Before Play"		English		1 RUL
Play	1962-63	English		10 Washington
Film	1963	English	2 RUL	1 Washington
Kilcool	1963	English	3 TCD	
"Before Come and Go"		English	2 RUL	2 RUL
Come and Go	1965	English	2 Stuttgart	4 Washington
Eh Joe	1965	English	1 Washington	6 Washington
Sans/ Lessness	c.1969	French (English)	1 Yale 2 Yale	 3 Yale
Breath	c.1969	English	1 Calder	1 Warner (Oxford)
Not I	1972	English	2 RUL	6 RUL
That Time	1974	English	1 RUL	7 RUL
Footfalls	1975	English	1 RUL	5 RUL

APPENDIX II

THE STRUCTURING OF *SANS/LESSNESS**

1. MONTAGE: Beckett's ordering of the text (Holograph by kind permission of Samuel Beckett and Francis Warner)

2. SENTENCE "FAMILIES"

*SEE ALSO: Beckett's description of the material (pp. 154–5 above) headed "Key".

MONTAGE

I

Sentences	Paragraphs
A3, A8, C9, A2	I
A9, D3, E9, B9, F2	II
F10, C6, D8	III
E6, D7, C1, F9, A5	IV
B4, C4, B1	V
F3, E4, C7, B7, F2, B6	VI
A4, C2, E3, C10, F5, E5, F4	VII
A1, C8, A6, B2, D5, A8	VIII
C5, F9, B5, D10, B3, D6, F1	IX
A10, E8, D9, E10	X
F6, B10, F7, A7	XI
D4, E7, D1, E1, C3, D2	XII

II

Sentences	Paragraphs
C4, D6, A2	I
B8, B10, F2, F7	II
E6, B2, F8, B4	III
D1, B3, A9, A5, E2, E9	IV
A1, F4, D6, C9, F6, B5, D7	V
C3, C10, E5, F3, F5, E8	VI
~~A4~~, ~~E1~~, D5, E3, D3	VII
A10, D9, F9, B1, A8, E4, C6	VIII
A3, E7, D2	IX
A4, B7, F1, C5, D[illegible], B9	X
C2, A6, D8, F10, D4	XI
C7, C1, C8, E10	XII

SENTENCE "FAMILIES"

A 1 In four split asunder over backwards true refuge issueless scattered ruins.
2 Blacked out fallen open four walls over backwards true refuge issueless.
3 Ruins true refuge long last towards which so many false time out of mind.
4 Slow black with ruin true refuge four walls over backwards no sound.
5 Four square true refuge long last four walls over backwards no sound.
6 True refuge long last issueless scattered down four walls over backwards no sound.
7 True refuge long last scattered ruins same grey as the sand.
8 Scattered ruins ash grey all sides true refuge long last issueless.
9 Scattered ruins same grey as the sand ash grey true refuge.
10 Blacked out fallen open true refuge issueless towards which so many false time out of mind.

B 1 Ash grey all sides earth sky as one all sides endlessness.
2 All sides endlessness earth sky as one no stir not a breath.
3 Flatness endless little body only upright same grey all sides earth sky body ruins.
4 Grey sky no cloud no sound no stir earth ash grey sand.
5 Earth sand same grey as the air sky ruins body fine ash grey sand.
6 No sound not a breath same grey all sides earth sky body ruins.
7 Earth sky as one all sides endlessness little body only upright.
8 No sound no stir ash grey sky mirrored earth mirrored sky.
9 All sides endlessness earth sky as one no sound no stir.
10 Grey air timeless earth sky as one same grey as the ruins flatness endless.

C 1 Little body ash grey locked rigid heart beating face to endlessness.
2 Legs a single block arms fast to sides little body face to endlessness.
3 Heart beating little body only upright grey face features overrun two pale blue.
4 Little body same grey as the earth sky ruins only upright.
5 Ash grey little body only upright heart beating face to endlessness.
6 Little body grey face features slit and little holes two pale blue.
7 Little body little block heart beating ash grey only upright.
8 Little body little block genitals overrun arse a single block grey crack overrun.
9 Grey face two pale blue little body heart beating only upright.
10 Only upright little body grey smooth no relief a few holes.

D 1 Little void mighty light four square all white blank planes all gone from mind.
2 Light white touch close head through calm eye light of reason all gone from mind.
3 Four square all light sheer white blank planes all gone from mind.
4 Face to calm eye touch close all calm all white all gone from mind.
5 Blank planes sheer white calm eye light of reason all gone from mind.
6 Face to white calm touch close eye calm long last all gone from mind.
7 Blank planes touch close sheer white all gone from mind.
8 Blank planes sheer white eye calm long last all gone from mind.
9 Head through calm eye all light white calm all gone from mind.
10 Light refuge sheer white blank planes all gone from mind.

E 1 Never was but grey air timeless no stir not a breath.
2 Never but this changelessness dream the passing hour.
3 Never but in vanished dream the passing hour long short.
4 Never but in dream the happy dream only one time to serve.
5 Never but dream the days and nights made of dreams of other nights better days.
6 Figment light never was but grey air timeless no sound.
7 Never but imagined the blue in wild imagining the blue celeste of poesy.
8 Never but silence such that in imagination this wild laughter these cries.
9 Never was but grey air timeless no sound figment the passing light.
10 Figment dawn dispeller of figments and the other called dusk.

F 1 One step more one alone all alone in the sand no hold he will make it.
2 In the sand no hold one step more in the endlessness he will make it.
3 He will stir in the sand there will be stir in the sky the air the sand.
4 He will live again the space of a step it will be day and night again over him the endlessness.
5 One step in the ruins in the sand on his back in the endlessness he will make it.
6 He will go on his back face to the sky open again over him the ruins the sand the endlessness.
7 It will be day and night again over him the endlessness the air heart will beat again.
8 On him will rain again as in the blessed days of blue the passing cloud.
9 Old love new love as in the blessed days unhappiness will reign again.
10 He will curse god again as in the blessed days face to the open sky the passing deluge.

APPENDIX III

LESSNESS RESTRUCTURED

I

Sentences	Paragraphs
D10 B10 A9	I
B2 E10 A10	II
E1 D4 D8 E4 A4 C2 C8	III
E2 D1 B8 C6 C10	IV
A6 F3 E9 D9	V
B4 F4 A5 A8 A7	VI
F9 E6 D2 C5 F10 F2	VII
F5 A2 B3 F8	VIII
D7 F6 D3 E5 E3 B5	IX
B6 E8 E7 D6 F1 C1	X
C3 A1 B1 A3 F7 B7 D5	XI
C9 C7 B9 C4	XII

II

Sentences	Paragraphs
A9 F8 F8 E10 A7 C2 B2	I
A8 D8 B9	II
C10 E9 B1 B7 E3	III
E7 A1 B10	IV
D10 F5 D5 E1	V
E6 A2 A4 F3 C4 B5	VI
A10 B3 C6 F4	VII
B4 E2 E5 D7	VIII
D3 C5 C8 C7 F7 F9 D1	IX
D4 C3 C9 C1 B6 B8	X
A3 F1 D6 F6 D2 A5	XI
F2 E4 A6 F10 D9	XII

D10 Light refuge sheer white blank planes all gone from mind.
B10 Grey air timeless earth sky as one same grey as the ruins flatness endless.
A9 Scattered ruins same grey as the sand ash grey true refuge.

B2 All sides endlessness earth sky as one all sides endlessness.
E10 Figment dawn dispeller of figments and the other called dusk.
A10 Blacked out fallen open true refuge issueless towards which so many false time out of mind.

E1 Never was but grey air timeless no stir not a breath.
D4 Face to calm eye touch close all calm all white all gone from mind.
D8 Blank planes sheer white eye calm long last all gone from mind.
E4 Never but in dream the happy dream only one time to serve.
A4 Slow black with ruin true refuge four walls over backwards no sound.
C2 Legs a single block arms fast to sides little body face to endlessness.
C8 Little body little block genitals overrun arse a single block grey crack overrun.

E2 Never but this changelessness dream the passing hour.
D1 Little void mighty light four square all white blank planes all gone from mind.
B8 No sound no stir ash grey sky mirrored earth mirrored sky.
C6 Little body grey face features slit and little holes two pale blue.
C10 Only upright little body grey smooth no relief a few holes.

A6 True refuge long last issueless scattered down four walls over backwards no sound.
F3 He will stir in the sand there will be stir in the sky the air the sand.
E9 Never was but grey air timeless no sound figment the passing light.
D9 Head through calm eye all light white calm all gone from mind.

B4 Grey sky no cloud no sound no stir earth ash grey sand.
F4 He will live again the space of a step it will be day and night again over him the endlessness.
A5 Four square true refuge long last four walls over backwards no sound.
A8 Scattered ruins ash grey all sides true refuge long last issueless.
A7 True refuge long last scattered ruins same grey as the sand.

F9 Old love new love as in the blessed days unhappiness will reign again.
E6 Figment light never was but grey air timeless no sound.
D2 Light white touch close head through calm eye light of reason all gone from mind.
C5 Ash grey little body only upright heart beating face to endlessness.
F10 He will curse God again as in the blessed days face to the open sky the passing deluge.
F2 In the sand no hold one step more in the endlessness he will make it.

F5 One step in the ruins in the sand on his back in the endlessness he will make it.
A2 Blacked out fallen open four walls over backwards true refuge issueless.
B3 Flatness endless little body only upright same grey all sides earth sky body ruins.
F8 On him will rain again as in the blessed days of blue the passing cloud.

D7 Blank planes touch close sheer white all gone from mind.
F6 He will go on his back face to the sky open again over him the ruins the sand the endlessness.
D3 Four square all light sheer white blank planes all gone from mind.
E5 Never but dream the days and nights made of dreams of other nights better days.
E3 Never but in vanished dream the passing hour long short.
B5 Earth sand same grey as the air sky ruins body fine ash grey sand.

B6 No sound not a breath same grey all sides earth sky body ruins.
E8 Never but silence such that in imagination this wild laughter these cries.
E7 Never but imagined the blue in wild imagining the blue celeste of poesy.
D6 Face to white calm touch close eye calm long last all gone from mind.
F1 One step more one alone all alone in the sand no hold he will make it.
C1 Little body ash grey locked rigid heart beating face to endlessness.

C3 Heart beating little body only upright grey face features overrun two pale blue.
A1 In four split asunder over backwards true refuge issueless scattered ruins.
B1 Ash grey all sides earth sky as one all sides endlessness.
A3 Ruins true refuge long last towards which so many false time out of mind.
F7 It will be day and night again over him the endlessness the air heart will beat again.
B7 Earth sky as one all sides endlessness little body only upright.
D5 Blank planes sheer white calm eye light of reason all gone from mind.

C9 Grey face two pale blue little body heart beating only upright.
C7 Little body little block heart beating ash grey only upright.
B9 All sides endlessness earth sky as one no sound no stir.
C4 Little body same grey as the earth sky ruins only upright.

A9 Scattered ruins same grey as the sand ash grey true refuge.
E8 Never but silence such that in imagination this wild laughter these cries.
F8 On him will rain again as in the blessed days of blue the passing cloud.
E10 Figment dawn dispeller of figments and the other called dusk.
A7 True refuge long last scattered ruins same grey as the sand.
C2 Legs a single block arms fast to sides little body face to endlessness.
B2 All sides endlessness earth sky as one no stir not a breath.

A8 Scattered ruins ash grey all sides true refuge long last issueless.
D8 Blank planes sheer white eye calm long last all gone from mind.
B9 All sides endlessness earth sky as one no sound no stir.

C10 Only upright little body grey smooth no relief a few holes.
E9 Never was but grey air timeless no sound figment the passing light.
B1 Ash grey all sides earth sky as one all sides endlessness.
B7 Earth sky as one all sides endlessness little body only upright.
E3 Never but in vanished dream the passing hour long short.

E7 Never but imagined the blue in wild imagining the blue celeste of poesy.
A1 In four split asunder over backwards true refuge issueless scattered ruins.
B10 Grey air timeless earth sky as one same grey as the ruins flatness endless.

D10 Light refuge sheer white blank planes all gone from mind.
F5 One step in the ruins in the sand on his back in the endlessness he will make it.
D5 Blank planes sheer white calm eye light of reason all gone from mind.
E1 Never was but grey air timeless no stir not a breath.

E6 Figment light never was but grey air timeless no sound.
A2 Blacked out fallen open four walls over backwards true refuge issueless.
A4 Slow black with ruin true refuge four walls over backwards no sound.
F3 He will stir in the sand there will be stir in the sky the air the sand.
C4 Little body same grey as the earth sky ruins only upright.
B5 Earth sand same grey as the air sky ruins body fine ash grey sand.

A10 Blacked out fallen open true refuge issueless towards which so many false time out of mind.
B3 Flatness endless little body only upright same grey all sides earth sky body ruins.
C6 Little body grey face features slit and little holes two pale blue.
F4 He will live again the space of a step it will be day and night again over him the endlessness.

B4 Grey sky no cloud no sound no stir earth ash grey sand.
E2 Never but this changelessness dream the passing hour.
E5 Never but dream the days and nights made of dreams of other nights better days.
D7 Blank planes touch close sheer white all gone from mind.

D3 Four square all light sheer white blank planes all gone from mind.
C5 Ash grey little body only upright heart beating face to endlessness.
C8 Little body little block genitals overrun arse a single block grey crack overrun.
C7 Little body little block heart beating ash grey only upright.
F7 It will be day and night again over him the endlessness the air heart will beat again.
F9 Old love new love as in the blessed days unhappiness will reign again.
D1 Little void mighty light four square all white blank planes all gone from mind.

D4 Face to calm eye touch close all calm all white all gone from mind.
C3 Heart beating little body only upright grey face features overrun two pale blue.
C9 Grey face two pale blue little body heart beating only upright.
C1 Little body ash grey locked rigid heart beating face to endlessness.
B6 No sound not a breath same grey all sides earth sky body ruins.
B8 No sound no stir ash grey sky mirrored earth mirrored sky.

A3 Ruins true refuge long last towards which so many false time out of mind.
F1 One step more alone all alone in the sand no hold he will make it.
D6 Face to white calm touch close eye calm long last all gone from mind.
F6 He will go on his back face to the sky open again over him the ruins the sand the endlessness.
D2 Light white touch close head through calm eye light of reason all gone from mind.
A5 Four square true refuge long last four walls over backwards no sound.

F2 In the sand no hold one step more in the endlessness he will make it.
E4 Never but in dream the happy dream only one time to serve.
A6 True refuge long last issueless scattered down four walls over backwards no sound.
F10 He will curse God again as in the blessed days face to the open sky the passing deluge.
D9 Head through calm eye all light white calm all gone from mind.

APPENDIX IV

Beckett's analysis of *Not I*
Copy of holograph (R.U.L. MS. 1227/7/12/1)
by kind permission of
Samuel Beckett and Reading University Library

Analysis

Birth ... [illegible] – premature – no love – [illegible]

field ... aetat. 65 – picking cowslips to make a ball – [illegible] – stop & stare into space – [illegible] – [illegible]

[illegible] ... first [illegible] – [illegible] (mention [illegible]) – [illegible] so far –

(Cut)

[illegible] – amplify

So far . . [illegible] – [illegible] of skull – [illegible]

buzzing . . [illegible]

brain – . . [illegible] – first thought – [illegible]

✓ [illegible]

memory . . [illegible] – field – [illegible] – added to walking

speculations – . perhaps something she had to say – (how it had been e.g.) – [illegible] – [illegible] – walking all her days – stop & stare into space – amplify

walking – ✓

punishment / suffering ... [illegible] punishment – [illegible] suffering – [illegible] – amplify – [illegible] suffering – buzzing

interruptions ✓ [illegible] – what? – who? – what? – [illegible] – buzzing – [illegible] – [illegible]

✓ [illegible] – [illegible] – [illegible]

[illegible] . . ✓ [illegible] – [illegible] – how she survived

[illegible] . . ✓ [illegible] – [illegible]

[illegible] ✓ [illegible]

APPENDIX V

Beckett's synopsis of *Not I*
Copy of typescript (R.U.L. MS. 1227/7/12/10)
by kind permission of
Samuel Beckett and Reading University Library

MS 1227/7/12/10

NOT I - synopsis

1. Premature birth
Parents unknown
No love at any time
At age of 70 in a field picking cowslips suddenly finds herself in the dark

2. No feeling apart from buzzing in her head and awareness of a ray of light
Mind still active in a way
First thought: she is being punished for her sins
Dismissed as she realises she is not suffering
Second thought: perhaps she should groan (to please tormentor)
Failure to utter a sound
All silent but for the buzzing
Motionless but for eyes opening and shutting
Mind questions this in view of life scene 1 (field)
Hears a voice largely unintelligible

3. Accent suggests it is hers
Life scene 2 (shopping centre)
Tries to delude herself voice not hers
Renounces as she feels lips moving
Fear that feeling may come back but for the moment mouth alone

4. Next thought: such distress can't continue
Description of same: unintelligible irrepressible voice, consternation of mind
Prayer for voice to stop: unanswered
Life scene 3 (Croker's Acres)
Brain grabbing at straws (e.g. God's mercy)
Life scene 1 (field) again
Perhaps something she should tell? Life scene 4 (courtroom), life scene 1 (field) and no from within

5. Something she should think? No as before
Life scene 5 (rushing out to tell)
Distress worse: description of same
Prayer for all to stop: unanswered
Life scene 1 (field) again

APPENDIX VI

Beckett's list of the quotations in *Happy Days*
Two pages from a production notebook
for *Glückliche Tage*, Schiller Theater, Berlin, 1971
(RUL MS. 1396/4/10)
by kind permission of
Samuel Beckett and Reading University Library

64

1 " – – – – – – – – oh woe is me
To have seen what I have seen, see what I see.

" Oh what a noble mind is here o'erthrown . ."

2 – – – – – – – O fleeting joys
Of Paradise, dear bought with lasting woes (adam)
BK. 10 741/2 Paradise Lost loc. ?

3 " – – Beauty's ensign yet
Is crimson in thy lips & in thy cheeks
And death's pale flag is not advanced there "

4 Fear no more the heat o' the sun
Nor the furious winter's rages
Thou thy worldly task hast done,
Home art gone & ta'en thy wages:
Golden lads & girls all must,
Like chimney-sweepers, come to dust (Guiderius)

5 " And moody madness laughing wild
Amid severest woe . . "
Thomas Gray : On a Distant Prospect of Eton Coll.

6 Paradise enow

7 " I say confusedly what comes uppermost "
R. Browning

8 Some say that ever 'gainst that season comes
Wherein our Saviour's birth is celebrated,
The bird of dawning singeth all night long.
And then, they say, no spirit can walk abroad,
The nights are wholesome;

66

9 Hail, holy light! Offspring of heaven first-born
Paradise Lost Bk. III line 1

10 In some melodious plot
Of beechen green & shadows numberless
(Keats: Ode to a Nightingale)

11 She never told her love (Viola)
But let concealment, like a worm i' the bud
Feed on her damask cheek; she pined in thought
~~and sick & yeeld~~ 12th Night II. 4
and, with a green & ~~yellow melancholy~~,
She sat, like patience on a monument,
Smiling at grief."

~~Go, forget me, why should sorrow
O'er that brow a shadow fling?~~
12 Go, forget me — and tomorrow
Brightly smile & sweetly sing.
Smile — though I shall not be near thee,
Sing — though I shall never hear thee.
(Charles Wolfe 1791-1823)

14 Gather ye rosebuds while ye may
Old Time is still a-flying
and this same flower that smiles today
Tomorrow will be dying.
Herrick: To the Virgins to make much of Time

13 I call to the eye of the mind
W. B. Yeats The Hawk's Well
a well long choked up & dry
~~(Half confusedly proud comes uppermost)
(Robert Browning)~~
and boughs long stripped by the wind.
and I call to the mind's eye
Pallor of an ivory face,
Its lofty dissolute air
a man climbing up to a place
The salt sea wind has swept bare

APPENDIX VII

1. CHART OF *NOT I* MSS.

2. TEN TYPESCRIPTS OF *PLAY*.

3. COMPLETE DRAFTS OF *THAT TIME* & *FOOTFALLS*.

NOT I

The drafts of *Not I* are investigated under six headings:

A — A description of the material (the extent of it)
B — The development of the stage directions
C — Addenda and notes (Beckett's afterthoughts on completing a draft)
D — "Question" (charting the progress of the recurring question that is finally established as: "what? . . . who? . . . no! . . . she!")
E — Selected verbal alterations in each draft
F — A selection of additional vocabulary in each draft

Other categories for investigation might well have been chosen, but the above gives a comprehensive view of the material, without daunting the reader with excessive detail. Reading each column downwards, from top to bottom, presents the information for each draft as compactly as possible:

	HOLOGRAPH I	HOLOGRAPH II
R.U.L. MS. NO.	1227/7/12/1	1227/7/12/1
A DESCRIPTION	3/4 page. Headed Paris 20.3.72 Entire text crossed out.	4¼ pages. Full text. Dated at close: Paris 1.4.72. Reverse of pp.4/5 numbered pp.6/7 and headed "Addenda". P.7 contains note on movement. Dated at close: Paris 21.4.72. Further unnumbered MS. sheet, headed "Analysis": (breakdown of full text with suggestions for improvement, some of which is drafted in addenda.)
B STAGE DIRECTIONS	NONE	Written sideways in margin of p.1 and crammed into top of page, above holograph 1. MOUTH: "~~back~~ *up* stage audience R, convenient level, faintly lit from close up and below, as little as possible of rest of face." AUDITOR: No podium. "downstage audience L. tall, upright figure"; "dead still throughout except for single brief movement where indicated ~~right~~ *stage right*." instructions for "ad-lib" before curtain up.
C ADDENDA AND NOTES	NONE	Addenda passages lettered A - H. <u>Movement</u>:"This consists in simple *sideways* raising of *Listener's* arms clear of sides and their falling back with if possible just audible thud of hands on thighs.xxx It ~~is less at~~ *lessens with* each recurrence and xxx scarcely perceptible at third. There is just enough ~~silence to~~ *pause to* contain it as MOUTH recovers from vehement refusal to ~~abandon~~ *relinquish* third person."
D QUESTION	NONE	What?...I?...no...no!...she
E SELECTED VERBAL ALTERATIONS	birth into the world...this world ...of a ~~small~~ *tiny* baby ~~boy or girl~~ *in a small* ... what?...girl? small ~~place~~ *hole* ~~on the coast~~ in the ~~downs~~ *bog* coming up to sixty this...what?...~~65~~? walking in a field with my youngest grandchild ~~looking~~ *searching* for cowslips and ~~she~~ *I* found ~~her~~ *my* self in the dark for ~~she~~ *I* could still hear the buzzing in ~~her~~ *my* ears	tiny ~~baby~~ *little thing*...5 pounds...in a ~~small~~ *remote godfor*...what?...girl?... tiny ~~baby~~ *little* girl ~~dead silent thought~~ *thought silent as the grave*
F SELECTED VERBAL ADDITIONS	that *early* April morning light	the *old* buzzing then working down *the whole frame* the face *alone...face and mouth* keep on *trying*

	TYPESCRIPT I 1227/7/12/2	TYPESCRIPT II 1227/7/12/3
A	1½ pages. First attempt at fair copy of holograph, with MS. alterations. Ends on realisation not suffering: "*not a twinge* ah ... for the moment."	4 pages (+ 1 page headed "A".) Full text typed from holograph, with MS. alterations. Stage directions added in MS. on p.1. Letters ABC in margins, where addenda passages to be inserted.
B	NONE	As holograph 2, except: MOUTH: "~~convenient level~~ ~~*unnaturally high level*~~ *8 ft above stage level* ~~as little as possible of rest of face~~ *upper face in shadow* AUDITOR: "*standing on invisible podium 4' high.*"
C	NONE	"A" (Addendum) Includes passage in which old woman finds her hand wet. Addendum ends: "head doesn't move but eyes ... Oh very much so ... hundred degrees at least."
D	As before except "<u>she</u>"	what?...~~I~~ *who?...what?*...no...No!... <u>she</u>
E	any subsequent ~~time~~ *stage* none ~~whatsoever~~ *not the slightest* ~~perhaps~~ *no doubt* all part of the xxx wish to ... torment	~~done his devilish work~~ *pulled buttoned up his trousers* ~~nine~~ *eight* months ~~flood~~ *stream* ~~sensation so lessened~~ *feeling so dulled* ~~some little time later it is true~~ *long after* trying to...~~trying to wint~~ ~~*not knowing what*~~...~~*trying what*~~... *not knowing what...what she was trying* snatching at ~~comfort~~ *the crumb*
F	searching *aimlessly* for cowslips	"imagine" added many times (as in <u>Eh Joe</u>). *with the other waifs* *sudden flash* *on the rare occasions* *guilty or not guilty* *tender mercies...new every morning* *nothing she could say?* *before her time* *poking around*

	TYPESCRIPT 3 1227/7/12/4	TYPESCRIPT 4 1227/7/12/5
A	5 pages. Full text with MS. alterations. Stage directions typed, p.1. A-H lettered in margins.	5 pages. Full text with MS. alterations. Headed in MS: Not I. 2 dots separate the phrases, increasing pace of flow.
B	AUDITOR: "dead still throughout but for *4* ~~single brief~~ *slight* movement*s* where indicated. *See note below.*" 4 movements are cued in margins, in longhand.	scream (*screams*) .. then listen ... (~~pause~~ *silence*) scream again (*screams again*) .. listen again (~~pause~~ *silence*.) Beside final typed directions Beckett has added (in longhand in margin) "grim truth".
C	"~~Note~~ *Movement* This consists etc." (note not completed). Addenda ABC typed into text and marked in margins. Addenda DEFGH marked in margins (at insertion points).	Text ends with movement note typed in. Beckett heads this in longhand, "Note 1." Below it he adds: "Note 2 'any': pronounce 'anny'".
D	what?...who?...what?...no...no!...she	what?..who?..what?..no..no!.. she!
E	what?...~~sixty-five~~...*seventy*...~~yes~~ *my God* ~~trousers~~ *breeches* ~~minute~~ *tick* ~~cowslip~~ ~~*flower bloom*~~ xxx *bell* since ~~she had uttered~~ ~~*heard-it*~~ *it had sounded* ~~unbroken~~ *steady* stream nothing she could ~~say~~ *tell?* ~~winter mostly~~ *always winter some strange reason* God... (~~long~~ *good* laugh.)	~~my~~ *good* God! ~~showered~~ *visited* ~~only a~~ *just the* face ~~flow~~ *stream* ~~women~~ *hag* on the way ~~back~~ *home..home!* .. a little mound
F	in margin, beside "distant bell": *in a cowslip bell/he* *no cry...just the tears* *how it was...could...what?...had been?* *...yes...something that would say...* *how it had been*	"kneeling" occurs for first time in list of postures, typed straight into text. "Croker's Meadows" also typed straight in, but altered to "acres" in longhand. *no love of any kind; stop and stare again;* meant to be suffering..*ha!* *no sound of any kind; mouth half open as usual;* but no *spared that*; couldn't pause *a second; drifting around...day after day;* to get her *going* breathing; lying *light failing* in her lap; *crawl back in;*

	TYPESCRIPT 5 1227/7/12/6	TYPESCRIPT 6 1227/7/12/7
A	6 pages. Full text with MS. alterations. MS. note p.1: "corrected". Title typed in. 2 dots separating phrases. Numbers in margins relating to: Incidence of buzzing (B1 - 7) Interruptions inviting "I" (1-22) Pauses (marked in red biro: 1-5)	6 pages. Full text. Fair copy with light MS. corrections. 2 dots separating phrases.
B	AUDITOR: *sex undeterminable with hood* MOUTH: ad-libbing *from text* as required Central image now mouth not face.	As Typescript 5 (revised version). Two MS. jottings on final page: 1) Consider pause for Mouth to stare ~~in pauses~~ *after "stare into space"* - *"stop and stare again"* - once or throughout. 2) For ad lib after curtain down: "there .. get on with it from there etc." For ad lib before curtain up: ?"~~whole body like gone~~"
C	Notes 1 and 2 typed in. Note 2 with MS. additions: "baby pronounce babby either " eether" (Suggestions in Note 2 are qualified by:"for example".) MS. note headed <u>Buzzing</u> divides text into 3 sections and notes 7 buzzing references, to be synchronized with movement of light, 7 sentences on reverse of final page (no heading) in red biro. Also (on same page): List of 22 Interruptions inviting "I".	<u>Note 1</u> altered: "this consists in ~~simple~~ *slight* sideways raising of arms from sides and their falling back. ~~with if feasible just audible thud of hands on thighs~~." <u>Note 2</u> Pronunciation details typed in, then cancelled.
D	As before. (Second "she" entered in margin, but cancelled.)	what?...who?..~~what?..no~~..no!..SHE! (last occasion "she..SHE!")
E	~~birth~~ *out* ~~visited~~ ~~*inflicted*~~ *vented* ~~exactly~~ *actually* insentient ~~snatching at straws~~ *grabbing at the straw* ~~one~~ *quick* grab just the ~~face~~ *mouth* ~~trying~~ *straining* to hear ~~gone mad~~ *like maddened* *sudden* flash ~~in the dark~~ in ~~court~~ *the dock* ~~merciful~~ God *is love* face ~~buried~~ in the grass	"dulled" underlined twice (p.1) and "numbered" in margin; alteration <u>not</u> made.
F	"imagine" added twice more. vowel marked in margin "vow-ell" quick grab and on *nothing there* *and can't stop* *stand up woman* *nothing she could tell...try something else* *whole* body like gone then *forgiven* back in the - *dull* roar *what she was trying...what to try* how she *had* lived	the buzzing *so called* all that *steady stream* old hag already *sitting staring at her hand*

There are two further versions of *Not I* at Reading University library.[1] The first of these is a six page stencilled text with manuscript alterations, described by Beckett as the 'script' on the envelope in which he presented the material to the library. The text is almost identical with the corrected version of Typescript 6, but has some minor variations from both Typescript 6 and from the Faber text. The second version is a nine-page photocopy of an uncorrected typescript, possibly an early proof. It is entitled *Not I* and appears to be based on Typescript 5, but does not include all the alterations made in the latter. The first page is headed, surprisingly, 'Act One' and the ensuing pages are numbered 1.1 to 1.8.

PLAY

The draft material for the ten typescripts of *Play* (which is held at Washington University, St. Louis) is too detailed to present in chart form. The ensuing discussion outlines the main stages in the development of the text, in which Beckett reworks his initial idea for the play (discussed in Chapter 7). Although close reading is inevitable, it enables a detailed comparison of Beckett's working method to be made over three plays, in conjunction with the complete drafts of *That Time* and *Footfalls*.

Typescript 1

In the first typescript of *Play* the heads are at first labelled H S1 and S2, only becoming M W1 and W2 in its final pages. Considerable care in shaping the text is apparent, particularly in the evolution of the chorus. The opening chorus does not appear until the end of the H, S1 and S2 section of the typescript, and is lettered 'A and D' in Beckett's hand. In Typescript 2 this chorus is typed out at A, the opening of the text. The brief second chorus is a manuscript afterthought, written above the text on the first page of Typescript 1. It is lettered B and E, as follows:

	S 1	I said to him, Give her up —	
(B)	S 2	One morning as I was sitting —	→ & (E)
	H	We were not long together —	

Beckett's lettering thus establishes A and D as Chorus I and B and E as Chorus II (respectively the long and short choruses found at the opening and close of the play). A manuscript addition establishes another small chorus at C, immediately following a blackout:

H } When first this change –
S 1 } Mercy Mercy –
S 2 } To say I am –

The structure of the play is thus laid down as a pattern of linked choruses, resembling the Japanese Noh play, as we have seen in Chapter 4. Choruses A and D with B and E frame the text and C comes as a brief central chorus, marking the abrupt change in the content of the narrative.

Only one blackout is indicated at this stage; it is added in manuscript at C, the central point of the text. Marginal notes above and below the blackout direction calculate the number of speeches made by each voice in each half of the text (i.e. before and after the blackout); they are totalled by Beckett as follows:

23
—
S 1 8+4=12
S 2 8+4=12
H 7+5=12

The precise total of twelve speeches for each voice is not present, as we have seen, in the final text of *Play*, but does occur (spread over three sections of text rather than two) in *That Time*.

There are only two directions for light in Typescript 1. The first is written in manuscript following the brief opening chorus and reads: 'Full light and voices'. The second is a manuscript addition after the blackout direction at C, and reads: 'Diminished light and voices'. There are no instructions for the movement of the light between speeches, but its personality is already strongly felt:

S 1. Get off me. (*Pause. Light full on. In a scream.*)
Get off me! (*Pause. Light down. Low.*) Is it that I do not tell the truth?...

The decrease of light within this speech in response to S 1's cry is a much weaker concept than the arbitrary demanding unheeding characterization of light, the unblinking eye of the final text. There are no further stage directions in Typescript 1 and no mention of repeating the play. The last three pages of the typescript are a second attempt at drafting the text after Chorus C, with the heads renamed as W 1, W 2 and M.

A greater explicitness than in the later drafts is apparent in Typescript 1. S 2, for example, enquires of the light:

What do you do when you go out? Winnow what I have said?

In the second attempt at writing this passage, 'winnow' has become 'sift'. But 'winnow' has set an image of the light sifting the information it elicits and Beckett hesitates between the two words in succeeding drafts, finally (in Typescript 5) opting for the less direct 'sift'.

Typescript 2

Detailed stage directions begin in Typescript 2. There are to be 'Three white boxes' and the heads are still partially characterized, as in 'Before Play': 'Age: in their thirties. Appearance: indifferent.' Voice directions are added in manuscript. For the opening chorus they are to be 'just audible, ~~unintelligible~~ **probably unintelligible**'. Light directions for the movement from head to head are placed between speeches and eight blackouts are now indicated: there are to be two blackouts at the opening (one after each chorus) and another two at the end of the first section of narrative, before and after chorus C. Four more blackouts occur at the end of the play, three coming before, between and after the two choruses and the final one after the man has repeated: 'We were not long together.'

Linguistically the search for allusive vocabulary begins in Typescript 2 as, for example, in W 2's speech: 'He stinks of ~~you~~ **bitch**'. A range of judicial language is also introduced, emphasising the man's broken contract: 'I ~~said~~ **swore**'; '~~threatened to~~ **swore she would**'; '~~I had to admit~~ **there was no denying**'; ~~take my life~~ ~~settle my hash~~ **swing for me**'; '~~came out with the whole thing~~ **confessed**'.

Typescript 3

Typescript 3 includes a rewrite of the second half of the text which is headed 3A. The rewrite cuts and splits up the long speeches of each character, so that the text loses its monologue effect. Each speech in 3A is ticked, presumably when it has been shaped to Beckett's satisfaction. The words 'just play' first emerge in 3A. In 3 the man had said 'I know now, all that was just a game.' This passage does not appear in earlier versions, but the second version of Typescript 1 does have two manuscript additions ('Oh I know now —' and 'I know now etc.') showing that the speech was already written at this stage.

The three rewritten pages of Typescript 1 are puzzling, since they, rather than any other preceding draft, seem to have been the model for 3A. It seems probable, therefore, that these pages are misplaced with Typescript 1 and should be placed just before 3A in the draft sequence. A comparison of the following sentence elucidates:

Typescript 1
S 1. She had money, I imagine. Though she lived quietly.
Typescripts 2, 3 and 4
W 1. She had means, I imagine. Though she lived quietly.
Typescript 1 (last 3 pages)
W 1. She had means, I imagine, though she did not spend.
Typescript 3A
W 1. She had means, I fancy, though ~~she did not spend~~ **lived like a pig.**

Once again the resonant phrase has taken several drafts to evolve. The correct arrangement of the drafts appears to be Typescripts 1, 2, 3, 4, followed by the last three pages of Typescript 1 and in turn by 3A.

Typescript 4
Typescript 4 is headed 'Corrected Ehrenbachhöhe August 1962'. The speeches are numbered throughout. The text has grown considerably over successive drafts, since the total of thirty-six speeches counted in Typescript 1. The text up to the central blackout at C is now thirty speeches and the remaining text twenty-seven speeches. There are extensive changes in the opening stage directions. The boxes, for example, become urns, and a long manuscript insertion gives detailed instructions for light and voice:

Their speech, throughout act, will be provoked by spotlights.

~~*Transfer of light*~~.

All spots on faces alone.

Transfer of light from one face to another immediate. No blackout xxx except where indicated.

Extortion of speech by light not immediate. At every solicitation a silence of 4 or 5 seconds before voice begins. ***Except on 5 occasions where longer delay indicated.***

Faces ~~*expressionless*~~ ***impassive*** throughout. Voices toneless except ~~where~~ ***on few occasions where*** ~~*otherwise*~~ ***expression*** *indicated.*

The basic text and paragraph structure of Typescript 4 have, as has been suggested, more in common with Typescript 3 than the alterations of 3A. But the text is considerably revised in manuscript, with such additions as:

'***Adulterers, take warning. Never admit***' or 'not forgotten ***coming and going on the earth***'. Vocabulary revisions add depth, such as the punning on the word 'shade' in 'just a ~~little~~ ***shade***' while the women's jealousy is implicitly suggested in the man's fantasy of their getting together over a cup of '~~china~~ ***green*** tea'. The hiccups are inserted into this draft and the concept of the roller appears in some detail as a further insertion:

W 2 Or is it your idea of mercy, to silence me . . . in my stride? It is like dragging a roller, on a scorching day. The strain to get it moving, momentum coming, then stop, and strain again. And you perhaps pitying me thinking, Poor thing, she needs a rest.

Since this passage has already been seen (improved and split up) in the last three pages of Typescript 1 and in 3A, it provides further proof that the two latter are subsequent versions.

Each head is given a speech (inserted in manuscript into Typescript 4) that points to its current situation as a bad joke:

W 2 Are you listening to me? [ ] Is **there** anybody listening to me? [ ] Is there anybody looking at me? [ ] Is **there** anybody bothering about me at all?

W 2 Well . . . one cannot have lived as long as I have, here I mean, telling the same old disaster, day after day, in the only way one knows, the old earthy way, and not sometimes wonder if it is not all falling, if it has not fallen, from the beginning, on empty air. [ ] Something is being asked, that seems clear, speech is all one has to give, so one speaks. [ ] So one reasons, when one reasons, in the old earthy way. [ ] But is something being asked. [ ] Perhaps nothing is being asked. [ ] Yes, one cannot have lived here as long as I have, giving in vain the only thing to give, and not say sometimes to oneself, Perhaps no one is asking me for anything at all. [ ] Yes.

M 3Are you ~~a~~ **deaf?** A mere eye? ~~As deaf as an eye?~~ Lip reading? Or not interested? Not interested in words. Just looking at my face. Looking for something in my face. In my eyes. Or not even that. A mere eye. Quite unintelligent. Opening and closing on me. [ ] Am I as much as being seen?

Typescript 5

In Typescript 5 the tripartite structure of the play emerges for the first time. The opening narrative has the vocabulary corrections made in Typescript 4 typed into the text. This section ends at C, but instructions for the blackout and brief central chorus at C are not given. The second part of the narrative in Typescript 5 (from C onwards) begins as a corrected version of Typescript 4, but it is a false start and ends after only half a page. A further attempt, based on the shortened paragraphs of 3A, follows. Typescript 5 improves upon 3A, moreover, by splitting the text into still shorter units. Beckett has clearly realized that a more rapid movement of light from head to head would have the effect of concentrating audience attention and be dramatically more effective.

A brief blackout is indicated in the middle of Woman 2's roller speech for the first time, thus dividing the play into three sections:

W 2 Like dragging a great roller, xxx on a scorching day. The strain . . . to get it moving, momentum coming — (*light off and back*) — kill it and strain again.

A further blackout is introduced at the end of the play, splitting up the man's final speech and emphasizing the closing question:

M Mere ~~eye lens~~ **eye**. No mind. Omening (sic) and closing on me. Am I as much — (*off and back*) — am I as musch (sic) . . . as being seen?

The vocabulary in the second part of Typescript 5 closely resembles that in 3A, while also introducing its own improvements on earlier versions. One such alteration shows Beckett working towards greater immediacy in the man's narrative:

M . . . . ~~She swore she would do away with herself if I didn't give her up. (*Hiccup*). Pardon.~~ **Give up that whore, she said, or I'll cut my throat — *(hiccup)* pardon — so help me God.**

Direct rather than reported speech gives expression to the linked themes of blackmail, sex and death. 'Her' becomes the much more satisfactory personalized image: 'that whore', while a mere social apology 'pardon' is developed into a prayer to the Almighty. It is a typical example of Beckett's linguistic craftsmanship, showing his capacity to breathe life into the flatter parts of his dramatic speech as the drafts progress.

Typescript 6

The play's title appears for the first time in Typescript 6: 'PLAY/An Act' and several important developments occur in the stage directions. The three heads, for example, are further depersonalized: ('Age and appearance indifferent') whereas their age had been specified as 'in their thirties' in previous drafts. A much altered manuscript note on the title page finally decides the matter as follows:

xxx ~~age and appearance so abstracted~~
Faces ~~so petrified beyond age and expression~~ so lost to age and aspect as to ~~be scarcely more differentiated than the urns as~~ seem almost part of urns. But masks forbidden.

The play largely takes the form of the published text in draft six, with directions for the 'repeat' appearing for the first time and the two further blackouts introduced in draft 5 now established in the text, making ten in all. The idea of a single spotlight also emerges for the first time in the opening directions:

Their speech, ~~throughout act~~, **throughout** *will be provoked by spotlights.* ***a spotlight ~~directed~~ projected on faces alone (see note p.)***[2]

Vocabulary alterations are again towards greater immediacy. The marvellous line 'Not even a *squeeze* of lemon' is jotted on the title page and sexuality is further introduced in the man's 'Then I got frightened and ~~owned up~~ **made a clean breast of it'**. The idea of his being overcome by the situation is made more apparent in 'I simply could ~~not~~ **no longer'**, while the alteration of a verb in a speech of Woman 1 suddenly spotlights the horror of her predicament: 'Silence and darkness were all I ~~asked~~ **craved'**.

Richard Admussen raises an interesting point by observing that the French translation of *Play* came as Beckett was still working on the English version: '*Comédie,* originally entitled 'Que Comédie', (of which there are four manuscript versions giving evidence of at least ten separate reworkings,) was translated in April and May of 1963 and seems to have been based on the sixth of the ten English versions.' He goes on to comment that: 'Since the original developed along with the translation, there may well have been influence of one language upon the other, although no patterns are readily decipherable.'[3] An analysis of draft 6 compared with the French versions by a comparative linguist would be of interest in ascertaining any such influence.

Typescript 7

Typescript 7 is headed 'SB corrected'. It includes most of the revisions of Typescript 6 and makes some further changes in the stage directions. The peremptory 'masks forbidden' of 6, for example, becomes 'no masks'. A final 'Note on light' is included, to accompany that on the rhythm of the chorus established in Typescript 2. In the closing direction 'Repeat play exactly' the word 'exactly' is hesitantly crossed out, though it reappears in the ensuing drafts. A note on the title page states 'Erskine for Arsene throughout', while vocabulary alterations follow the now familiar pattern of increasing resonance. Ideas of God and purgatory, for example, now characterize the following: 'all I held most ~~dear~~ **sacred**' and '~~tolerable~~ **endurable** moments'; and 'lolling on air-~~cushions~~ **pillows**' introduces a sexual element, to parallel that already present in the latter part of the line: 'in the stern . . . sheets'.

Typescript 8

The corrected version of Typescript 7 closely resembles the Faber text. Typescript 8 is dated 'Ussy december 1963'. It incorporates most of the revisions made in draft 7, though 'Arsene' is retained throughout, despite the 'Erskine' note in 7. The text of Typescript 8 is minimally altered, though such changes as do occur are important. In the opening directions, for example, the urns finally become 'grey' not white and the tempo throughout is to be very 'rapid'. In order to achieve this effect, the response to light is speeded up, as it is in the published text:

The reaction to light is instantaneous. No pause between stimulus and reflex (speech) except where indicated.

A final note on the urns is introduced in 8, to accompany those on light and chorus. There is also a manuscript note in French on the urns (jarres) indicating, presumably, the progress of Beckett's translation of the play.

Typescript 9

Typescript 9 is a carbon of draft 8. There are few alterations, but a surprising one occurs in the opening directions. Beckett has here decided to ignore the 'instantaneous' response to light of draft 8 and return to the form of draft 7, where there is 'a pause of about two seconds before utterance is achieved.' The latter note is written into draft 9 as a manuscript alteration, but reduces the pause to 'about one second'. 'Erskine' is inserted in manuscript throughout the text.

Typescript 10
Draft 10, the final typescript, is headed 'Ussy december 1963' and has a prefatory note: 'Conform with Faber proofs and script sent to George 12.1.64.' George Devine directed the first English production of *Play* for the National Theatre at the Old Vic on 7 April 1964. The text is a retyping of draft 7, incorporating only some of its revisions. Many differences from the Faber text thus occur, hence the note to 'conform' with Faber proofs (which seem to have been based on the corrected version of draft 7.)[4] Draft 10 has, for example, 'large white urns' and 'masks forbidden' in the opening directions, both requiring emendation.

Draft 7 is thus seen to be be a crucial text, from which stem two distinct versions: Drafts 8 (and 9) are a fair copy of draft 7 and include most of its revisions; draft 10 is a further copy of draft 7 that omits most of its revisions. Of the last four drafts of *Play*, therefore, the last least resembles the Faber text. On the other hand the published text sometimes derives from *both* versions of draft 7. The Faber stage directions, for example, contain notes on chorus and light corresponding exactly with those in drafts 7 and 10 but not in drafts 8 and 9; Faber also contains a note on the urns only found in drafts 8 and 9. The arrangement of blackouts following the opening chorus is a further example:

Typescripts 7 and 10.
Blackout. 5 seconds. Spots on 3 faces. 5 seconds. Voices.

Typescripts 8 and 9.
Blackout. 3 seconds. Spots on 3 faces. 3 seconds. Voices.

Faber Text.
Blackout. 5 seconds. Spots on 3 faces. 3 seconds. Voices.

The chart on p. 267 comparing the last four typescripts with the Faber text indicates the double derivation of the text more fully:

A note on the repeat of *Play* is held at Washington University with draft 10. It is described in manuscript as: 'made after National Theatre production' (of April 1964). It does not appear, therefore in the 1964 Faber text, but, with slight variations, it is the note that appears in the 1968 edition.

The ensuing accounts of the drafts of *That Time* and *Footfalls* include descriptions of the original manuscript of both plays as well as the typescripts that followed them. It is thus necessary to incorporate rather more quotation and commentary in the course

TYPESCRIPT 7	TYPESCRIPTS 8 and 9	TYPESCRIPT 10	FABER TEXT 1964-68
Arsene (title page *suggests changing to* Erskine)	Arsene (8); Manuscript changes to Erskine (9)	Arsene	Erskine
Identical ~~large~~ white urns	identical grey urns	identical large white urns	identical grey urns
~~talk~~ *chat*	talk	~~talk~~ *chat*	talk (1964) chat (1968)
Manuscript inclusion of direction for light to flick on and off man, without voice	Direction typed into text	Direction omitted	Direction included
I have ~~come~~ *dropped in*	I have dropped in	I have come	I have dropped in
He swore we should	He said we should	He swore we would	He swore we should
~~tolerable~~ *endurable* moments	endurable moments	tolerable moments	endurable moments
a)Not even a ~~slice~~ *squeeze* of lemon	a)Not even a squeeze of lemon	a)Not even a squeeze of lemon	a)Not even a squeeze of lemon
b) " " " ~~slice~~ *squeeze* of ~~lemon~~	b) " " " " " –	b) " " " " " "	b) " " " " " –
none whatsoever	none whatsoever	none whatever	none whatsoever
great roller	heavy roller	heavy roller	great roller
Pardon	Par-Pardon	Pardon	Par-Pardon (1964) Par – don (1968)
of both. They being one	of both, they being one	of both. They being one	of both. They being one
à la rigueur	at a pinch	à la rigueur	at a pinch
air~~-cushions~~ *pillows*	air-cushions	air cushions	air-cushions (1964) air-pillows (1968)
there, all there	there, all there	there,	there, all there
Repeat play exactly	Repeat play exactly	Repeat play exactly	Repeat play exactly (1964) Repeat play (1968)
~~Mobile~~ *pivoting* spot	Mobile spot	pivoting spot	Mobile spot
Note on "Rhythm of Chorus" – Spacing identical with Faber	"Chorus" note spacing differs from Faber	Note on "Rhythm of Chorus" – Spacing identical with Faber	"Chorus" note (as 8 and 9) spacing as 7 and 10
No urn directions	Directions for urns	No urn directions	Directions for urns
Final directions for light as Faber, except minor word changes	Omission of section of final light directions present in Faber	Final directions for light as Faber, except minor word changes	Final directions for light as 7 and 10, except minor word changes

of discussing the progress of this material than occurs with the typescripts of *Play*.

THAT TIME

Description of draft material

That Time was begun in Paris on 8.6.74. and the play was worked on steadily (as subsequent dating shows) for the ensuing month, since typescript 5 is dated 10.7.74 at the close. The seventh and final typescript is, however, dated more than a year later: 'Paris August 1975'. The manuscript and seven typescripts are all at Reading University Library.[5] The same library has two further typescripts (headed by Beckett 'Continuity') which are concerned with the ordering of speeches for each voice[6] and two manuscript pages, one containing lighting directions and the other also dealing with speech order.[7]

Manuscript

The thirteen page holograph of *That Time* opens with three pages of notes on the projected play, followed by eight pages of text, in which the voices are each written as separate monologues. Two final pages contain further notes on the play and some additional text for voices C and B. At the end of the last page a heading 'Directions' is followed by staging instructions and a note on the voices. The holograph is written throughout in Beckett's quickest hand and is at times very difficult to read.

From the manuscript to final typescript the main thrust of the text shows Beckett's concept to have been fairly clearly defined from the first. Nonetheless preliminary notes for the play show that there was a marked development in his ideas on image and sound. Beckett's initial concept for the stage image was:

<table>
<tr>
<td>Head on
white
pillow?</td>
<td>Old man (sitting) in dark. <s>Front</s>
Facing front, a little off centre.
Face alone lit faintly. Very white, long
white hair standing on end.</td>
<td>}</td>
<td>Face about 8′
above stage
level,
problem in
consequence.</td>
</tr>
</table>

His second thoughts (beside the right hand bracket) become the final choice of image, after increasing the height of the face above stage level to ten feet. The precise nature of the 'problem' anticipated is not identified in ensuing notes, but the image is extended in these notes by directions for the eyes:

No blinking. Eyes ~~wide~~ ***staring*** ***~~front~~ wide*** *~~open~~ as long as possible, then closed as long or longer.* } ***or: eyes open only in silence***

Again Beckett's second thoughts become the final choice and are developed further, later on the same page, when he comes to consider the voice:

End: voice stops. xxx Silence 5 secs. Eyes open. Silence 10 seconds. Curtain in silence on lit face eyes open.

Convention: brief breaks **(never exceeding 2 secs)** *in speech do not open eyes, which open only after 5 seconds silence followed by 10 seconds silence.* **2 at most** *such 15 sec. silences in course of play.*

Beckett's initial concept was to emphasise the passage of time by a 'Faint tick-tack through **-out** only *just* audible in silence', but he later decided against so obvious a device.

The threefold text is identified from the outset as being in a single voice 'Coming from left (A), right (B), and above (C).' Beckett notes that all three texts should contain a 'recurrence of element "time",' giving as examples 'the time they,' 'that time she,' 'one time **xxx we.**' The pronoun 'he' is to be avoided ('in ref. to ~~face~~ **old man'**) and the stories should, states Beckett, be 'overlapping,' for example:

A beginning stops B or C, but for a moment 2 together,
A may resist, B or C yield & A continue.

Like many earlier voices, the voice is to be 'low, flowing' and 'so low in places as to be unintelligible. Fading effect.' The voices are identified separately, thus:

not inter-exclusive {
A: factual, names, dates, places, confusion
B: mental, confusion of thought.
C: affective, " " sensation.

The preliminary notes also show Beckett to have had a specific duration in mind for the play. The text is to last:

15 min. at 220 words/min. = 3000 words
i.e. 3 recordings 1000 words ~~each~~ ***apiece.***

He goes on to consider the nature of the opening, closing and median silences and, in the second and third pages of the holograph, works out two possible alternatives for changing from one voice to another: 'by interruption, each interrupted and interrupting only once.'

The first draft of A's monologue is written in a continuous unparagraphed flow. It is more personal than the final version — naming two women, for example:

Where ~~is~~ **was** it you stayed then, all the houses gone,
was it that kip on the front where you used to —
no, that was another time, Dolly was with you then,
~~no matter, or was it Nelly,~~ **no matter,** only one night
in any case, after all those years.

A also recalls the 'old codger' unable to find his way back to the spot that he describes, after some hesitation, as 'Maguire's Folly' — and how he could not ask for directions: '~~bite your tongue off first~~ **die rather**'. He recalls how people stared at him: 'like something out of —'. By Typescript 1 this has become, self-consciously: 'like something out of Beckett.'

Voice B's text is written in paragraph form from the outset. The physical separation of the lovers, so marked in the final text, is present but not consistently maintained, as in paragraph seven when B recalls: 'that time walking hand in hand on the towpath.' Later, however, there is 'no ~~reaching out with the hands to~~ **feeling to** see were you flesh and blood no better than two wraiths if it wasn't for the odd coo out of you.' They 'always ~~stood~~ **stock** still **like in a daze'** with 'every now and again the ~~mouth~~ **lips** to say you **(R)** ~~loved each other~~ **piece'**

The deliberately anti-romantic image of the dead rat in the sunset colours the relationship of the lovers from the first. The 'rat or bird or whatever it was floating off into the sunset' is in fact juxtaposed with an earlier image of the girl, where the same word, 'floating' is used: 'picture came floating up and there you were', thus making a conscious parallel between images of love and of the death of love. The evanescence of love and of life itself is also present in the way the girl disappears after they have stood together on the towpath, watching the rat out of sight:

nothing moving only the water and the sun going down
till it went down and you vanished all vanished.

This memory seems to satisfy the narrating voice, who comments: 'that was more like it' as though he has here managed to reflect the past more accurately.

Voice B is dated at the close 'Ussy 17.6.74' and Voice C, also paragraphed from the start, was begun the following day. Beckett's birth is the beginning of death theme is nowhere more clearly stated than in a passage in Voice C describing:

You squirming like a worm on the same old spit
from the moment they cut your stalk.

The very last lines Beckett tries out in Voice C's text (which, in modified form, become the final lines of the play) are a further direct expression of the birth/death theme:

~~Come and gone come and gone~~ **come and gone**
born and died ~~in no~~ **born and died**
get all born and died in no time.

Voice C is preoccupied by his propensity for self-deception:

Was ~~it then~~ **that the time** you began **last infirmity**
not to know yourself from Adam began trying
not to know yourself from Adam no idea who it
was saying what you were saying whose ~~head~~ **skull**
it was you were pent up in whose mother etc.
had you the way you were.

C's solution to his identity problem is to try to pretend to himself that he does not know who he is; 'from Adam' links himself, the particular man, with 'all mankind' as in *Godot*. C's refusal to accept the self is strikingly evident in another passage:

did you ever say I to yourself in your life
come on xxx **now** did you ever say I to yourself
in your life

thus linking this play specifically with *Not I*, which immediately preceded it. C's avoidance of self leads directly to the fictionalizing in which the voices in *That Time* indulge, as, for example, the 'imaginary conversations' described by Voice A, which also emphasize the solitariness of the child.

Voice C, the old man, on being 'put out' of the Portrait Gallery goes 'the old rounds'. The image contains both the sense of the tramp wandering the streets of his childhood and of his mental circuit always returning, as does Krapp's, to the same thoughts. Voice C describes his deliberate attempt to break the pattern:

trying xxxx xxx how that would xxxx **work** how never
having been would work the old rounds, ~~turning you into~~
trying to turn you into it **tottering and muttering**
all over the parish till the words dried up and the
head dried up and the legs dried up ~~up~~ (sic) ~~or the~~
whoever they were or ~~they looked~~ **it gave up** ~~whatever~~
whoever it was.

This appears to link with C's culminating vision in the library, when everything turns to dust and also with Voice B's final passage, where he abandons the struggle 'to keep it out':

When you tried **and tried** and couldn't **any more**
no words left to keep it out so gave up there
by the window in the dark or moonlight gave up
and let it in

'It' ('**whatever it may have been**,' as Beckett observes in the margin) can refer both to a final acceptance of selfhood, or to the dust and silence that supervenes at the end of the play: 'pouring it on top of you a great white shroud.' Voice B even seems to welcome the end as it engulfs him: 'and not a whit the worse.' This compares interestingly with *Krapp's Last Tape* where Krapp, after trying for years to keep out the 'darkness' from his work finally realises, in a moment of revelation, that precisely this should be his subject. The darkness he has tried to eliminate is his own reality and thus his true subject. *That Time* as we have seen has special affinities with *Krapp's Last Tape*.[8] There is also a strong thematic link between *That Time* and O's fruitless flight from self perception in *Film*, only to drop his guard in sleep and awaken to confront himself.

The sense of being a marked man is present from the early stages of Voice C when, in the Portrait Gallery, the face appeared: 'that made you twist round to see who it was **xx there** in the room ~~with~~ **behind** you that you hadn't heard come in.' Here again is the sudden awareness of death, a waiting presence in the shadows, that Beckett introduced into rehearsals of *Krapp's Last Tape*.

The last two pages of the holograph are concerned with staging; they are condensed finally under the heading *DIRECTIONS*:

All in darkness except the Listener's face
Spotlit about 8' above stage level ~~*and*~~

midstage off centre
Old face — long flowing white hair as if
seen from above spread on a pillows (sic)
The voices A B C are his own coming
to him from both sides and above (see note)
They relay one another without any break
in general flow except when ~~pauses and~~ silences indicated.

There follows a crossed out note, which is rewritten in the left-hand margin:

The differentiation of A B C as shades of the same cld.
be sufficiently conveyed by diversity of sound and
theme. If not it may be indicated by selective recording.

Typescript 1
There is evidence of at least two separate revisions in Typescript 1, one in black ink the other in red pen. Some new material also occurs silently between MS. and typescript, as though Beckett were not merely making a typed draft of the manuscript, but composing on the typewriter at the same time. Thus the 'terminus' in the manuscript becomes a 'Doric terminus' with 'the colonnade falling to bits'. The most significant addition to Typescript 1 also occurs in this manner; Voice C's account of the 'old ones' in the library begins in the manuscript, but typed into Typescript 1 is the haunting new line: 'something the dust said.' The dust itself speaks to the old man when he opens his eyes. We are never told what it says, the experience as described is eloquent enough. The uselessness of human endeavour seems to be expressed in C's final vision of dust. Not life alone but all human knowledge and literary achievement as represented by the library, dwindles to nothing. The extreme pessimism compares with the apparent disintegration of romantic love in this play, into a 'dead rat caught in the reeds.'

Each voice is written separately in Typescript 1, as in the manuscript, but the text is now spaced into unpunctuated paragraphs. Alterations are in Beckett's usual manner of moving towards indirect statement: 'Dolly', for example, becomes 'she'; 'never clear what she looked like' becomes: 'no sight of the face' and physical contact now ceases between the lovers. The vocabulary becomes more pointed: '~~saying~~ **vowing** you loved each other'; '~~covered~~ **sheeted** with glass'; '~~raised~~ **hoisted** your head'; '~~large~~ **vast** oil'; 'a ~~lot~~ **bevy** of old ones'; '~~reading~~ **poring on** their books'; 'old ~~codger~~ **ruin**'.

Occasionally, too, the insertion of a phrase in Beckett's hand brings a passage to life: C's seat in the Portrait Gallery, for example, suddenly takes on overtones of the mortuary: 'sitting there **on the marble slab** with the portraits of the dead.'

Typescript 2

Typescript 2, is in three columns, one for each voice. Beckett enters each voice in a column in its order of speaking, leaving the rest of the column blank. On page 3, for example, Voice B speaks first, Voice C second and Voice A last, so the page is ordered thus:

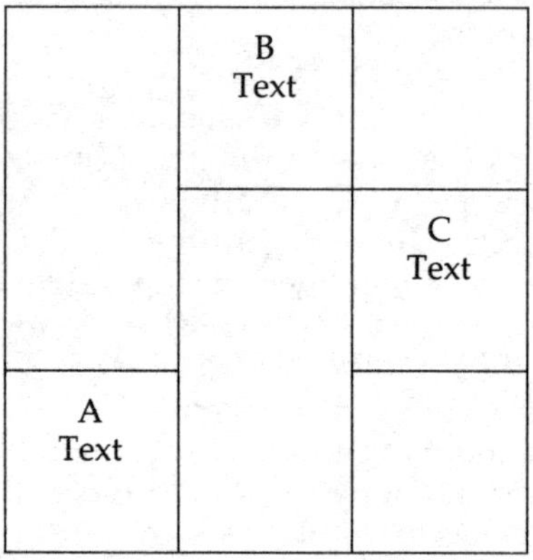

	B Text	
		C Text
A Text		

Beckett can both write manuscript alterations in the blank columns beside each passage of text and see the pattern of alternating voices, visually expressed on the page. Indeed the alternating technique is described by Voice A: 'making it up now one voice now another till you were hoarse and they all sounded alike.'

Beckett emphasizes the importance of continuity for each voice by underlining the first and last phrase in every paragraph. In the last three pages of text he is at first undecided what most of these phrases should be and simply types in the word 'overlap' before each section of text. He then substitutes an overlapping phrase in longhand as, for example, with two speeches for Voice C on page 7:

1 Sat down ~~and *overlap*~~ **on the first**
2 ~~*Overlap*~~ **vacant seat** and was taking a look round

Beckett also begins to structure the play in Typescript 2 by positioning the silences for the first time and realises the appropriateness of a silence being provoked by each voice. There are at this stage only twenty-four speeches in all:

A	B	C	B	C	A	C	A	B
C	C	A	A	A	B	B	B	C
A	B	*Silence*	B	C	*Silence*	C	A	*Silence*

Beckett structures the play so that a silence falls after each group of eight speeches and each voice speaks eight times in all. After some deliberation, directions for the median silences in the play are inserted on page 6 as follows:

Silence. 10 seconds. ***Faint sound of breathing.*** *After 3 seconds eyes open.*

The final silence follows these directions, but adds:

6 seconds. Smile. Curtain.

Among numerous vocabulary revisions in Typescript 2, 'Maguire's Folly' becomes 'Foley's Folly' on page one, but 'Madden's Folly' on page eight. The mundane 'wondering should it be rice or macaroni for your supper' (present since the manuscript in Voice B's text) is now struck out in favour of Confucius: 'or that old Chinaman born with ~~white~~ **long white** hair.' The Post Office episode in Voice C's text now takes place amid '**all xmas bustle**', thus accentuating further the old man's isolation. The spectacle of the old man in A's text becomes: '~~titter giggle~~ **gape** at the ~~old ruin~~ **scandal** huddled there.' 'Poring on their books' in C's text is altered alliteratively to 'poring on the page.'

Typescript 3

In Typescript 3 Beckett types each monologue onto a single foolscap sheet, sellotaping extra space onto the end of the sheets, so that the full flow of each voice can be seen at a glance. He then divides the text for each voice (which is no longer paragraphed, but typed in a continuous stream) into twelve parts, thus arriving at the thirty-six speeches in all, of the published text. He numbers the speeches in the left-hand margins, but the position of the silences is not indicated.

Typescript 4

Typescript 4 is Beckett's first attempt to interleave the three monologues. Each paragraph is numbered, beginning A1 C1 B1. After twelve paragraphs Beckett writes Ⓢ in the left-hand margin, to indicate the first silence, and places a second Ⓢ after paragraph 24. Other marginal notes (headed 'E') refer to the eyes. At this stage Beckett thought that the eyes should remain open longer after the first silence; thus they are not closed until paragraph 15, whereas paragraph 13 is the eventual choice. The order in which the voices are to speak is not yet fixed. Beckett contemplates reversing B12 and C12, for example, which would end the play on the line: 'little or none (**nothing**) the worse little or none (**nothing**).'

Vocabulary changes in Typescript 4 tend to be sombre or ironic in tone. 'Terminus', for example, becomes 'the end of the line'; when A describes 'talking to yourself', '**who else**' is inserted drily; even the nettles where the child hides have an unusual capacity for harm, they are now '**giant** nettles.' Paragraph B4 has the most chilling additional text: 'to keep the void from pouring in on top of you **the still (shroud)**'.

Typescript 5

In Typescript 5 both the title and the preliminary stage directions are present for the first time since the manuscript. Beckett makes certain additions to the directions, making the location of the face more ambiguous, for example:

*Old **white** face, long flaring white hair as if seen from above spread on a pillow. **No pillow**.*

He also adjusts the directions for both voices and silences and an increasingly aural emphasis is found: 'vowing every now and again you loved each other **just a murmur**'; 'or back with a shrew to its hollow tree **and not another sound hour after hour not a sound.**' A developing harshness in the language is also noticeable: '~~shocking~~ **loathsome** appearance'; 'fellow ~~men and women~~ **bastards**'; 'for all the ~~reprobation abhorrence~~ **loathing** you were getting.'

The voice order is indicated by the letters A B and C, typed into the left-hand margins and the thirty-six paragraphs are also numbered in longhand. The pattern, after marginal reordering of the central section, becomes:

	A	C	C	A		C	C	A	B		B	A	B	A	
silence	C	A	A	C	*silence*	B	A	C	C	*silence*	A	B	C	B	*silence*
	B	B	B	B		A	B	C	A		C	A	B	C	

Typescripts 6 and 7

By Typescript 6 the paragraph order and resulting pattern has become that of the published text:

	A	A	A	C		C	C	C	B		B	B	B	B	
silence	C	C	C	A	*silence*	B	B	B	C	*silence*	A	A	A	A	*silence*
	B	B	B	B		A	A	A	A		C	C	C	C	

At the end of the play the pattern remains unbroken, like the silence, whereas in the two earlier sections the regularity of the pattern is interrupted and the silence is broken. Beckett continues to redraft the note on the voices in Typescript 6, until it reaches the form of the published text in Typescript 7. The latter is the final draft. It incorporates the alterations made in Typescript 6 and contains small additional differences, which seem to have been composed directly onto the typewriter. The text finally stabilises in Typescript 7, which is virtually identical with the Faber first edition of 1976.

Continuity

There are two further texts of the play, a typescript and a carbon[9] both headed 'continuity'. Beckett appears to have worked separately on both, while finalising the speech order. The typescript was worked on first. Calculations in red biro on page 4 of the typescript show Beckett juggling with several voice combinations and eventually approving a different arrangement from the published text. These calculations appear to have been completed on a separate sheet, also in red biro, (MS1639) where, the voice order is reworked further, in conjuction with the carbon text and the arrangement of the published text decided on.

Beckett completes his ordering of the text in MS 1639 by numbering and lettering each paragraph and marking the silences by lines drawn across the page. Since the voice order in Typescript 6 is already that of the published text, it seems certain that Beckett worked on the 'continuity' sheets after writing Typescript 5, which also contains extensive marginal calculations. Vocabulary evidence supports this view, since the 'continuity' texts contain several phrases found in Typescript 5 but omitted from later drafts.

Lighting Cues

One other page of manuscript notes requires consideration with the drafts of *That Time*. This is a second page of RUL MS 1639 (headed *That Time*) which consists of lighting cues for the play, with page references to the first Faber edition. It thus seems clear that the two sheets comprising MS 1639 were written at different times: the calculations in red biro between Typescripts 5 and 6, and the lighting notes during the production of the play. There are no directions for lighting in the published text, so these notes are of interest in establishing Beckett's intentions. Added above the lighting cues, moreover, one striking note reflects beyond *That Time* towards an understanding of the reductive nature of Beckett's dramatic technique:

> To the objection visual component too small, xxx xxxx xxxxx out of all proportion with aural, answer: make it xxx xxxx xx **smaller, on the principle that less be more**

The lighting directions follow; they require '~~strong~~ **full** light' on the face when the eyes are open, but for this to 'fade to half ~~opening intensity~~ **full**' after the eyes have closed. In all speeches that precede the intervention of silence the lights are to fade up again, so that the audience sees Listener's eyes open and close in full light, after which it is reduced to 'half full' once more. In each case the fade down is to be completed during the speech in which the eyes close. At the end of the play light is to come up in the penultimate speech, so that Listener is in full light throughout the completion of the narrative.

FOOTFALLS

Description of draft material

The manuscript of *Footfalls* was begun in Berlin on 2 March 1975. At that time the play was headed: *Footfalls/It all?*. The date at the close of the manuscript is Paris 1.10.75. There are two attempts at writing V's monologue. The second of these (dated 'Paris 25.10.75.') was written after completion of the first draft. There are five typescripts following the holograph, numbered 1, 2, 2A, 3 and 4. The Beckett Archive at Reading University holds all the drafts, together with the Faber page proofs, corrected by the author.[10]

Manuscript

From its conception the play is in three scenes, although the numbers I and II (in the sense of separate scenes) do not appear until the manuscript is revised. The third scene is headed 'Text for III' from the outset.

The opening directions in the manuscript contain an idea that is never developed, listing three characters for the play:

V: Woman's Voice from dark ~~backstage~~
~~*S: Speaker from dark*~~
M: Mary

Since the character of S is crossed out and has no text at all, Beckett seems to have had immediate second thoughts and decided on two characters only. It is possible that M was initially conceived of as a divided role, with Mary's past and present to be represented separately.

There are no costume directions for Mary in the manuscript, merely a note: 'Both voices low' followed by lighting and pacing directions. At this stage the lighting strip covers the 'whole xxx **visible width** of forestage.' The opening dialogue at first writing is very short. Mary makes only two offers of assistance to her mother (an injection and a change of position) and then resumes pacing. The text ends on V's question:

V: Can you not stop ~~turning~~ **revolving** it all ~~over?~~
M: (*pacing*) It?

Just before the pacing is resumed, however, Beckett places an omission mark in the right-hand margin and (on an inserted sheet headed '1A') writes some additional dialogue, in which Mary proposes further aid:

M: Rearrange your pillows? (*Pause.*) Change ~~the~~ **your** drawsheet? (*Pause.*) Pass you the urinal? (*Pause.*) The bed pan? (*Pause.*) ~~Tell you a story?~~ Dress your sores? (*Pause.*) Tell you a ~~story~~ **bedtime story?**
V: ~~Yes. But not just yet~~. **It is too soon.**

The offer of a 'bedtime story' prepares the way for the story of Mrs. Winter and her daughter Emily that Mary tells in Scene 3 of the MS. In the remaining dialogue on the '1A' sheet the first discussion as to their respective ages occurs between M. and V. Beckett initially makes V 'Seventy-nine, eighty', but on second thoughts amends this to exactly ten years older. It is noticeable that each only knows the other's age, emphasising their interdependence. It is as if each exists only in the other. The question of Mary's age is treated humorously:

V: I had you late in life.
M: Could you not have waited?
V: I ~~lost control of myself~~ **forgot myself** ~~for~~ a moment.

Beckett's first attempt at the second scene, V's monologue, is full of the kind of concrete detail noticeably absent from the final text:

She is in the old home, the same where she was fooled into this world by the old family physician, a general practitioner named Haddon, long gone to his account.

When did this begin? Shall we say. ~~In girlhood~~ xxxx Well before puberty?

Beckett's first idea, as with the preliminary drafts of *Come and Go*, was to grant Mary some kind of sexual experience:

Though on the plain side, **as you may see** she has had admirers, male and female, but none outstanding, ~~as far as~~ **that** one knows. ~~That~~ **Indeed that** she is still a maid is almost certain.

V describes Mary's contemporaries as 'playing hockey, or otherwise revelling in life', while her daughter simply paced 'with tread more measured than at sentry-go.' Her movement is described elaborately:

See with what grace she wheels, now deasil, now withershins, and, when she halts, how always facing ~~fron~~ **the wall,** to gaze before her with unseeing eyes.

Perhaps the most interesting aspect of the first draft is the ambiguity of V's own situation. Her monologue opens with the observation:

Now I am one who may not predecease her,
Chilling prospect, for her physical health is fair.

Since Mary refuses to leave the house she is not even liable to external accident:

she has not been abroad now for — let me calculate — over 30 years. So no help from that quarter.

However a parenthesis later in the monologue states that the mother has 'incidentally long gone to her account.' Thus the fact that she 'may not predecease' her daughter suggests that V, though technically dead, remains a living presence in Mary's head and that their suffering is mutual. Not only does Mary have to endure the constant recapitulation of conversations between her mother and herself — hearing, endlessly, her mother's voice, but V, far from being left in peace having 'gone to her account' has, in her turn, to suffer active participation, alive still in her daughter's mind. If, as Beckett suggested in rehearsal,[11] both women are ghosts, their continued unhappiness as each reflects on the other has affinities with Sartre's *Huis Clos*.

By the manuscript revision of V's monologue Beckett has decided, contrary to his usual practice of increasing ambiguity, that it is necessary to make certain aspects of V's situation more explicit. Thus the monologue now begins:

I walk here now. (*Pause.*) Rather I come and sit. (*Pause.*) At nightfall. (*Pause.*) My voice is in her head. (*Pause.*) She thinks she is alone. (*Pause.*) ~~See how How~~ **See how** ~~firm~~ **still** she stands, **facing the wall.** (*Pause.*) How calm, outwardly ~~clear, if a little grey, the complexion~~. (*Pause.*) She has not been out since girlhood. (*Pause.*) She hears in her head, she has not been out since girlhood. (*Pause.*) **Not out since girlhood. (Pause.)**

The text in substance remains the same in the first Faber edition of the play. All subsequent editions, however, omit the lines stating that V's voice is in her daughter's mind, Beckett having decided in rehearsal that they were too explicit.

Beckett cuts the passage about V being 'long gone to her account' from the revision of her monologue, though the doctor is now described as being 'dead too'. It is not clarified whether 'too' refers specifically to either woman, or both. Among other vocabulary changes in the manuscript revision of V's text, the archaisms 'deasil' and 'withershins' are cut, while 'hockey' expands into 'hockey and lacrosse'.

The third scene in the manuscript carries a preliminary note: 'Punctuated by steps'. Beckett is now visualizing Mary's movement as an integral part of the text. The 'Text for III' flows more easily than the two earlier scenes and has no major extension or revision on separate sheets. The text already has much its final form, reminiscence from Mary, followed by her narration of the story of Emily and Mrs. Winter. 'Epilogue', originally the first word of Mary's monologue, is crossed out in favour of 'Appendix'. Scene 3 is intended to give a longer perspective on the earlier scenes, a later view of events. How much later is at first precisely specified. Mary begins: 'Some 10 years later' but, after a pause, corrects herself: 'Some 5 years later, when it was as though she had never been, **but had she? (*Pause*) Had she? (*Pause*) Some five years later,when it was as though she had never been,** she began to walk.' Despite the specific figures, an immediate note of ambiguity is introduced through Mary's self-questioning. All we have been told is brought into question, the events about to be described may not have occurred at all.

Mary is said to enter the church by the South door 'always locked at that hour' and to walk 'up and down at normal walking pace, neither fast nor slow, the corresponding transept.' Later in the monologue she describes how she: 'began to walk, along the south xxx transept, to and fro . . .'. Direct reference to the South transept is most interesting in relation to the later text. In Typescript 1 the first reference becomes, ambiguously, 'the corresponding arm' but the South transept again appears later in the monologue. Typescript 2 makes no changes, but in 2A ambiguity is deliberately introduced at each reference:

up and down, ~~the corresponding arm~~ **up and down, His poor arm.**

~~along the South transept~~ **up and down, up and down,** ~~His~~ **that poor arm.**

In Typescript 3 'his poor arm' loses the capital H and remains thus in both Faber editions (the separate text of 1976 and the *Ends and Odds* version of 1977.) This is especially interesting since Typescript 4 returns to the capital H and the Grove Press American edition follows this version, thus identifying the arm as an arm of the cross, to which shape churches are traditionally built.

The pacing figure is described in the manuscript version of Scene 3 as 'a tangle of rags', passing before 'a ~~candle~~ **candelabrum'**, 'like moon through ~~cloud~~ **cloud** (*Pause*) Or mist.' It walks 'at certain periods of the years'. In the Mrs. Winter story Emily's state is described specifically as '~~Terribly~~ **Dreadfully** unhappy.' In the first Faber edition of the play, this becomes the more ambiguous 'Dreadfully — ' but the ensuing English and

American editions of *Ends and Odds* adopt a compromise: 'Dreadfully un-'. The first draft of the story contains a good deal of unfamiliar material:

Emily: At the end? Mrs. Winter: Well yes I suppose if you like, what difference does that make? (*Pause*) '. . . the love of God, and the fellowship of the Holy Ghost, be with us ~~you~~ all, ~~now and for~~ evermore Amen, You said Amen xxxxx I heard you distinctly. (*Pause.*) Emily: ~~Yes, I was just back then. I was~~ **I was there at the end.** ~~Just there then~~ (*Pause*).

The holograph is followed by a page of manuscript jottings on the diminution of image and sound in the play. Beckett at first considers 'only progression failing light' but on second thoughts decides that the 'only regressions' in the play should be 'sound, light and pacing.' The positive implications of progression characteristically give place to regression, but whereas the earlier note diminished light alone, Beckett's second thoughts are to lower the sound levels also and to reduce the number of lengths paced by Mary. He considers how many lengths should be paced in each section and decides on a steady reduction ('10+' in Section A, '7 approx' in Section B and '4' in Section C.) There are thus to be 21 lengths in all, each of seven paces, which Beckett totals as 149 steps.[12]

Beckett considers shading the colour of the image from white (1) through light grey (2) to dark grey (3) and black (4) to correspond with the diminishing sound of footsteps, from loud (1) 'less loud' and 'still less loud' (2 and 3) to silence (4). But this jotting is crossed out, as is a note on diminishing voices that still identifies three characters:

1. S V M Voices ~~clear~~ **over audible**
2. S V " ~~lower~~ **normally audible**
3. M " just audible.

An ink-framed note stands out on the page of jottings, an explicit description of the play's structure, in which the empty strip is identified as the final scene:

A Dying mother
B Mother back
C ~~Epilogue~~ **appendix**
D Empty strip

Scenes two and three in the manuscript end with the phrase 'it all' which at this stage is the play's alternative title. By Typescript 1 the phrase has become a refrain that ends all three scenes. It is part of a process of rhythm and echo that Beckett builds up in the drafts of *Footfalls*. The echo effect includes the tone of voice of mother and daughter 'both low throughout' and the way they repeat each other's words and phrases. By the end of the manuscript Emily even speaks Mrs. Winter's lines as well as her own, thus clarifying for an audience that her mother's voice is in her mind and that the narrated story is an objectification of her own experience. In succeeding drafts the echo effect becomes part of a diminuendo of sound (created by diminishing the chime) and this is paralled by a reduction of visual image, as pacing and light are decreased. The gradual diminution creates a strong impression of cyclic progression. The pacing figure becomes steadily more memorable as she is seen to be fading, so that the echo of her presence exists strongly for the audience in her final absence from the stage.

Typescript 1
Typescript 1 largely follows the holograph, but is heavily amended. Additional directions state the number of lengths Mary is to pace and the idea of dwindling sound (already contemplated in the holograph jottings) is now tried out to mark the scenes. After Scenes 1 and 2, for example, the directions read: 'Sound **a little fainter'** and 'sound **a little fainter still'.** More is told about the doctor:

A general practitioner named Haddon, ~~dead soon after to die. With not long to live~~. **Long past his best. (*Pause*) Not long to live.**(*Pause*.) **Made rather a mess of it (*Pause*).**

Mary's description is also slightly extended:

Though always ~~on the~~ plain ~~side~~ **and dull** she once had ~~an admirer~~ **a swain**

Some advances towards ambiguity do occur, however, in Scene 3. The date is less specific; 'some five years later' becomes 'some few years later' and, at the end of the story, Emily is increasingly doubtful of her presence:

I ~~was~~ **may have been** there at the **very** end.

After typing the story Beckett hit on the idea of abbreviating Mrs. Winter's name and adds in the margins a sequence of dialogue between Emily and 'Mrs. W'.[13]

There is little manuscript alteration in Typescript 2, but full stage directions (largely as in the published text) appear for the first time. In Scene 1 the offer of a 'bedtime story' for V is crossed out in favour of 'Pray with you?' and the comedy over Mary's birth increases:

V: I had you late in life.
M: Not late enough.

In Scene 3 Emily is once more definite about her presence at the end: 'I was there at the very end.'

Typescript 2A

Typescript 2A seems to be a duplicate of the printed text of Typescript 2, but with extensive further amendments in which Beckett's ideas on the play are largely crystallized into their final form. 2A is thus the most seminal of the typescripts. Here Mary becomes May and Emily, Amy. Directions crystallize: May's 'flimsy grey gown' becomes a 'shabby grey wrap'; the strip of light is precisely located for the first time: 'a little off centre audience right'; the steps become a 'clearly audible **rhythmic** pad'. The rhythm of voice and steps is thus clearly stressed, counterpointing the steady diminution of light and sound. The nature of the 'sound', hitherto unspecified, is also decided on in Typescript 2A:

Faint gong. ~~When~~ ***Pause as echoes die.***

Thematically an emphasis on suffering that seems to have echoes of Calvary is extended further in 2A. It first appeared in Typescript 1 with the insertion of such phrases as: 'Sponge you down? (*Pause.*) Moisten your lips' and V's apology to her daughter for bringing her into the world: 'Forgive me again'. In an insertion in 2A, V's plea for forgiveness is repeated and May suggests praying for her mother: '~~Tell bedtime story? Pray for you?~~ **(*Pause*). Pray with you? (*Pause*). For you?'** A note of compassion is developed also in the repetition of the word 'poor' that sounds steadily through succeeding drafts: 'in your poor mind' (manuscript, Scene 3); 'His poor arm' and 'that poor arm' (insertions in 2A) and 'moisten your **poor** lips' (Typescript 3). In the reference to 'His poor arm', we are made aware of the cruciform structure of the church, as well as the unquiet spirit that continues to enter the building through a locked door. The 'locked' door first appears in 2A; hitherto it had been 'closed'. An ironic reference to the cross also enters the text in 2A, when V's reference to 'hockey' is finally abandoned in favour of 'lacrosse'. Beckett even extended the image of the cross in rehearsal. He decided it was necessary to have a shaft of light upstage, behind May's strip, so that when the lighting dimmed between sections, the audience would not think the play was over and begin applauding. But a single shaft of light looked accidental, so Beckett laughingly suggested during rehearsal in Berlin that there would be no mistake if a horizontal bar of light should cross the vertical.[14]

May's sardonic response to V's 'I had you late in life' is finally cut from 2A. After considering 'Better never' Beckett seems to have felt that the comic tone of the response would undercut the sombre mood developing in Scene 1 and May makes no response at all. In Scene 2 there is a steady reduction in personal contact for May; all references to her 'admirer' and to Dr. Haddon are cut. In Scene 3 vocabulary changes advance towards the final text: May's monologue is now the 'sequel'; reference to a specific number of years becomes, more ambiguously, 'a little later'; the 'appearance' becomes the 'semblance'; 'rags' become 'tatters' and 'evensong' is changes to 'vespers'. The romantic passage describing the candle flames is also amended:

~~a~~ **the** candelabrum, how ~~the~~ **its** flames, ~~the~~ **their** light ~~of the flames~~ . . . like moon through **passing** cloud. ~~(*Pause.*) Or mist~~.

The ambiguity of Amy's story is considerably increased by the omission of the sequence in which she describes 'being there at the very end.'

In a manuscript note at the beginning of 2A Beckett states:

8 bouts of pacing (3+2+3+0)
approx 19 lengths: 133 steps in all.

He then jots the number of lengths to be paced per scene in the margins throughout the typescript, totalling the footsteps at the end of each scene. After adding two extra lengths to Scene 3 the final total becomes 21 lengths — as suggested in the notes attached to the original manuscript. The number of footsteps (21 x 7) is then correctly calculated in the margin as 147. In 2A Beckett

introduces the idea that the final length should be accomplished in two stages, after a long pause. In earlier drafts Mary never completed the final length, but merely took three steps and then halted facing the audience.

Typescript 3

Typescript 3 is a retyping of the amended 2A text, in which the vocabulary receives further polishing and there are some interesting amendments to the stage directions. The reduction in pace of May's footsteps from scene to scene is introduced here, for example. They are to be a little slower each time, paralleling the diminishing light and sound. The gong now gives place to a 'single chime', the 'urinal' in Scene 1 becomes a 'warming pan' and some of the striking vocabulary of the final text also appears for the first time: '~~stock~~ **stark** still'; 'passing ~~cloud~~ **rack**'. The phrase 'will you never have done' is to be repeated where it occurs at the end of Scenes 1 and 3, thus drawing attention to the cyclic nature of May's obsession:

> Will you never have done? **(*Pause*). Will you have never done ...** revolving it all?

Typescript 4

The ensuing history of the text is complicated, as might be expected from the discrepancies between editions already noticed. The amended Typescript 3 appears (with further small alterations) to have been the basis for the first Faber text (the separate edition of 1976) which was published to coincide with the play's first production (at the Royal Court Theatre, London) in May 1976. Small alterations from Typescript 3 are found in the Faber page proofs for the first edition and these are largely incorporated into Typescript 4. Typescript 4 also contains important changes made during rehearsal of the first production of the play, which was directed by Beckett himself. Rehearsal alterations included changing from seven to nine steps per length, restoring the capital H in 'His poor arm' and altering the church door from 'South' to 'North' because, as Beckett explained to the actress Hildegard Schmahl when rehearsing the play subsequently in Berlin:

> South door is too warm, North door is colder. You feel cold. The whole time, in the way you hold your body too. Everything is frost and night.[15]

Typescript 4 became the basis for the Grove Press (New York)

Ends and Odds text of 1976. However, close comparison between Typescript 4 and the second Faber edition (*Ends and Odds*, 1977) shows the latter to be a hybrid version, containing material from the first Faber edition and some but not all of the rehearsal changes found in Typescript 4. There are several small discrepancies in punctuation and length of pauses between the Faber *Ends and Odds* version and Typescript 4 and a few major differences: In Scene 1, for example, the Faber *Ends and Odds* text reads 'five six seven wheel' while Typescript 4 has 'seven eight nine wheel' and in Scene 3 the Faber text repeats the words 'Sequel' and 'The semblance', whereas in Typescript 4 they occur once only. There are also differences in pacing directions between the two versions: In Typescript 4 Scene 1 May resumes pacing earlier than in the Faber *Ends and Odds* text, while the reverse happens in Scene 3. In the Faber text May begins pacing immediately after her first word: 'Sequel', whereas in Typescript 4 she does not begin to move until after the line: 'None at least to be heard.'

Although the Grove Press *Ends and Odds* text largely follows Typescript 4, there are again some discrepancies. In Scene 1, for example, Typescript 4 twice introduces the word 'again':

Would you like to change your position **again?**
Pray with you? (*Pause.*) For you? **(*Pause*) Again.**

The Grove Press edition stresses the word still further by, on four occasions, introducing three dots before it is spoken. Of the three versions (the Faber first and second editions and the Grove Press *Ends and Odds* version) the latter appears to be the one most faithful to the text that Beckett arrived at in rehearsal.

Studying Beckett's working method over three plays and a large number of drafts increases understanding and appreciation of his creative process. His careful planning, his rigorous and repeated self-analysis while structuring a text, his steady enrichment of language, have all been evident as matters of general practice. At the same time, as we have seen, the content of the text tends to move from direct to indirect statement, leaving the greatest possible latitude to the audience's imagination.

NOTES

Chapter 1 — Introduction

1 *New York Times*, 6 May 1956, Section 2 (x), pp.1,3.
2 *En attendant Godot*, ed. Colin Duckworth, London 1966, p.xlv.
3 Quoted by A. J. Leventhal in *Samuel Beckett : an exhibition* (ed. James Knowlson) London, 1971, p.14.
4 I am grateful to Deirdre Bair for this information (*Samuel Beckett*, pp.204, 235-6).
5 Letter to George Reavey 22 July, 1937.
6 In 3 notebooks and loose sheets; material in possession of Ruby Cohn.
7 Letter to Thomas McGreevy 4 August, 1937.
8 Reproduced in *Just Play : Beckett's Theater*, Ruby Cohn, Princeton 1980, pp.295-305.
9 Unpublished manuscript Reading University Library (MS.1227/7/16/8) p.123.
10 *Disjecta*, ed. Ruby Cohn, London 1983, pp.171-172; translation by Martin Esslin.
11 *Disjecta*, p.173.
12 *Disjecta*, p.172.
13 My own views on the play are expressed in *Waiting for Godot*, Longman, 1981; co-editor with Nicholas Zurbrugg.
14 Reading University Library MS.1227/7/4/1.
15 *Éleuthéria*, pp.1-3. (RUL MS. 1227/7/4/1.)
16 Ibid, p.13.
17 *T.C.D. : A College Miscellany*, 14 November 1929, Vol 36, p.42.

Chapter Two — Pattern

1 Harold Hobson 'Samuel Beckett, Dramatist of the Year', *International Theatre Annual*, No. 1, London 1956, p.153.
2 *Molloy, Malone Dies, The Unnamable*, John Calder, 1959, p.84. (Hereafter *trilogy*).
3 'Dante . . . Bruno. Vico . . Joyce', *Our Exagmination round his Factification for Incamination of Work in Progress*, London, 1961, p.14.
4 *Samuel Beckett*, London, 1976.
5 See *Epilogue*, pp.207-210.
6 Turret Books, London 1971, ed. James Knowlson (Item 376).
7 See especially pp.181–2.

Chapter 3 — Lessness: A Study in Structure

1 I am indebted to Samuel Beckett and Francis Warner for permission to quote from material in Francis Warner's possession. Additional draft material and 'key' to *Sans/Lessness* are in the Beinecke Rare Book and Manuscript Library, Yale University, whose assistance I gratefully acknowledge.

2 Ruby Cohn, *Back to Beckett*, Princeton, 1973, p.265.

3 *trilogy*, p.418.

4 See Appendix II for the sentences and paragraph order. 'Key' is on pp. 154-5.

5 *Back to Beckett*, p.263.

6 James Knowlson, *Light and Darkness in the Theatre of Samuel Beckett*, London, 1972.

7 In ordering the 60 sentences into paragraphs I discovered that in order to make the figures agree with those Beckett gave to Ruby Cohn (p.16 above) two separate draws for paragraphs are necessary (as with the two draws for arranging the sentences.) The numbers 3, 5 and 7 should thus be written on TWO pieces of paper (not four) and the numbers 4 and 6 should be written on THREE pieces of paper (not six). The 60 sentences then divide precisely into 12 paragraphs, when two draws are held, and produce a new version of *Lessness*.

8 First publication: *Sans*, Paris, 1969; *Breath*, New York, 1969.

9 *trilogy*, p.397.

10 W. B. Yeats, *Collected Plays* London, 1934, p.593.

11 *The Works of George Herbert*, edited by F. E. Hutchinson, Oxford, 1941, p.42.

12 W. B. Yeats, *Collected Poems* London, 1933, p.396.

13 *trilogy*, p.398.

14 Zeno of Elea (c.490-430 B.C.) Greek philosopher, who devised a number of arguments (subsequently related by Aristotle) demonstrating the unreality of motion. Attributed to him is the argument that it is impossible to reach the end of an infinite series in a finite time. e.g. If a heap of millet is divided in half, and half of one heap is added to the other, followed by half the remaining quantity (and so on . . .) although the second heap is seen to increase, the transfer of all the millet to a single heap cannot be completed in a finite universe. (See W. D. Ross, *Aristotle's Physics*, Oxford, 1936, pp. 71-85).

Chapter Four — Form and Content; the Circle

1 'Dante. . .Bruno.Vico..Joyce', p.14.

2 *Proust and 3 Dialogues with Georges Duthuit*, London, 1965, p.88.
3 *Samuel Beckett: an exhibition*, p.23.
4 '. . . The death of friends, or death/Of every brilliant eye/That made a catch in the breath —/Seem but the clouds of the sky/ When the horizon fades; W. B. Yeats, *Collected Poems*, pp.224-225.
5 'An Imaginative Work!', *Dublin Magazine*, Vol.11, July-September 1936, pp.80-81; 'MacGreevy on Yeats', *Irish Times*, 4 August, 1945, p.2; 'Hommage à Jack B. Yeats, '*Les Lettres nouvelles*, No. 14, April 1954, pp.619-620.
6 R. M. Angus 'Connections between the Works of Samuel Beckett and Jack B. Yeats' (unpublished M.Phil. dissertation, University of Oxford, 1969.)
7 See Yasuko Stucki, 'Yeats's Drama and the Nō. A Comparative Study in Dramatic Theories', in *Modern Drama*, Vol.9, May 1966, pp.101-122.
8 See F. A. C. Wilson, *W. B. Yeats and Tradition* Methuen, 1968, pp.140-147.
9 See Francis Warner, 'The Absence of Nationalism in the Work of Samuel Beckett', *Theatre and Nationalism in Twentieth Century Ireland*, ed. Robert O'Driscoll, Toronto, 1971, pp.192-204.
10 Janet Hitchman, *Such a Strange Lady. An Introduction to Dorothy L Sayers (1893-1957)* New English Library 1975, p.87.
11 *International Theatre Annual*, No. 1, London, 1956, p.153.
12 *Play* (Faber 1964) p.19.
13 'Dante . . . Bruno. Vico . . Joyce', p.21.
14 This analysis of *Play* was made in 1972 and appeared in *Modern Drama* (Vol.XIX No.3) Toronto 1976. In 1982, on looking at Beckett's rehearsal notebook for his 1976 production of *Play* (*Spiel*) in Berlin (RUL MS.1976) I found that Beckett himself had divided the play so as to emphasise the groups of speeches. He notes the 32 speeches in Part One and totals the remaining speeches into two groups containing 36 speeches each, leaving a final 9 speeches to form an epilogue, out of which a new movement (the repeat) grows.
15 *Samuel Beckett: an exhibition*, p.92.
16 Compare 'Texts for Nothing (VIII)' (in *No's Knife*, London, 1967, p.109): 'I'm a mere ventriloquist's dummy.'
17 *trilogy*, p.344.
18 *trilogy*, p.397.
19 First published London, 1976.
20 See Pilling, 'The Conduct of the Narrative in Samuel Beckett's Prose Fiction', unpublished doctoral dissertation, University of London, 1971.
21 Cohn, *Back to Beckett*, Princeton, 1973, p.266.
22 *Dante. . .Bruno.Vico..Joyce*, p.22.
23 *Samuel Beckett: an exhibition*, p.98: '. . .written, according to Beckett, at about the same time as *Acte sans paroles II*' (i.e. 1956).

24 See *Proust and 3 Dialogues*...pp.45-53 in which Beckett discusses the 'multiplicity of Albertine'.
25 See Appendix IV.
26 Tom F. Driver, 'Beckett by the Madeleine' (*Columbia University Forum*, IV, Summer 1961), p.23.

Chapter 5 — Cyclic and Linear Patterning

1 See *En attendant Godot*, ed. Duckworth, chapter 5, for a detailed discussion of structure. The Act1/Act 2 repetitions are usefully charted on p.1xxxiv and the geometrical shape of the overall structure on p.xcii.
2 Ihab Hassan, *The Literature of Silence, Henry Miller and Samuel Beckett*, New York, 1967, p.176.
3 James Knowlson, 'From *Godot* to *Footfalls*' (Radio 3 talk given on 23 May 1976) B.B.C. Archive Recording.
4 Charles Marowitz, *Encore*, March/April 1962, p.44.
5 Compare 'To find a form that accommodates the mess' (p. 48, above).
6 Walter D. Asmus 'Beckett Directs Godot', *Theatre Quarterly* Vol.V No. 19, London, 1975, p.23; translated by Ria Julian.
7 See Esslin, 'Samuel Beckett and the Art of Broadcasting', *Encounter*, London, September 1975, p.38.
8 R.U.L. MS. 1396/4/5, p.1.
9 *Performance I*, No.2 (New York, April 1972), p.112.
10 *Beckett's Happy Days: A Manuscript Study* (Ohio, 1977), p.15.
11 *The Literature of Silence*, p.176.
12 See Esslin, *Encounter*, September 1975, pp.38-9.
13 Richard N. Coe, *Beckett*, London 1964 (Revised 1968) p.90.
14 See Chapter 9 for discussion of the play's origins.
15 Schiller Theater, Berlin, 5 October 1969.
16 'Martin Held talks to Ronald Hayman', *Times* (Saturday Review) 25 April 1970.
17 *Murphy*, p.172.
18 *Gambit International Theatre Review*, Vol.7, no.28, London 1976, p.61.
19 R.U.L. MS. 1396/4/10.
20 *Beckett's Happy Days: A Manuscript Study*, p.4.
21 See note 14, p.290, above. Beckett refers to time as an 'impossible heap' in *Endgame.*
22 *The Poems of Charles Wolfe*, London, 1903, p.5. 'Go, forget me — why should sorrow/O'er that brow a shadow fling?'
23 *Radio 1*.
24 *Poems in English*, London 1961, p.41.
25 'Maunu' in the original French version.
26 *trilogy*, p.418.
27 *Beckett and Broadcasting* (Abô, Finland, 1976) p.127.

28 *trilogy*, p.397.
29 *Eh Joe and other writings*, p.31.
30 See p. 35 above.
31 Compare the poem 'Roundelay', 1976 *Collected Poems in English and French*, London 1977, p.35:
'. . . Steps sole sound/long sole sound/on all that strand/at end of day'.
32 Compare *The Unnamable*, p.364: '. . . when steps are heard on graves as the saying is, genuine hell.'
33 *Footfalls* (Faber 1976) p.9. Subsequent editions have a sequence of *nine* steps instead of seven.
34 *Journal of Beckett Studies* No 2, (John Calder, 1977) pp.83-84.
35 I am indebted to Dorothy Bednarowska for this observation.
36 4 June, 1976: *New Statesman*, 6 August 1976, p.178.
37 Walter Pater, *The Renaissance*, London, 1924, p.140.

Chapter 6 — Drafting the Text

1 Washington University Libraries, St. Louis, Missouri has '6 MSS. in notebook' of *Bing* and 2 MSS. and 1 ts. of *Ping*. R. Federman and J. Fletcher publish ten ts, drafts of *Bing* in *Samuel Beckett: His Works and His Critics* (California, 1970) pp.325-343.
2 TCD M S.4663. Beckett's explanatory note with the MS. reads: 'This seems to be 1st draft of 2nd act, much of which subsists in final version in 1 act.' Draft dated at the close 16 February 1956.
3 'Été 56' notebook. (RUL MS. 1227/7/7/1).
4 RUL MS. 1227/7//16/7.
5 RUL.MS. 1227/1/1/2 (letter dated 7 October 1964).
6 *En attendant Godot*, ed. Colin Duckworth, London 1966, p.xlviii.
7 *Angels of Darkness*, New York, 1972, p.17.
8 *En attendant Godot*, p.xlvi.
9 *En attendant Godot*, p.xlviii.
10 Ibid, pp.xlv-vi.
11 Federman and Fletcher, Appendix 1, p.323.
12 Letter to the author, dated Paris 22 March, 1974.
13 *En attendant Godot*, p.lvii.
14 Ibid, pp.l-li.
15 Ibid, pp.lx-lxi.
16 Ibid, p.lxii.
17 Ibid, p.lxvii.
18 *The Village Voice Reader*, New York, 1962, pp.182-186.
19 The same library contains a 42 page typescript of Beckett's English translation of *Fin de partie*, with MS. alterations.
20 *Fin de partie*, ed. Fletcher, London, 1970, p.8.
21 Letter to the author, January 1978.
22 *Village Voice Reader*, New York, 1962, p.184.
23 *Fin de partie*, p.8.

24 'The Beginning of Endgame', (*Modern Drama* Vol 9, No.3, December 1966) pp.321-2.
25 *Fin de partie*, p.9.

Chapter 7 — Developing Ambiguity

1 RUL MSS. 1227/7/16/4 and 5.
2 This edition contains a reprinting of the English and French texts of the play as well as the German version.
3 RUL MS. 1227/7/16/5.
4 RUL MS. 1227/7/16/4.
5 'Unpleasant laugh' in *Type of Confidence* version.
6 RUL MS. 1227/7/16/5.
7 The colour emphasis is made still more explicit in the Washington drafts (TSS1 and 3) where Beckett colours in the arms, thus: Ru (left) in blue biro, Vi (centre) in red biro and Flo (right) in green biro.
8 *Cascando and Other Short Dramatic Pieces* (Grove Press, 1968) pp. 65-69. (This text incorporates the additional dialogue at the opening of the play, but not at the close.)
9 *Come and Go*, Calder and Boyars, 1967.
10 *Watt*, p.248. Compare *All That Fall* p.37: 'The trouble with her was she had never been really born!' See p.107, above, for a fuller discussion of this point.
11 Shakespeare, *Twelfth Night*, I.5.
12 *Songs of Experience*, 1794; *Poetical Works of William Blake*, ed. John Sampson, Oxford 1913, p.95.
13 *Das Oxforder Buch Deutscher Dichtung*, Oxford 1920, pp.77-8.
14 The same music was used in the Claddagh recording (CCT3) that Beckett made with Jack Macgowran.
15 '*Krapp's Last Tape*: the evolution of a play, 1958-75', *Journal of Beckett Studies*, I, London 1976, p.55.
16 RUL MS. 1227/7/16/6.
17 Empty square brackets denote an omission from the ms.
18 *Fin de partie*, ed. Fletcher, London, 1970, p.74.
19 Samuel Beckett Papers, Washington University Libraries, St. Louis.
20 'The MSS. of Beckett's *Play*, (*Modern Drama* Vol 16, Toronto, June 1973) p.24.
21 TCD MS. 4664.
22 Letter to James Knowlson, 24 September 1974.
23 Holograph begun 20 March 1972 and completed 1 April 1972.
24 RUL MS. 1227/7/12/1.
25 See Appendix IV.
26 See Appendix V.
27 *Fin de partie*, p.9.
28 *Fin de partie*, p.95.

29 Alan Schneider 'Waiting for Beckett', *Beckett at Sixty*, London 1967, p.38.
30 *Village Voice Reader*, New York, 1962, p.185.
31 'Beckett by the Madeleine', *Columbia University Forum*, 4, No.3 (1961) p.23.

Chapter 8 — Genesis: Sound and Screen

1 *Encounter*, September 1975, pp.38-39.
2 Jean-Jacques Mayoux, 'Le Théâtre de Samuel Beckett' *Études Anglaises*, T.X., No.4, Paris, Oct-Dec 1957, p.350.
3 RUL MS. 1227/7/7/1.
4 *Beckett and Broadcasting*, Abô Akademi Vol 51, No 2, Finland, 1976, p.31.
5 *All That Fall*, p.31.
6 See pp. 85–6, above.
7 See transcript of Jung's lectures (published by the Analytical Psychology Club, London, 1936) p.107.
8 T.C.D. MS.4663.
9 *Encounter*, September 1975, p.42.
10 See Clas Zilliacus 'Samuel Beckett's *Embers*: "A Matter of Fundamental Sounds" ', *Modern Drama* Vol 13 (September 1970) p.220.
11 'Le Théâtre de A Jusqu'à Z', *L'Avant-Scène* No.313, Paris, 15 juin 1964, p.8.
12 *Embers*, p.39; compare Shakespeare, *Merchant of Venice*, V I: 'How far that little candle throws his beams!/So shines a good deed in a naughty world.'
13 *Samuel Beckett*, London, 1976, p.101.
14 'Denis Devlin', *transition*, no.27, April-May 1938, p.293.
15 Quoted by Enoch Brater in 'Dada, Surrealism, and the Genesis of *Not I*', *Modern Drama*, Vol XVIII 1975, p.53.
16 *Ends and Odds*, London, 1977.
17 Minuit *Revue Périodique* No.16, Paris, Novembre 1975, pp.2-12.
18 MSS.1396/4/43 and 44.
19 Produced and directed by Martin Esslin for BBC Radio 3, to mark Beckett's seventieth birthday.
20 R.U.L. MS. 1227/7/7/1.
21 *Beckett and Broadcasting*, p.100.
22 *Beckett*, London 1973, p.120.
23 Martin Esslin, *Encounter*, September 1975, p.42.
24 1st performance, BBC archives; a cassette of the second performance can be obtained from London University Audio-Visual Centre.
25 Minuit *Revue Périodique*, No.5, Septembre 1973, pp.31-35.

26 Letter to the author 28 June 1974.
27 *Stereo Headphones*, No.7, Ipswich, 1976, edited and published by Nicholas Zurbrugg.
28 Harvard Theatre Collection; letter dated 21 September 1962.
29 Voix 1 dated (start and finish) 1 December 1961. Voix 2 dated 3 December 1961 (start) and 18? December 1961 (close).
30 *Beckett and Broadcasting*, p.136.
31 Ibid, p.130.
32 *Evergreen Review*, No.30, New York, May — June 1963, pp.47-57.
33 The Faber text omits from the first speech of Voice: '[then rest...it's the right one...this time...I have it...] I've got it... Woburn...'; also from the second speech of Voice with Music: 'we're there...[nearly]...I'm there...'. In the typescript, Opener says in his second speech 'I open the other' where Faber has 'the door'. Faber ends with 'Curtain' where the typescript simply has 'End'.
34 *Beckett and Broadcasting*, p.129.
35 *Cascando*, p.44.
36 *trilogy*, p.418.
37 *Beckett and Broadcasting*, p.131; letter dated 12 March 1974.
38 R.U.L. MS. 1227/7/6/1.
39 Grove Press, New York. Washington University, St. Louis has a carbon copy of a typescript and six pages of typed notes, with diagrams and additions in Beckett's hand. These were sent to Grove Press in May 1963 and used for the first American edition. Apart from some very minor word changes and a rearrangement of the opening paragraphs, this typescript and notes are identical with the Faber text of 1967. Ensuing page references are to the Faber edition.
40 On page 1 of the preliminary notes, the characters are described as E and H (presumably 'He' or 'Him'.)
41 Compare the opening of *Molloy* (*trilogy*, p.7.)
42 Presumably images *of* O.
43 *Film*, p.41 (in *Eh Joe and Other Writings*.)
44 London, 1941; Penguin edition 1953, pp.128-130.
45 London, 1958: Republished 1967 in *No's Knife, Collected Shorter Prose*, 1945-1966, p.141.
46 All references are to the Collins edition, 1953, chapter 10, pp.72, 73.
47 H. E. Berthon, *9 French Poets 1820-1880*, London 1953, pp.75-76.
48 A simultaneous translation could fit the known dates. The English holograph was completed on 1 May 1965, but the subsequent typescripts are undated. The French translation was begun on 28-6-65 and completed on 3-7-65. It is written in the same blue ink as the note in French in Typescript 3 of the English version.

Chapter 9 — 'Vaguening': Stage and Sans

1 RUL MS. 1396/4/6.
2 Minuit *Revue Périodique* No. 8, Paris, 1974.
3 RUL MSS. 1396/4/7, 8 and 9.
4 RUL MSS. 1554/1, 2 and 3.
5 There is one small variation. In the published text (p.69) A says: 'Qu'est-ce que vous avez à me regarder comme ca?' There is no 'me' in the second typescript (p.5).
6 *Collected Shorter Plays*, Faber, 1984.
7 "Bid us sigh on from day to day,
And wish, and wish the soul away;
Till youth and genial years are flown,
And all the life of life is gone?" (James Thomson "To Fortune").
Poetical Works, ed. J.L. Robertson, Oxford, 1965.
8 B presumably intended.
9 Broadcast 10 December, 1957.
10 R.U.L. MS. 1227/7/7/1.
11 Beckett Collection, Humanities Research Center, University of Texas at Austin, which also contains the four typescripts and further letters to Schwartz.
12 Beckett's eightieth birthday on 13 April 1986 is clearly one reason for the change of date.
13 R.U.L., MS. 1396/4/16, p.45. See also Knowlson, *Light and Darkness in the Theatre of Samuel Beckett*, London, 1972.
14 R.U.L. MS. 1227/7/10/1.
15 *Journal of Beckett Studies*, No.1, London, 1976, p.54.
16 TCD MS. 4661 (Calypso notebook).
17 In *Beckett*, ed. Tom Bishop and Raymond Federman, Editions de l'Herne, Paris 1976, pp.15-23.
18 RUL MS. 1396/4/41.
19 RUL MS. No. 1396/4/42.
20 *Ends and odds* Grove Press, 1976 and Faber 1977 (*Theatre II*); *Collected Shorter Plays*, Faber, 1984 (*Rough for Theatre II*).
21 *L'Avant-Scène* No.313, Paris, 1964, p.8.
22 Reply to author's questionnaire, January 1978.
23 First version R.U.L. MS. 1227/7/7/1; all remaining drafts are in The Ohio State University Libraries at Columbus.
24 *Beckett's Happy Days; A Manuscript Study*, Ohio, 1977, p.33.
25 Stage I merely mentions 'a parasol'; Stage II has 'a collapsible (and collapsed) striped parasol'.
26 See Appendix VI.
27 Compare Belacqua's 'fleam in the neck', *More Pricks Than Kicks*, p.172.
28 Charles Wolfe, C19 Irish poet.
29 R.U.L. MS. 1396/4/10, p.66 (See Appendix VI.)
30 *Proust and 3 Dialogues*, p.28.
31 Ibid, p.15.

32 Robert Browning, *Paracelsus*, 3.372.
33 Ditto. Beckett frequently writes: '*Pause. Do.*' instead of '*Long Pause.*'
34 *Beckett's Happy Days; A Manuscript Study*, p.43.
35 Manuscript note preceding Typescript I of *Fin de partie*, The Ohio State University Libraries.
36 John Calder, *Gambit*, Vol.4, No 16, London, 1970, p.6.
37 Ibid, pp.8-9.
38 The six statement groups of *Sans* are headed: A. Effondrement du refuge; B. Terre; C. Homme; D. Refuge Oublié; E. Passé — Futur Nié; F. Passé — Futur Affirmé.
39 'Beckett Symposium', *New Theatre Magazine*, Vol XI, No 3, Bristol 1973, p.12.

Chapter 10 — Working Method

1 *Beckett's Happy Days: A Manuscript Study*, Ohio, 1977, p.2.
2 Omission marks denote phrases for inclusion in the text jotted on the blank facing page.
3 'Him' is written over the word 'God' in the last line.
4 1 May 1970.
5 *Beckett and Broadcasting*, Abo (Finland), 1976, p.31.

Chapter 11 — Stagecraft

1 Lyttelton Theatre, 7 April 1976.
2 Kenneth Tynan, *Tynan on Theatre*, London, 1964, p.38.
3 Letter to Barney Rosset (Clas Zilliacus, *Beckett and Broadcasting*, Abo, Finland, 1976) p.3.
4 *Fin de partie*, ed. Fletcher, London, 1970, pp.17-18.
5 'Voices, Patterns, Voices — Samuel Beckett's Later Plays', *Gambit*, Vol 7, No 28, London, 1976, p.95.
6 Robert O'Driscoll (ed.) *Theatre and Nationalism in Twentieth Century Ireland*, Toronto, 1971, p.182.
7 Letter to the author from John Beckett, 10 May 1975.
8 Interview with Israel Shenker, *New York Times*, 6 May 1956, Section 2 (x) p.3.
9 R.U.L. MS. 1396/4/10, p.9.
10 Charles Marowitz 'Paris Log', *Encore*, March/April 1962, p.44.
11 *Theatre Quarterly*, Vol III, No 2, London, 1973, p.20.
12 *The Arts in Ireland*, Dublin, 1973, p.28.
13 *Theatre Quarterly*, July-Sept. 1973, p.20.
14 'Beckett as Director', *Gambit*, Vol 7, No 28, London, 1976, p.62.
15 'What's it meant to mean?': An approach to Beckett's Theatre', *Critical Quarterly*, Vol 18, No 2, p.31.
16 e.g. *Les Aveugles* (1890) *Pelléas et Mélisande* (1892) *La Mort de Tintagiles* (1894).
17 Denis Bablet, *Edward Gordon Craig* (translated Daphne Woodward), London, 1966, p.54.
18 Zilliacus, *Beckett and Broadcasting*, p.203.

19 Quoted from the BBC Archives by Martin Esslin, *Encounter*, September 1975, p.40.
20 Zilliacus, *Beckett and Broadcasting*, p.89.
21 *En attendant Godot*, (ed. Duckworth), London, 1966, p.xxii.
22 *The Renaissance*, London, 1924, p.140.
23 *Proust and 3 Dialogues*, p.91.
24 'My Collaboration with Samuel Beckett', *Beckett at Sixty*, London, 1967, p.21.
25 'Beckett as Librettist', *Music and Musicians* (May issue), London, 1977, p.5.
26 *Gambit*, Vol 7, No 28, London, 1976, p.43.
27 Letter to George Devine, 9 March 1964 (*Samuel Beckett: an exhibition*, ed. James Knowlson), London, 1971, p.92.
28 Michael Davie '' 'Le Grand Sam' Plays It Again'', *Observer Review*, 2 May 1976, p.36.
29 Programme note to National Theatre production of *Play* at the Old Vic, 7 April 1964.
30 Discussion following the National Theatre production of *Happy Days* on 7 April 1976.
31 Zilliacus, *Beckett and Broadcasting*, p.128.
32 *Modern Drama*, Vol 18, 1975, p.53.
33 *Molloy*, p.50.
34 Antonin Artaud *Le Théâtre et son double* (Paris, 1938) Translated by Victor Corti, London, 1970, p.35.
35 *Seraphim's Theatre* (essay, included in English translation of *The Theatre and Its Double*) p.100.
36 Letter to the author, January 1978.
37 TCD MS. 4664, (reverse of pp.11-12).
38 *The Literature of Silence*, New York, 1967, p.206.
39 *Modern Drama*, September 1970, p.223.
40 *The Theatre and Its Double*, p.27.
41 *Gambit*, (ed. John Calder) Vol 7, No 28, London, 1976, p.41.
42 Letter dated 18 September 1970. R.U.L. MS. 1227/1/2/14.
43 *Observer Review*, 2 May 1976, p.36.
44 'Beckett Directs *Happy Days*', *Performance* I, No. 2, New York 1972, p.114.
45 R.U.L. MS. 1396/4/10; see Chapter 5, pp.59-60.
46 R.U.L. MS. 1396/4/10, pp.80-83.
47 National Theatre discussion, 7 April 1976.
48 Letter to the author, January 1978.
49 San Quentin Drama Workshop, *Samuel Beckett inszeniert Krapp's Last Tape mit Rick Cluchey*, Heft 2, Publikation 5, Berlin, November 1977, p.16.
50 'Beckett Directs *Happy Days*', (*Performance*, Vol 1, No 2), New York, 1972, p.116.
51 *Theatre Quarterly*, Vol V, No 19, London 1975 (translation by Ria Julian) p.21.

52 'Theatre and the Visual Arts', *Yeats Studies* No 2, ed. R. O'Driscoll and L. Reynolds, Shannon, 1971, p.135.
53 R.U.L. MS. 1396/4/11 (pp.13-14).
54 *Journal of Beckett Studies* No. 2, London, Summer 1977, p.85.
55 *Samuel Beckett: an exhibition*, p.92.
56 Frankfurt, 1970. (*Journal of Beckett Studies* I, p.52).
57 Letter to the author, January 1976.
58 Letter to the author, 26 January 1973.
59 The status of Beckett's production changes is a complex question that is currently causing much critical debate. In *Krapp's Last Tape*, for example, Beckett's repeated cutting of the Baring Gould hymn 'Now the day is over' and his introduction of the 'hain' into productions both represent definite authorial changes of mind as to how the play should be performed, but are not reflected in English editions of the text.
60 *Film* (Illustrated Scenario, with an essay by Alan Schneider) Faber, 1972, p.85.
61 Letter to James Knowlson, 18 May 1972.
62 *Journal of Beckett Studies* I, London, 1976, p.56.
63 Letter to James Knowlson, 30 April 1974.
64 Enoch Brater, *Modern Drama*, Vol 18, 1975, p.50.
65 '*Film* and The Religion of Art', *Beckett The Shape Changer — A Symposium*, ed. Katharine Worth, London 1975, p.167.
66 *Watt*, p.69.

Chapter 12 — Conclusions 1956–76

1 *transition*, No 27, Paris, 1938, p.290.
2 'Beckett By The Madeleine', Columbia University Forum, 1961, p.23.
3 *En attendant Godot*, (ed. Duckworth), p.xxvi.
4 Katharine J. Worth *Revolutions in Modern English Drama*, London, 1972, pp.146-147.

Epilogue — The Latest Plays

1 All published in *Collected Shorter Plays of Samuel Beckett*, Faber, 1984.

I. TELEVISION 1977–84

1. First published by Grove Press, New York, 1976.
2. R.U.L. MS. No. 2100.
3. See Chapter 2, pp.11-13.
4. *Collected Shorter Plays*, p.293.
5. Martin Esslin, lecture at the Edinburgh Festival, August 24th 1984.
6. Produced by Süddeutscher Rundfunk and first transmitted on 19 May 1983.

II. THEATRE 1979–84

1 New Series, Vol 1, No 3, Summer 1979 (Gambier, Ohio).
2 *Murphy*, London, 1938, p.172.
3 *For To End Yet Again*, John Calder, London, 1976, p.11.
4 It was first published in 1981 by Grove Press, New York.
5 See Chapter 8, p.107
6 First published by Grove Press, New York, in 1981.
7 10 January 1983, pp.26-27.
8 *How It Is*, Calder, 1964, p.118.
9 *How It Is*, p.123.
10 *Journal of Beckett Studies*, No 2, London, 1977, p.85.
11 TCD MS. 4664; see Chapter 7, pp.91-2.
12 Conversation with the author, Paris, 4 September, 1986.
13 Ibid.

Appendix VII

1 R.U.L. MSS. 1226/7/12/8 and 1227/7/12/9.
2 No page number given. A final 'note on light' is not in fact present until draft seven.
3 'The Manuscripts of Beckett's *Play*', *Modern Drama*, Vol 16, June 1973, p.25.
4 Some of the corrections in draft 7 do not enter the Faber text until the 1968 edition (see chart p.267). The 1964 text has more in common with drafts 8 and 9.
5 R.U.L. MSS. 1477/1-8.
6 R.U.L. MSS. 1477/9-10.
7 R.U.L. MS. 1639.
8 See Chapter 4, p.38.
9 R.U.L. MSS. 1447/10 (typescript) and 1447/9 (carbon).
10 R.U.L. MSS. 1552, 1-7.
11 Beckett's rehearsal comment to the actress Rose Hill in London in 1976 was: 'Do it like one ghost talking to another.'
12 149 appears to be an error for 147 (21×7).
13 In the published text this sequence begins 'to put it mildly' and ends 'I was not there.'
14 'Beckett suggests jokingly that it be made into a cross, then it can't be a mistake.' (*Journal of Beckett Studies*, 2, p.91).
15 *Journal of Beckett Studies*, No 2, London 1977, p.85.

INDEX

THE IRISH LITERARY STUDIES SERIES

ISSN 0140-895X

1. *Place, Personality and the Irish Writer*. Edited by Andrew Carpenter
   ISBN 0-901072-63-X 200pp. 1977 out of print
2. *Yeats and Magic: the Earlier Works*. Mary Catherine Flannery
   ISBN 0-901072-69-9 iv, 166pp. 1978 out of print
3. *A Study of the Novels of George Moore*. Richard Allen Cave
   ISBN 0-901072-58-3 272pp. 1978
4. *J.M.Synge and the Western Mind*. Weldon Thornton
   ISBN 0-90172-89-3 170pp. 1979
5. *Irish Poetry from Moore to Yeats*. Robert Welch
   ISBN 0-901072-93-1 248pp. 1980
6. *Yeats, Sligo and Ireland*. Edited by A.Norman Jeffares
   ISBN 0-86140-041-0 x, 270pp. 1980
7. *Sean O'Casey, Centenary Essays*. Edited by David Krause and Robert
   G.Lowery ISBN 0-86140-008-9 x, 258pp. 1981
8. *Denis Johnston, A Retrospective*. Edited by Joseph Ronsley
   ISBN 0-86140-078-X xii, 276pp.+ 8pp. illus. 1981
9. *Literature and the Changing Ireland*. Edited by Peter Connolly
   ISBN 0-86140-043-7 x, 230pp. 1982
10. *James Joyce: An International Perspective*. Edited by Suheil Bushrui &
    Bernard Benstock ISBN 0-86140-084-4 xiv, 302pp. 1982
11. *Synge: The Medieval and the Grotesque*. Toni O'Brien Johnson
    ISBN 0-86140-104-2 viii, 210pp. 1983
12. *Carleton's* Traits and Stories *and the 19th Century Anglo-Irish Tradition.*
    Barbara Hayley ISBN 0-86140-118-2 xiv, 432pp. 1983
13. *Lady Gregory, Fifty Years After*. Edited by Ann Saddlemyer and
    Colin Smythe ISBN 0-86140-112-3 xiv, 464pp. 1987
14. *Woman in Irish Legend, Life and Literature*. Edited by S.F.Gallagher
    ISBN 0-86140-159-X 158pp. 1983 OS, we hope to reprint
15. *'Since O'Casey', and Other Essays on Irish Drama*. Robert Hogan
    ISBN 0-86140-115-8 176pp. 1983
16. *George Moore in Perspective*. Edited by Janet Egleson Dunleavy
    ISBN 0-86140-120-4 174pp.+ 16pp. illus. 1984
17. *W.B.Yeats, Dramatist of Vision*. A.S.Knowland
    ISBN 0-86140-117-4 xvi, 256pp. 1983
18. *The Irish Writer and the City*. Edited by Maurice Harmon
    ISBN 0-86140-174-3 x, 204pp. 1984
19. *O'Casey the Dramatist*. Heinz Kosok
    ISBN 0-86140-168-9 xiv, 410pp. 1985
20. *The Double Perspective of Yeats's Aesthetic*. Okifumi Komesu
    ISBN 0-86140-158-1 200pp. 1984

21. *The Pioneers of Anglo-Irish Fiction, 1800-1850.* Barry Sloan ISBN 0-86140-205-7 xxxvi, 278pp. 1986
22. *Irish Writers & Society at Large.* Edited by Masaru Sekine (IASAIL-Japan Series 1) ISBN 0-86140-226-X x, 252pp. 1985
23. *Irish Writers and the Theatre.* Edited by Masaru Sekine (IASAIL-Japan Series 2) ISBN 0-86140-234-0 viii, 246pp. 1986
24. *A History of Verse Translation from the Irish 1789-1897.* Robert Welch ISBN 0-86140-249-9 xii, 200pp. 1988
25. *Kate O'Brien, A Literary Portrait.* Lorna Reynolds ISBN 0-86140-239-1 133pp.+ 8pp. illus. 1987
26. *Portraying the Self; Sean O'Casey & the Art of Autobiography.* Michael Kenneally ISBN 0-86140-250-2 xvi, 268pp. 1988
27. *W.B.Yeats and the Tribes of Danu: Three Views of Ireland's Fairies.* Peter Alderson Smith ISBN 0-86140-257-X 350pp. 1987
28. *Theatre of Shadows: from* All that Fall *to* Footfalls. *Samuel Beckett's Drama 1956-76.* Rosemary Pountney ISBN 0-86140-407-6 xx, 310pp. 1998 pbk of 1988 ed.
29. *Critical Approaches to Anglo-Irish Literature.* Edited by Michael Allen & Angela Wilcox ISBN 0-86140-285-5 x, 194pp.+ 8pp. illus. 1988
30. *'Make Sense who May': Essays on Samuel Beckett's Later Works.* Edited by Robin J.Davis & Lance St.J.Butler ISBN 0-86140-286-3 x, 176pp. 1989
31. *Cultural Contexts and Literary Idioms in Contemporary Irish Literature.* Edited by Michael Kenneally (Studies in Contemporary Irish Literature Series 1) ISBN 0-86140-230-8 viii, 370pp. 1989
32. *Builders of My Soul: Greek and Roman Themes in Yeats.* Brian Arkins ISBN 0-86140-304-5 xxii, 242pp.+ 4pp. illus. 1991
33. *Perspectives on Irish Drama and Theatre.* Edited by Jacqueline Genet and Richard Allen Cave ISBN 0-86140-309-6 xiv, 184pp. 1991
34. *The Great Queens: Irish Goddesses from the Morrigan to Cathleen ní Houlihan.* Rosalind Clark ISBN 0-86140-290-1 x, 278pp. 1992
35. *Irish Literature and Culture.* Edited by Michael Kenneally ISBN 0-86140-313-4 x, 196pp.+ 8pp. illus. 1992
36. *Irish Writers and Politics.* Edited by Okifumi Komesu and Masaru Sekine (IASAIL-Japan Series 3) ISBN 0-86140-237-5 viii, 350pp. 1991
37. *Irish Writers and Religion.* Edited by Robert Welch (IASAIL-Japan Series 4) ISBN 0-86140-236-7 xiv, 242pp. 1992
38. *Yeats and the Noh.* Masaru Sekine & Christopher Murray ISBN 0-86140-258-8 xviii, 182pp.+ 16pp.illus. 1990
39. *Samuel Ferguson: the Literary Achievement.* Peter Denman ISBN 0-86140-326-6 viii, 230pp. 1990
40. *Reviews and Essays of Austin Clarke.* Edited by Gregory A. Schirmer ISBN 0-86140-337-1 xx, 388pp. 1995
41. *The Internationalism of Irish Literature and Drama.* Edited by Joseph McMinn ISBN 0-86140-339-8 x, 362pp. 1992

42. *Ireland and France, A Bountiful Friendship: Literature, History and Ideas*. Edited by Barbara Hayley and Christopher Murray
ISBN 0-86140-341-X xii, 222pp. 1992
43. *Poetry in Contemporary Irish Literature*. Edited by Michael Kenneally (Studies in Contemporary Irish Literature Series 2)
ISBN 0-86140-310-X xvi, 460pp. 1995
44. *International Aspects of Irish Literature*. Edited by Toshi Furomoto, George Hughes et al. (IASAIL-Japan Series 5)
ISBN 0-86140-363-0 xii, 430pp. 1996
45. *A Small Nation's Contribution to the World*. Edited by Donald E.Morse, Csilla Bertha, and Istvàn Pàlffy
ISBN 0-86140-375-4 xiv, 248pp. 1993
46. *Images of Invention. Essays on Irish Writing*. A.Norman Jeffares
ISBN 0-86140-362-2 xii, 352pp. 1996
47. *Literary Inter-Relations: Ireland, Egypt, and the Far East*. Edited by Mary Massoud ISBN 0-86140-377-0 x, 440pp. 1996
48. *Irish Writers and their Creative Process*. Edited by Jacqueline Genet and Wynn Hellegouarc'h ISBN 0-86140-384-3 viii, 150pp. 1996
49. *Rural Ireland, Real Ireland?* Edited by Jacqueline Genet
ISBN 0-86140-385-1 246pp. 1996
50. *Mrs S.C.Hall: A Literary Biography*. Maureen Keane
ISBN 0-86140-394-0 viii, 260pp. 1997